Constructing a Microprogrammed Computer

Second Edition

```
;=========================================================
        ; Fetch machine instruction, increment pc
fetch:  a.pc c.mar
        a.pc add b.1 c.pc rd


;=========================================================
        ; Decode instruction

        a.mdr add b.0 c.ir neg@L1
L0:     a.ir sll b.1 c.dc neg@L01
L00:    a.dc sll b.1 c.dc neg@L001
L000:   a.dc sll b.1 c.dc neg@L0001
        br@L0000
```

Anthony J. Dos Reis

10 9 8 7 6 5 4 3 2

Preface

Constructing a Microprogrammed Computer (*CMC*) will provide you with a detailed examination of a complete computer system. It covers number systems, digital circuits, microprogramming, and programming in machine language, assembly language, C, and C++. Its companion volume, *C and C++ Under the Hood* (*CUH*), further examines C and C++ and culminates with an introduction into system programming in C (implementing machine interpreters, assemblers, linkers, and file display programs).

One distinguishing characteristic of *CMC* is that it will give you plenty to do. Thus, you will learn not only by reading but also by doing. For example, *CMC* not only examines and evaluates four instruction set architectures, but also guides you through their microcode implementations.

To get the latest version of the software package, send an email to `cmc2edition@gmail.com`. You will then immediately receive an automatic reply with a link to the site at which you can download the latest version of the software package. The software package runs on Windows, Mac OS X (both the pre-m1/m2 Macs and the m1/m2 Macs), Linux, and Raspberry Pi.

The following enhancements have been incorporated into the second edition:

- The assembler syntax has been updated to the more modern syntax that matches the assembler syntax used in *CUH*.

- The second edition covers new material: text and binary files, computer endianness, debugging, the new optimal instruction set, fast decoding of opcodes, C++, linking, and virtual memory.

- The debugging facility of the `sim` program has been substantially improved. It now includes both microlevel and machine-level debugging and several new commands. In addition, the trace output now provides more information. The second edition has been updated to reflect these enhancements to the debugger.

- A new chapter (Chapter 10) on fast decoding of opcodes and C++ is included. In addition, two new chapters (on linking and virtual memory) in PDF form are included in the software package.

- A hex-ASCII file display program (`see`) is now included in the software package. It is used by this edition to examine the internal structure of text and executable files.

- Binary microcode for each instruction set is provided so students can try out each instruction set before implementing it in microcode. These files are encrypted so they cannot be used to determine the microcode implementations of the instructions sets.

Anthony J. Dos Reis
SUNY New Paltz
dosreist@newpaltz.edu

Table of Contents

4 Simple Digital Circuits

5 Complex Digital Circuits

6 Microlevel of the LCC

7 Microprogramming the Basic Instruction Set

8 Stack Instruction Set

9 Register Instruction Set

10 Optimal Instruction Set and Fast Opcode Decoding

11 Linking (in the software package in PDF form)

12 Virtual Memory (in the software package in PDF form)

1 Number Systems

Decimal, Binary, and Hexadecimal

Decimal is a *positional number system*. It is so called because in a decimal number the contribution of each digit to the value of the number depends not only on the digit but on its position in the number. For example, consider the three-digit decimal number 123:

$$\frac{1 \quad 2 \quad 3}{100 \quad 10 \quad 1} \quad \text{weights}$$

Each position has a weight. In a whole number, weights start with 1 and increase from right to left by a factor of 10 from each position to the next. The value of the number is given by the sum of each digit times its weight. Thus, the value of 123 is

$$1 \times 100 + 2 \times 10 + 3 \times 1$$

The 1 digit contributes $1 \times 100 = 100$ to the value of the number; the 2 digit contributes $2 \times 10 = 20$ to the value of the number, the 3 digit contributes $3 \times 1 = 3$ to the value of the number. Although the 3 digit is greater than the 2 digit, the 2 digit contributes more to the value of the number than the 3 digit because its weight is ten times that of the 3 digit.

We call decimal the *base-10* number system because it uses 10 distinct symbols and because weights increase by a factor of 10 from each position to the next. *Binary* is the *base-2* positional number system. It uses two distinct symbols (0 and 1), called *bits*. In binary, position weights increase by a factor of 2 from each position to the next. For example, consider the five-bit binary number 01101:

$$\frac{0 \quad 1 \quad 1 \quad 0 \quad 1}{16 \ 8 \ \ 4 \ \ 2 \ \ 1} \ \text{weights}$$

Its value is given by the sum of each digit times its weight:

$$0 \times 16 + 1 \times 8 + 1 \times 4 + 0 \times 2 + 1 \times 1 = 13 \text{ decimal}$$

It is easy to determine the decimal value of a binary number: Simply add up the weights corresponding to the 1 bits. In the binary number above, the weights corresponding to 1 bits are 8, 4, and 1. Thus, the value of the number is $8 + 4 + 1 = 13$ decimal.

We call a sequence of eight bits a *byte*. For example, 1111000010101010 consists of two bytes: 11110000 and 10101010. To *complement* a bit means to flip it. That is, change a 1 bit to 0, and a 0 bit to 1.

Hexadecimal (or hex for short) is the *base-16* positional number system. It uses 16 symbols: 0 to 9 and A, B, C, D, E, and F in upper or lower case (the lowercase forms are more convenient for keyboard input because their entry do not require the shift key). The values of A, B, C, D, E, and F and their corresponding lowercase forms equal decimal 10, 11, 12, 13, 14, and 15, respectively.

Weights in a hexadecimal number increase by a factor of 16. For example, consider the three-digit hex number 2C5:

$$\frac{2 \quad C \quad 5}{256 \quad 16 \quad 1} \text{ weights (in decimal)}$$

Its value is given by

$$2 \times 256 + C \times 16 + 5 \times 1$$

The hex digit C is 12 in decimal so the expression above using only decimal is equal to

$$2 \times 256 + 12 \times 16 + 5 \times 1 = 512 + 192 + 5 = 709$$

The following table shows the decimal numbers from 0 to 15 and their binary and hex equivalents.

Decimal	Binary	Hex
0	0000	0
1	0001	1
2	0010	2
3	0011	3
4	0100	4
5	0101	5
6	0110	6
7	0111	7
8	1000	8
9	1001	9
10	1010	A (or a)
11	1011	B (or b)
12	1100	C (or c)
13	1101	D (or d)
14	1110	E (or e)
15	1111	F (or f)

Since we will be working quite a bit with binary and hex, *it is essential that you memorize this table.*

If you append a 0 on its right side of a binary whole number, the weight of each digit increases by a factor of 2. Thus, the value of the number doubles. For example, 3 in binary is 0011. If we append a 0, we get 00110, which is 6 decimal. If we append another 0, we get 001100, which is 12 decimal. Adding a 0 on the left side does not affect the value of a number. For example, 0110 equals 00110.

Similarly, if you append a 0 on the right side of a hex whole number, its value increases by a factor of 16 (since the weight of each digit increases by a factor of 16). For example, A is 10 decimal, and A0 is 160 decimal.

Rule: Adding a 0 on the right side of a positional whole number multiplies its value by its base.

Numbering Bits

The bits in a binary number are numbered right to left starting with 0. For example, in an eight-bit number, the rightmost bit is bit 0; the leftmost bit is bit 7:

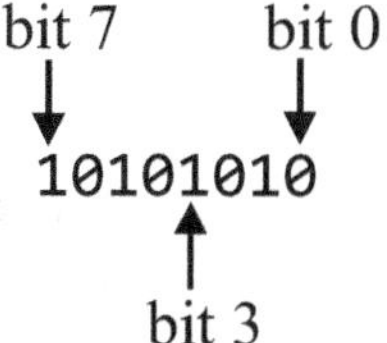

With this numbering scheme, there is a nice correspondence between a bit's number and its weight: Bit i has weight 2^i. For example, bit 3 in the binary number above has the weight $2^3 = 8$. Thus, it contributes 8 to the value of the number.

The leftmost bit and the rightmost bit in a binary number are called the *most significant bit* (abbreviated msb) and the *least significant bit* (abbreviated lsb), respectively.

Adding Positional Numbers

Let's quickly review how we add two decimal numbers. Consider the following addition:

```
    1  carries
   157
 + 238
   395
```

We start in the right column. Adding 7 and 8, we get 15. The result is two digits. So we record the right digit 5 at the bottom of the column and carry the left digit 1 to the next column. Thus, in the next column we add 1, 5, and 3 to get 9. The result is a single digit so we do not carry into the next column. Finally, we add 1 and 2 in the left column to get 3 for that column.

To add two binary numbers, we take exactly the same approach as we take with decimal. For example, consider the following addition of the binary numbers 0011 and 0011:

```
    11  carries
   0011
 + 0011
   0110
```

When we add the right column, we get 10 binary (2 decimal). The result is two bits. So we record the right bit 0 and carry the left bit 1 to the next column. Thus, in the next column, we add 1, 1, and 1 to get 11 binary (3 decimal). So we record the right bit 1 and carry the left bit 1 to the next column, where we add 1, 0, and 0 to get 1. Finally, in the leftmost column, we add 0 and 0 to get 0.

Let's now add the hex numbers 1B and 37:

```
   1  carries
   1B
 + 37
   52
```

Adding B (11 in decimal) and 7, we get 12 hex (18 decimal). We record the 2 digit and carry 1 to the next column, where we add 1, 1, and 3 to get 5.

Representing Negative Numbers

Signed numbers within a computer are usually represented in the *two's complement* system. Before we discuss two's complement, let's make a simple observation. Suppose a computer represents numbers using only 4 bits. If our computer adds 0001 to 1111, what is the result? Here is the addition:

```
1 111    carries
  1111
+ 0001
  0000
```

We get zero with a carry out of the leftmost column. Since we are assuming the computer uses only four bits to represent numbers, this carry out not included in the result. Thus, the result is 0000.

Rule: Adding 1 to a binary number with a fixed number of bits all of which are 1 results in all zeros.

Let's now experimentally determine the two's complement representation of -3. We want the binary form of -3 that when added to the binary form of $+3$ gives a sum of zero. Let's see if complementing (i.e., flipping) all the bits in the binary form of $+3$ is the desired representation of -3:

```
  0011  = +3
+ 1100  = +3 with each bit flipped
  1111
```

We do not get zero so 1100 is not -3. But recall our preceding rule: Adding 1 to all 1's gives zero. Thus, because flipping the bits of $+3$ gives all 1's when added to $+3$, flipping the bits *and* adding 1 should give us the representation that produces zero when added to $+3$. Let's try it. Flipping the bits of $+3$ and adding 1, we get

```
  1100  = +3  with each bit flipped
+ 0001  add 1
  1101  Is this −3?
```

Is 1101 the representation of -3 that we want? Let's add it to $+3$ to see if it gives zero:

```
1 111    carries
  0011  = +3
+ 1101  Is this −3?
  0000
```

We, indeed, get zero with a carry out of the leftmost position. Thus, 1101 is the correct representation of -3 in the two's complement system.

Rule: To negate a binary number in the two's complement system, flip its bits and add 1.

The binary number system that can represent both positive and negative numbers and in which a number is negated by flipping its bits and adding 1 is called the *two's complement system*. We call the negation of a number the *two's complement* of that number. For example, the two's complement of 0011 (+3) is 1101 (−3). The two's complement of 1101 (−3) should get us back to is 0011 (+3). Indeed, it does:

```
    0010  = −3 with each bit flipped
+      1
    0011  = +3
```

To add two's complement numbers, we simply add them using the standard adding procedure. It does not matter if one is positive and one is negative. For example, lets add +1 and −3. The result should be the two's complement number for −2:

```
    0001  = +1
+   1101  = −3
    1110  = −2
```

To confirm that 1110 is −2, take its two's complement to see if you get +2. That is, flip the bits in 1110 and add 1. The result is indeed 0010 (+2), which confirms that 1101 is −2.

In the two's complement system, −1 is represented with all 1's. Let's confirm this by taking the two's complement of +1. We flip the bits in +1 and add 1. We get

```
    1110  = +1 with each bit flipped
+      1
    1111  = −1
```

Rule: In the two's complement system, all 1's represents −1.

In the two's complement system, the leftmost bit of a number indicates the sign of the number: A 1 bit indicates the number is negative; a 0 bit indicates the number is non-negative (i.e., zero or positive). Note that in the two's complement system, the bits to the right of the sign bit do *not* represent the magnitude of the number. For example, 1111 in the two's complement system is −1. The three bits to the right of the sign bit, 111 (7 decimal), is *not* the magnitude of the number.

Signed and Unsigned Numbers

If the number representation used for a number allows for positive and negative numbers, we say the number is a *signed number*. Otherwise, it is an *unsigned number*. Because unsigned numbers have no sign, they represent only non-negative numbers. For example, the value of the unsigned number 1111 is 15 in decimal, but as a two's complement signed number, its value is −1. Note that the number 1111 can be either an unsigned number or a signed number.

What makes a binary number signed or unsigned is how it is treated. For example, suppose you compare 1111 and 0010 and conclude that 1111 is bigger (because 1111 represents 15 and 0010 represents 2). Then the numbers are unsigned because you are treating them that way. But if you conclude 0010 is bigger (because 0010 represents 2 and 1111 represents −1), then the numbers are signed.

From this point on, when we use the term "signed number," we mean a number in the two's complement system.

Range of Signed and Unsigned Numbers

There are two patterns that can be represented by a single bit: either 0 or 1. With two bits, either bit can be 0 or 1. Thus, there are $2 \times 2 = 2^2 = 4$ patterns: 00, 01, 10, 11. With three bits, there are $2 \times 2 \times 2 = 2^3 = 8$ patterns: 000, 001, 010, 011, 100, 101, 110, 111. Generalizing, with n bits we get 2^n patterns.

If we represent unsigned numbers with four bits, we can have $2^4 = 16$ patterns. If we use these 2^4 patterns to represent the sequence of non-negative numbers starting with 0, we can represent the numbers 0 to $2^4 - 1$ (we go up to $2^4 - 1 = 15$, not 2^4, because we are starting from 0). Generalizing, with n bits we can represent unsigned numbers from 0 to $2^n - 1$. For example, with eight bits, we can represent unsigned numbers from 0 to $2^8 - 1 = 255$. The following table shows the range of four-bit signed and unsigned numbers:

Unsigned	Value	Signed	Value
0000	0	1000	−8
0001	1	1001	−7
0010	2	1010	−6
0011	3	1011	−5
0100	4	1100	−4
0101	5	1101	−3
0110	6	1110	−2
0111	7	1111	−1
1000	8	0000	0
1001	9	0001	1
1010	10	0010	2
1011	11	0011	3
1100	12	0100	4
1101	13	0101	5
1110	14	0110	6
1111	15	0111	7

With two's complement signed numbers, the left bit indicates the sign (0 for non-negative numbers or 1 or negative numbers). Suppose we represent numbers with four bits. For the negative numbers, the sign bit is 1, leaving only three bits to specify the negative number. With three bits, we can specify $2^3 = 8$ numbers. Thus, starting from −1, we can represent the numbers −1 down to −8. For the non-negative numbers, the sign bit is 0, leaving only three bits to specify the number. Thus, as with the negative numbers, we can represent $2^3 = 8$ non-negative numbers. But we start from 0, not 1. Thus, we can represent the numbers 0 to 7 (not 1 to 8). The table above shows the four-bit unsigned and signed numbers in ascending order along with their values in decimal. Note for the signed numbers, the negative numbers go down to −8, but the non-negative number go up to only +7. The numbers go one further in the negative direction than in the positive direction because the negative numbers start from −1, but the non-negative numbers start from 0.

The following table shows the ranges of unsigned and signed numbers with n bits for several values of n.

n	Unsigned	Signed
1	0 to 1	−1 to 0
2	0 to 3	−2 to 1
3	0 to 7	−4 to 3
4	0 to 15	−8 to 7
5	0 to 31	−16 to 15
6	0 to 63	−32 to 31
7	0 to 127	−64 to 63
8	0 to 255	−128 to 127
9	0 to 511	−256 to 255
10	0 to 1023	−512 to 511
12	0 to 4095	−2048 to 2047
16	0 to 65535	−32768 to 32767
k	0 to 2^k-1	-2^{k-1} to $2^{k-1}-1$

Do not attempt to memorize this table. Instead, learn the value of 2^n for n from 1 to 16. Once you know these powers of 2, it is easy to figure out the ranges of unsigned and signed numbers with n bits for the values of n in the table. For example, 8 bits has 256 patterns (because $2^8 = 256$). Thus, 8-bit unsigned numbers range from 0 to $2^8 - 1 = 255$. For signed numbers, half of the 2^8 patterns are for negative numbers, and half are for non-negative numbers. Half of 2^8 is $2^7 = 128$. Thus, 8-bit signed numbers range from -128 to 127. Here are the powers of 2 you should know:

n	2^n
1	2
2	4
3	8
4	16
5	32
6	64
7	128
8	256
9	512
10	1,024 (aka 1K)
11	2,048 (aka 2K)
12	4,096 (aka 4K)
15	32,768 (aka 32K)
16	65,536 (aka 64K)
20	1,048,576 (aka 1M)
30	1,073,741,824 (aka 1G)

Converting Between Binary and Hex

It is trivial to convert between binary and hex once you know the binary numbers from 0000 to 1111 and their hex equivalents. To convert a binary number to hex, break up the binary number into groups of four bits, starting from its right end. Then substitute the hex equivalent for each four-bit group. For example, to convert 11010111000001100, we first break it up into four-bit groups:

```
1   1010   1110   0000   1100
```

We then substitute the hex equivalent for each four-bit group:

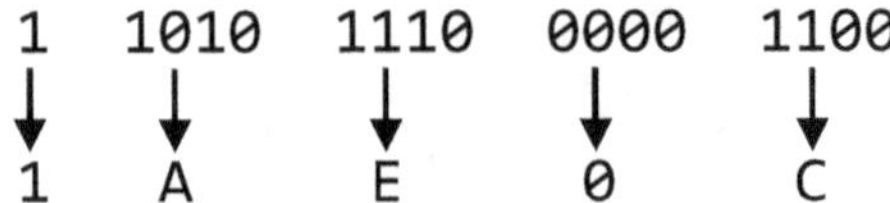

Thus, 11010111000001100 binary is equal to 1AE0C hex. To convert hex to binary, we simply substitute the four-bit binary equivalent for each hex digit. For example, to convert A5 to binary, substitute 1010 for A and 0101 for 5 to get 10100101.

Converting Decimal to Binary

If we repeatedly divide a number by 10 until we get a 0 quotient, the remainders will be the digits that represent that number in decimal. For example, let's divide 123 by 10 repeatedly:

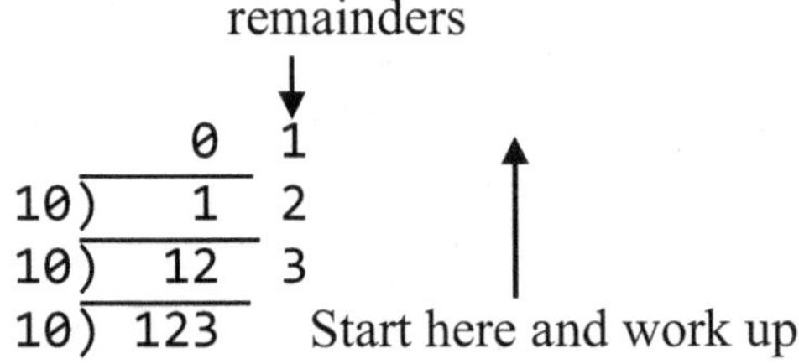

As you can see, the remainders are the digits that make up the decimal number. If, instead, we repeatedly divide by 2, then the remainders will be the bits that make up the binary number equal to 123 decimal:

```
            0   1
   2)   1   1
   2)   3   1
   2)   7   1
   2)  15   0
   2)  30   1
   2)  61   1
   2) 123        Start here and work up
```

Reading the remainders from the top down, we get the bits that make up the binary number equal to 123 decimal. Thus, 123 decimal = 1111011 binary. Let's check our answer by converting it to hex and then to decimal. 1111011 = 111 1011 = 7B hex = 7×16 + 11 = 123 decimal. You can similarly convert numbers to hex by dividing repeatedly by 16.

Zero and Sign Extension

Suppose we have a one-byte binary number that we want to extend to two bytes (recall that a byte is eight bits). We can do this in two ways. We can add eight zeros on the left or add eight copies of the sign bit on the left. For example, to extend 11111110, we can add eight zeros to get

```
0000000011111110
```

or we can replicate the sign bit (i.e., its leftmost bit) of 11111110 to get

```
1111111111111110
```

The former approach is called *zero extension*; the latter approach, *sign extension*.

If a negative signed number is zero-extended, it changes its value. 11111110 (which is equal to −2) zero-extended to 16 bits is 0000000011111110 (which is equal to +254). If, however, it is sign-extended, its value remains −1.

Rule: Always sign-extend signed numbers.

If an unsigned number with 1 in its leftmost position is sign-extended, its value changes. For example, if the unsigned number 11111110 (254) is sign-extended to 16 bits, we get 1111111111111110 (65534). However, if we zero-extend an unsigned number, its value remains the same.

Rule: Always zero-extend unsigned numbers.

Problems

1) Convert the following unsigned binary numbers to decimal:

    010111110110111, 11111111, 1000000000

2) Convert the binary numbers in the preceding problem to hex.

3) Add 8000 hex (−32768 decimal) and ffff hex (−1 decimal). Represent the computed result using 16 bits. What is the sign of the computed result? What is the sign of the true result? Why is there a discrepancy between the computed result and the true result?

4) What is the range of 12-bit unsigned numbers and 12-bit two's complement signed numbers?

5) What is the range of 5-bit two's complement numbers? 9-bit? 11-bit?

6) Convert the following decimal numbers to binary and hexadecimal:

    1023, 1024, 1025, 255, 16

7) Convert the following hexadecimal numbers to binary:

   5567 ABABAB, F03, 3579BDF, 2468ACE, FCC

8) Convert the following hexadecimal numbers to decimal:

   A0, B0, C0, D0, E0, F0, 400, 10000

9) Add the following pairs of binary numbers: Give your answers in both binary and hex.

```
0111111111111111      0111000111000111      0011111111111111
0000101010101011      0010101010101010      0000000000000001
```

10) Subtract the numbers in the preceding question.

11) Add the following pairs of hexadecimal numbers:

```
0FFFFFFFF             996
000000001             959
```

12) Subtract the numbers in problem 11. Give your answers in both hex and decimal.

13) Write −75 decimal as a 16-bit two's complement binary number.

14) What is the next (and final number) in this sequence: 1000, 22, 20, 13, 12, 11, 10?

15) Convert 0.111 binary to decimal. *Hint*: The weights of the three 1-bits from left to right are 0.5, 0.25, and 0.125 decimal.

16) Convert 0.5 decimal to binary. *Hint*: Multiply repeatedly by 2, removing the whole part after each multiplication. The whole parts make up the binary number.

17) Convert 0.75 decimal to binary. See hint in problem 16.

18) Convert 0.1 decimal to binary. See hint in problem 16.

19) Convert the following octal (base 8) numbers to decimal: 123, 777, 100.

20) Convert the following base 9 numbers to octal (base 8): 123, 777, 100.

2 Machine Language

Introduction

Machine language is the only language the computer hardware can "understand." Thus, if you write a program in any language other than machine language, it first has to be translated to machine language before it can be executed by the computer. A machine language instruction is a binary number. Thus, a machine language program consists of a sequence of binary numbers. The collection of machine instructions a computer supports is called the computer's *instruction set*.

Each type of computer has its own machine language. IBM mainframe computers have one type of machine language. PCs that run Windows have another type of machine language. In this book, we will study the LCC (**L**ow **C**ost **C**omputer). The LCC is a modification and extension of the computer model presented in Patt and Patel's book, *Introduction to Computing Systems*. It is a *microprogrammed computer*. That is, within its central processing unit (CPU), there is a read-only memory, called *microstore*, that contains a *microprogram*. The microprogram consists of a sequence of microinstructions that determines the machine language of the LCC. Thus, by changing the microprogram, we can change the machine instructions that the LCC supports.

With high-level languages like C++, we often refer to the instructions that make up a program as "code." Similarly, we refer to the microinstructions that make up a microprogram as *microcode*. In subsequent chapters you will learn how to write the microcode that defines a machine language instruction set. By doing so, you will gain a clear understanding of the operation of the LCC at the microlevel. In addition, you will get a sense of what constitutes a good instruction set.

All the data, instructions, and addresses inside a computer are in binary. It is hard to read binary (for us—not for the computer), and binary numbers require a lot of space on the printed page. For this reason, in most of this book, we use hexadecimal to represent the binary numbers within the LCC.

Structure of the LCC

The two principal units of the LCC are the *central processing unit* (CPU) and *main memory* (see Fig. 2.1). Within the CPU are the *arithmetic/logic unit* (ALU) and the *control unit*. The ALU is the unit that performs high-speed computations. The control unit is the control center for all the components of the computer. Within the control unit is the microstore that holds the microprogram that determines the machine instruction set. Also, within the CPU are storage areas, called *registers*, named pc (program counter), ac (accumulator), sp (stack pointer), and ir (instruction register). Each of these registers can hold one 16-bit number. The pc (program counter) "points to" the machine instruction in memory to be executed next. The ac register accumulates the results of computations. The sp (stack pointer) register points to the top of the stack that resides in memory. The ir (instruction register) holds the machine instruction that the CPU is executing. We will elaborate on the function of each of these registers shortly.

Memory is an array of $2^{16} = 65536$ cells, each of which can hold one 16-bit number. The memory cells are numbered starting with 0. The number of a cell (i.e., the number that identifies a particular cell) is called the *address* of that cell. The number *inside* the memory cell is the *contents* of that cell.

The *word size* of the LCC is 16 bits. That is, the computational circuits in the CPU of the LCC operate on units of data that are 16 bits wide. For example, the adder circuit in the CPU can add two 16-bit numbers.

In the LCC, each memory cell can hold one word (i.e., 16 bits). For this reason, we say its memory is *word addressable*. That is, successive addresses correspond to successive words. Memory on most computers, however, is *byte addressable*. That is, successive addresses correspond to successive bytes.

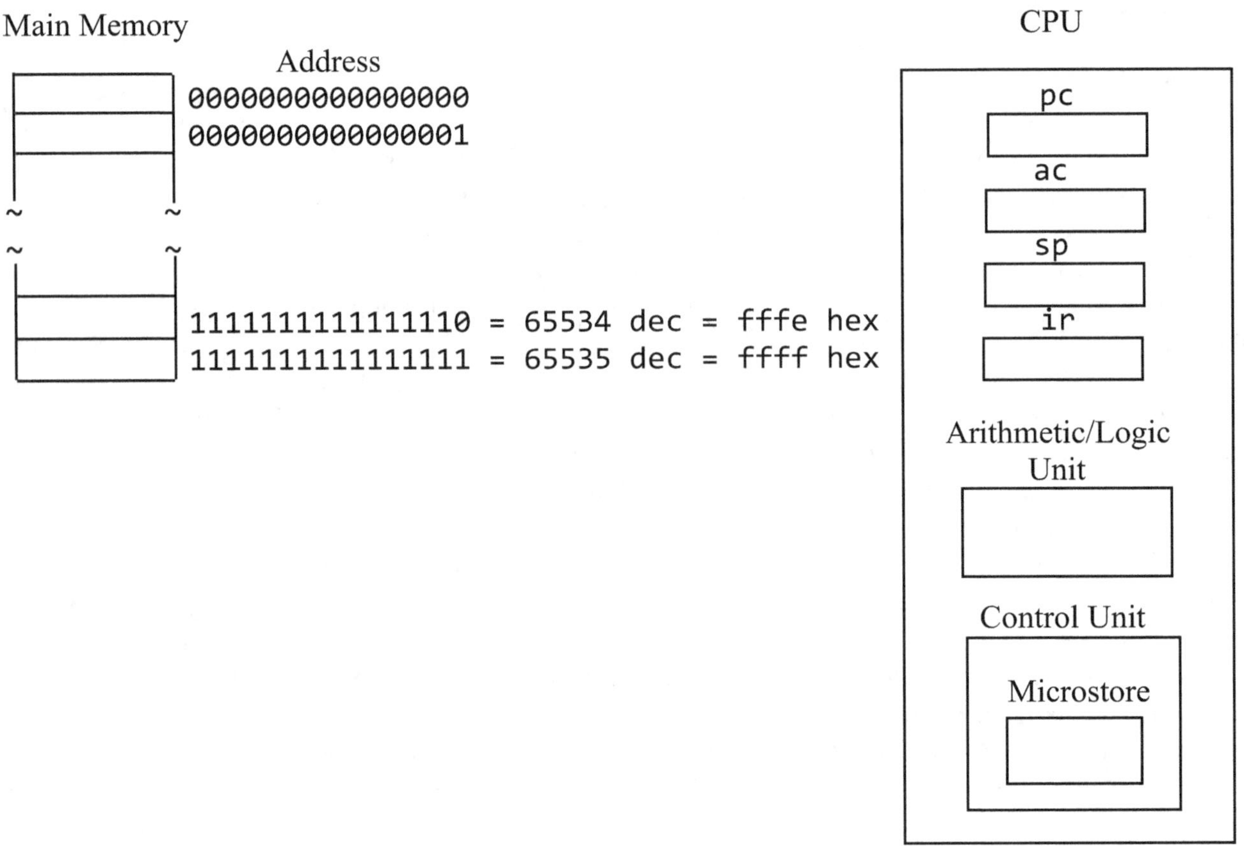

Figure 2.1

To execute a machine language program, the computer user enters a command to the operating system (OS) specifying the name of the file that holds the machine language program. The OS responds by loading the program into memory starting at some address, referred to as the *load point*. To keep our discussion as simple as possible in this introduction, let's assume the load point is 0, and execution always starts at that address.

After the OS loads the program into memory, it loads the pc register with the load point (we are assuming it is the address 0). The CPU then executes the loop in Fig. 2.2 (a *loop* is a sequence of operations that are repeatedly executed). The first time the loop is executed, the pc register contains 0. Thus, in step 1, the CPU fetches the instruction from the memory cell at the address 0 and loads it into the ir. In step 2, it increments the pc register to 1. In step 3, it *decodes* the instruction (i.e., determine its opcode). In step 4, it executes the instruction it fetched in step 1, which is now in the ir. On the next iteration of the loop, the CPU fetches the instruction at the address 1—not 0—because the pc register now contains 1 (because of step 2 in the preceding iteration). Each time the CPU performs step 1, it gets the next instruction from memory because step 2 in the preceding iteration increments the pc register. Thus, the CPU executes instructions one after another in order of memory address. This process continues until a halt or branch machine instruction is executed. A halt machine instruction halts the execution of the program and causes a return to the OS. The branch machine instructions do not halt execution. Instead, they cause the CPU to go to a new location and start executing instructions from there. For example, a branch instruction at address 10 can cause the CPU to go back to address 0 and execute instructions in memory order starting again from there.

1. *Fetch* the instruction the `pc` register "points to." That is, the CPU loads the `ir` with the instruction in the memory cell whose address is in the `pc` register. The CPU does not remove the instruction from its memory cell. Instead, it makes a copy of it. Thus, the contents of the memory cell that the `pc` register points to are unaffected.

2. *Increment* the `pc` register.

3. *Decode* the instruction in the `ir`.

4. *Execute* the instruction in the `ir`.

Figure 2.2

Simple Machine Language Program

As we mentioned above, the microprogram within the CPU determines the set of machine instructions the computer can execute. In this chapter, we will use the LCC with a microprogram that defines an instruction set we call the *basic instruction set*. It is an instruction set that is easy to understand and use. Thus, it is a good instruction set to use as we start to investigate the operation of the LCC.

Let's examine a simple machine language program that uses the basic instruction set. It consists of six instructions, each occupying one word in memory, and three data words. Let's assume this program is loaded into memory starting at the address 0. Here is a description of each word of the program along with its address:

Address (hex)	Description of Instruction
0:	Load a copy of the number in memory at address `0006` into the `ac` register.
1:	Add a copy of the number in memory at address `0007` to the `ac` register.
2:	Store the number in the `ac` register into the memory location at address `0008`.
3:	Display in decimal the number in the `ac` register.
4:	Move the display cursor to the beginning of the next line on the screen.
5:	Halt.
6:	First number (`0002` hex)
7:	Second number (`0003` hex)
8:	Location into which the sum is stored

The instruction at address 0 is a `ld` (load) instruction. Here is the instruction *in binary*:

```
ld opcode   12-bit memory address (006 hex)

0000  000000000110
```

The first four bits (0000) is the *opcode*. The opcode specifies the operation to be performed. 0000 is the opcode for the ld instruction. The next twelve bits—000000000110—zero-extended to 16 bits is the memory address of the number to be loaded into the ac register. When this ld instruction is executed, the CPU loads a copy of the number at this address into the ac register, overlaying whatever is there. The number at the address 0000000000000110 is 0000000000000010. Thus, the ld instruction loads 0000000000000010 into the ac register.

You may find it difficult to read the long binary numbers in the preceding paragraph. So let's describe the action of the ld instruction again, but this time using hex notation: The ld instruction above—0006 in hex—loads the ac register from the memory location at the address 6. This location contains 0002. Thus, the ld instruction loads 0002 into the ac register. The memory location at the address 6 is unaffected.

The next instruction is an add instruction. This instruction adds a copy of the number in the memory location at the address 0007 hex to the ac register:

```
add opcode   12-bit memory address (007 hex)

0010  000000000111
```

The next instruction is a st (store) instruction:

```
st opcode    12-bit memory address

0001  000000001000
```

It contains the st opcode (0001). The remaining 12 bits in the instruction is the address of the memory location into which a copy of the number in the ac register is stored.

The last three instructions in our machine language program are *trap instructions*. When executed, they cause a transfer of control to the OS. The OS then performs some service, depending on the *trap vector* (the rightmost eight bits of the trap instruction). After performing the requested service, the OS returns control to the instruction following the trap instruction unless the trap instruction requests a halt. Here is the sequence of trap instructions we need in our program:

```
opcode                trap vector        dout trap instruction

1111      0000        00000010           nl trap instruction
1111      0000        00000001           halt trap instruction
1111      0000        00000000
```

All the trap instructions have the same opcode (1111). However, the effect of each trap instruction differs and depends on its trap vector. For example, the first trap instruction above (whose vector is 00000010) displays in decimal the number in the ac register. The second trap instruction (whose vector is 00000001) moves the display cursor to the beginning of the next line. The third trap instruction (whose vector is 00000000) terminates the program. To distinguish the various trap instructions, we give each variation a unique name. For example, we give the `trap` instructions whose vectors are 00000010, 00000001, and 00000000 the names `dout` (decimal out), `nl` (new line), and `halt`, respectively.

To complete our program, we need two data numbers (2 and 3) following our six instructions and a third location to receive the sum of the addition:

```
0000000000000010
0000000000000011
0000000000000000
```

Here is the entire machine language program:

Address (hex)	Machine instruction (binary)	
0000	0000000000000110	(ld)
0001	0010000000000111	(add)
0002	0001000000001000	(st)
0003	1111000000000010	(dout)
0004	1111000000000001	(nl)
0005	1111000000000000	(halt)
0006	0000000000000010	(data)
0007	0000000000000011	(data)
0008	0000000000000000	(receives sum)

When executed, this program displays 5 (the sum of the two data words: 2 and 3). To try out this program, we have to create a file that contains the program in binary form. The easiest way to do this is to first create a text file that contains the program in hex form. We can represent each line of the program with a four-digit hex number. For example, the `dout` instruction,

```
1111 0000 0000 0010
```

in hex form is

```
f002
```

Let's create the file that contains the hex version of the program using any text editor—for example, `notepad` (Windows) or `nano` (OS X, Linux, or Raspberry Pi). The file name extension should be ".`hex`". Suppose we create a file named `e0201.hex` that contains the hex version of our program. We get

```
    e0201.hex
┌─────────────────┐
│ 0006   ;  ld    │
│ 2007   ;  add   │
│ 1008   ;  st    │
│ f002   ;  dout  │
│ f001   ;  nl    │
│ f000   ;  halt  │
│ 0002   ;  data  │
│ 0003   ;  data  │
│ 0000   ;  sum   │
└─────────────────┘
```

We have added a comment to each line that describes the contents of that line. A comment starts with a semicolon and extends to the end of the line.

Once we have a file containing the program in hex form, we can translate it to binary using the h2b program (or, equivalently, the hexbin program) in the software package for this book.

To get the latest version of the software package, send an email to cmc2edition@gmail.com You will get an immediate reply with the link to the software. Read 1READFIRST.txt in the software package for instructions on installation and use.

We invoke h2b (and the other programs in the software package for this book) from the *command line*. To get to the command line, start the command prompt program (Windows) or the Terminal program (OS X, Linux, or Raspberry Pi). Position the OS on the directory that contains the software package for this book using the cd command.

To translate e0201.hex to binary, enter on the command line

```
    h2b e0201.hex              (on Windows)
or
    ./h2b e0201.hex            (on Mac OS X, Linux, or Raspberry Pi)
```

h2b will then output the binary form of the program to the file named e0201.e. The output file name is the same as the input file name except for the extension—the output file name has the extension ".e" in place of ".hex". Now that we have our program in binary form, we can run it using the sim program (also in the software package for this book) which simulates the LCC. To run ex0201.e using the sim program, enter

```
    sim e0201.e               (on Windows)
or
    ./sim e0201.e             (on Mac OS X, Linux, and Raspberry Pi)
```

In response, the sim program executes the program in e0201.e and displays the following:

```
sim Simulator Ver 3.0 Copyright (c) 2022 by Anthony J. Dos Reis
Opening machine code file e0201.e
Opening microcode file b.m
Opening log file e0201.log
========================================== output
5


==================================================
Machine code size:            9
Machine instructions executed: 6
Microcode size:               71
Microinstructions executed:   35
```

The output that the machine language program in e0201.e produces appears between the two rows of equal signs. Preceding the output on the display are the names of the files that the sim program uses.

Following the output on the display are some statistics on the run. In this run, we can see that the size of our machine language program is 9, and 6 machine language instructions were executed. Each machine language instruction requires the LCC to execute a number of microinstructions. Thus, although only 6 machine language instructions were executed, 35 microinstructions were executed. The number of microinstructions executed is a measure of the execution time of the program.

The `sim` program also creates a ".log" file that is a record of what is displayed on the display screen. In addition, it includes a list of the source program (i.e., the `e0201.hex`). The ".log" file also includes a time stamp and your name. The first time you run the `sim` program, it will prompt you for your name. Thereafter, it will include your name in the ".log" files it creates.

Load Immediate Instruction

A `ld` instruction loads the `ac` register with a word from memory. Thus, it first fetches that word from memory. Then it loads it into the `ac` register. The `ldi` (load immediate) instruction also loads the `ac` register. But the word it loads comes from within the instruction itself. Thus, the `ldi` instruction does not have to perform the memory fetch operation that the `ld` instruction performs. For example, the following `ldi` instruction contains 000000000010 (002 hex) in its rightmost 12 bits:

$$\text{ldi opcode} \qquad \text{12-bit immediate operand}$$

$$1000 \qquad 000000000010$$

When the CPU executes this instruction, it extracts the 12 rightmost bits, zero-extends it to 16 bits to get 0000000000000010 (0002 hex), and then loads it into the `ac` register. The number loaded is in the instruction itself. Thus, as soon as the instruction is fetched by the CPU and placed in the `ir`, the operand is *immediately* available—it is sitting in the 12 rightmost bits of the `ir`. An operand that is in a machine language instruction is called an *immediate operand* because it is immediately available once the instruction is fetched and placed in the `ir`. The CPU treats the 12-bit immediate operand in a `ldi` instruction as an unsigned number. Thus, it cannot be a negative number. Because its only 12 bits in length, its range is only 0 to 4095 decimal (000 to fff hex).

Let's rewrite the program in `ex0201.hex` so that it uses the `ldi` instruction in place of the `ld` instruction. We get

```
     e0202.hex
8002    ; ldi
2006    ; add
1007    ; st
f002    ; dout
f001    ; nl
f000    ; halt
0003    ; data
0000    ; sum
```

The program is both shorter (because we do not need a data word for 2) and runs faster than the program in `e0201.hex` (because the `ldi` instruction is faster than the `ld` instruction).

Strings

A string in a computer is a sequence of characters, each represented by a code. The code that the LCC uses is ASCII (American Standard Code for Information Interchange). ASCII represents each character with a seven-bit number which is usually zero-extended to 8 bits. Here are the ASCII codes for several characters:

```
'A':   01000001  (41 hex, 65 decimal)
'a':   01100001  (61 hex, 97 decimal)
'B';   01000010  (42 hex, 66 decimal)
'b':   01100010  (62 hex, 98 decimal)
'0':   00110000  (30 hex, 48 decimal)
'1':   00110001  (31 hex, 49 decimal)
' ':   00100000  (20 hex, 32 decimal)
'\n': 00001010  (0A hex, 10 decimal)
'\r': 00001101  (0D hex, 13 decimal)
```

The uppercase letters are assigned numbers in ascending order, starting from 41 hex. The lowercase letters are assigned numbers in ascending order, starting from 61 hex. The code for each uppercase letter differs from the code for the lowercase version in only bit 5: In the uppercase letter, bit 5 is 0; in the lowercase letter, bit 5 is 1. The digits are assigned numbers in ascending order starting from 30 hex. `'\n'` is the *newline character*. `'\r'` is the *return character*. On systems other than Windows, just the `'\n'` character usually marks the end of each line in a text file. On Windows systems, the two-character sequence, `'\r'`, `'\n'`, marks the end of each line of a text file. For example, suppose a text file on a Windows system contains the following text:

```
AB
0 1
```

It is represented with the following sequence of ASCII codes (given in hex):

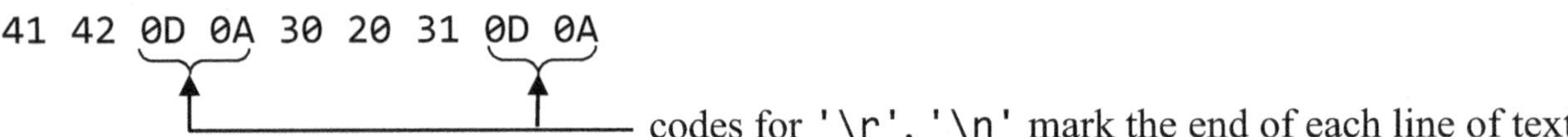

```
41 42 0D 0A 30 20 31 0D 0A
```

codes for `'\r'`, `'\n'` mark the end of each line of text

The newline, return, and space characters are called *whitespace* since they do not produce a displayable character in print on a paper. You see just the white background—hence the name "whitespace."

On the LCC, a string of characters is represented by the sequence of their ASCII codes, each occupying *one word*, followed by the *null character* (the character represented by all zero bits). For example, if the string "AB" is in memory starting at location 200 hex, the locations of memory starting at address 0200 contain the following codes:

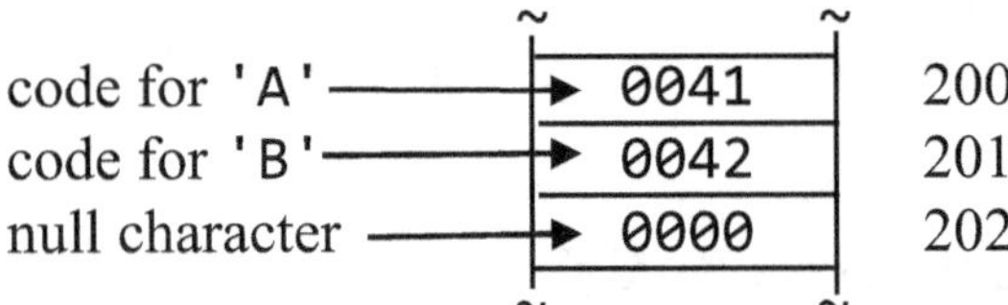

The null character marks the end of the string.

It is a good idea to memorize the ASCII codes for `'A'`, `'0'`, space, `'\n'`, and `'\r'`. That will allow you to quickly identify and decipher strings in their binary or hex representations.

To display a string on the display monitor, we use the `trap` instruction whose trap vector (i.e., the rightmost 8 bits in the `trap` instruction) is 00000110 (06 hex). When this `trap` instruction is executed, the `ac` register should have the address of the first character of the string. The `trap` instruction displays all the characters in memory starting from the address in the `ac` register until it reaches the null character. The name of this particular trap instruction is `sout` (for "string out").

Let's write a program that displays the string "hi\n". The ASCII codes for `'h'`,`'i'` and `'\n'` are 01101000 (68 hex), 01101001 (69 hex), and 00001010 (0a hex), respectively. At the bottom of our program, following the `halt` instruction, we need three words containing these codes followed by the null character. When the `sout` instruction is executed, the `ac` register should contain the address of the string. We use a `ldi` instruction to load the `ac` register with that address:

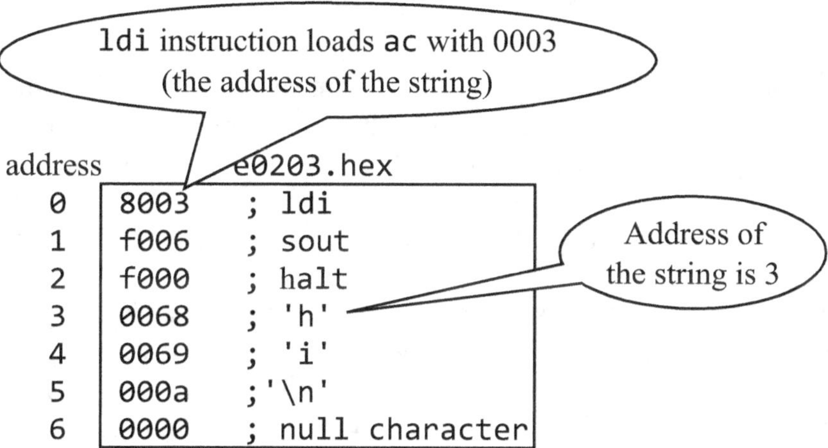

Branch Instructions

Machine instructions are normally executed serially in order of increasing memory address. For example, after the machine instruction at address 0 is executed, the machine instruction at address 1 is executed, then the machine instruction at address 2, and so on. However, a branch instruction can change this execution pattern. It does this by loading a new value (its rightmost 12 bits zero extended) into the `pc` register. Recall from Fig. 2.2, that the CPU executes a loop that repeatedly

1. fetches the instruction that the `pc` register points to
2. increments the `pc` register (so it is pointing to the next instruction in memory)
3. decodes the opcode (i.e., determine the opcode)
4. executes the instruction is just fetched.

Thus, when the `pc` register contains 2, the CPU fetches the instruction that is in memory at address 2 (assume a branch instruction is there), increments the `pc` to 3, and then decodes and executes the branch instruction. However, when the branch instruction is executed, it can change the address in the `pc` register. For example, it could change the address in the `pc` register to 0. Then when the CPU proceeds to fetch the next instruction, it fetches the instruction at address 0—not at address 3—because the `pc` register now contains 0. For example, consider the following program:

immediate operand will be sign extended to 16 bits

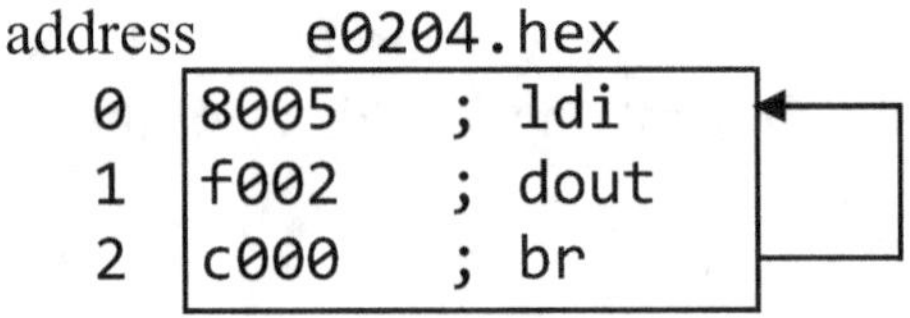

```
1000 000000000101    ; ldi
1111 000000000010    ; dout
1100 000000000000    ; br (unconditional branch)
```

address will be zero-extended to 16 bits

In hex format, it is

```
address    e0204.hex
  0   8005    ; ldi
  1   f002    ; dout
  2   c000    ; br
```

The first instruction (the `ldi` instruction) loads the `ac` register with 5. The second instruction (the `dout` instruction) displays the number in the `ac` register (5) in decimal. The third instruction (the `br` instruction) branches back to the address 0 (by loading the `pc` register with 0). Thus, the three instructions are again executed. Each time the `br` instruction is executed, the CPU branches back to address 0. Thus, the three instructions make up an *infinite* (i.e., never ending) *loop*. Try running this program. You will see it fills the screen with a never-ending stream of 5's.

The `br` instruction is an *unconditional branch*. That is, when it is executed the branch always occurs. The basic instruction set also has two conditional branch instructions: `brz` (branch on zero) and `brn` (branch on negative). The `brz` branches only if the value in the `ac` register is zero. The `brn` instruction branches only if the value in the `ac` register is negative. For example, in the following program, the `ldi` instruction initializes the `ac` register with 3. The first time the `brz` instruction is executed, it does not branch because the value in the `ac` register is not zero. The `dout` instruction then displays 3. The `sub` instruction subtracts 1 (the constant at the address 0006) from the `ac` register. So now the `ac` register contains 2. The `br` instruction then unconditionally branches back to the `brz` instruction. The same sequence of instructions, starting with `brz` instruction, is executed, but this time with 2 in the `ac` register (so 2 is displayed). The sequence is executed a third time with 1 in the `ac` register (so 1 is displayed). However, when the `brz` instruction is executed the fourth time, the `ac` register contains 0. Thus, the `brz` instruction branches to the `halt` instruction, terminating the program. The net effect of the program is to display "321" and then halt.

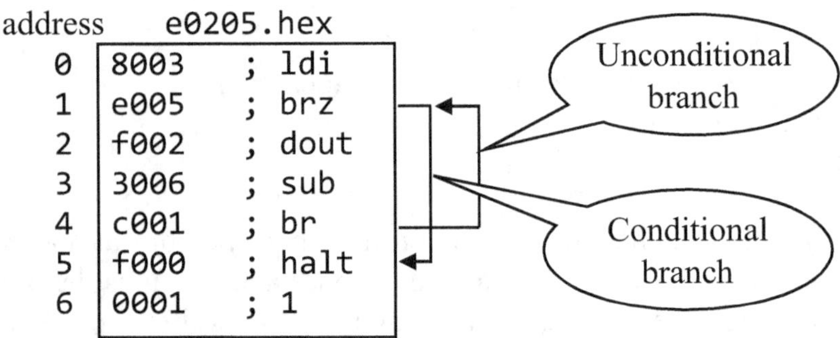


```
address    e0205.hex
  0   8003    ; ldi
  1   e005    ; brz
  2   f002    ; dout
  3   3006    ; sub
  4   c001    ; br
  5   f000    ; halt
  6   0001    ; 1
```

Trap Instructions

We have already seen four trap instructions: dout (decimal out), nl (newline), halt, and sout (string out) corresponding to the trap vectors 02 hex, 01 hex, 00 hex, and 06 hex, respectively. For example, here is the halt trap instruction in binary:

         opcode (f hex)   trap vector (00 hex)

              1111 0000 00000000

This instruction written in hex is f000. The trap instructions for dout, nl, and sout written in hex are f002, f001, and f006, respectively. Here is a complete list of the trap instructions:

Trap instruction	Name	Function
f000	halt	Terminate execution
f001	nl	Output newline to display
f002	dout	Display signed number in ac in decimal
f003	udout	Display unsigned number in ac in decimal
f004	hout	Display number in ac in hex
f005	aout	Display character in ac
f006	sout	Display string ac points to
f007	din	Read decimal number from keyboard into ac
f008	hin	Read hex number from keyboard into ac
f009	ain	Read character from keyboard into ac
f00A	sin	Read in string to address in ac register
f00E	bp	Breakpoint

Let's write a program that reads in a decimal number and displays its value in hex. Here's what you should see on the screen when you run the program if you input the decimal number 30:

```
30
1E
```

A properly designed program should prompt the user before reading in a number so the user is notified that the program is waiting for input. It should also label the output. A session should look like this:

```
Enter decimal number
30
Number in hex = 1E
```

But let's keep our program simple for now by omitting the label on the output and the prompt.

To read in a decimal number into the ac register, we use the din trap instruction. The din (decimal in) instruction reads the decimal number entered on the keyboard, converts it to a 16-bit binary number, and loads it into the ac register. Then to display the number in the ac register in hex, we use the hout trap instruction. It converts the number in the ac register to hex and displays it on the screen. Here is the program:

```
      e0206.hex
┌─────────────────────┐
│ f007    ; din       │
│ f004    ; hout      │
│ f000    ; halt      │
└─────────────────────┘
```

If you run this program, be sure to enter a decimal number after you start it. It does not prompt for the decimal number so the `sim` program will just wait for it indefinitely without giving you any notification that it is waiting for input.

Problems

1) Write and run a machine language program that adds decimal 1, 200, and 500 and displays the sum in decimal and hex each on a separate line.

2) Write and run a machine language program that adds decimal −1, −200, and −500 and displays the sum in decimal and hex each on a separate line.

3) Rewrite and run the program given in `e0206.hex` so that it prompts the user and labels the output.

4) Write and run a machine language program that reads in a character (use `ain`) and displays its ASCII code in decimal and hex. Prompt the user and label the output. Test your program with `'A'`, `'a'`, and `'0'` *Note*: When entering a character in response to the `ain` instruction, do not enclose the character in quotes. Also run your program and do not enter any character. Just immediately hit the Enter key (which inputs the newline character).

5) Write and run a machine language program that reads in a decimal number (use `din`). Output what is read in with `dout`, `udout`, and `hout`. Test your program with −1. Display each value on a separate line.

6) Write and run a machine language program that displays the numbers 1 to 10 each on a separate line. Use a loop.

7) Write and run a machine language program without using `sout` that displays your name.

8) Write and run a machine language program that reads in a positive decimal number and then displays "hello" that number of times each on a separate line.

9) Write and run a machine language program that reads in two decimal numbers and displays "bigger" if the first number is bigger than the second, "equal" if the two numbers are equal, or "smaller" if the first number is smaller than the second. Test you program with 5 and 3, 3 and 5, 3 and 3. Also test your program with 32767 and −1. *Hint*: Subtract and test the result with the `brn` and `brz` instructions.

10) Write and run a machine language program the computes and displays the sum of the first 15 positive odd numbers. Label the output.

3 Assembly Language

Introduction

Assembly language is a symbolic form of machine language. An assembly language instruction consists of symbols that represent the binary fields of a machine language instruction. Because it is symbolic, assembly language is easier to read, write, modify, and debug.

Here is a machine language program from chapter 2 (it loads the `ac` register from address 6, adds from address 7, stores the sum at address 8, and displays the sum in the `ac` register). Next to the machine language program is its corresponding assembly language program (which is in the file `e0301.a`). Note that for files containing an assembly language program, we use the file name extension "`.a`":

<table>
<tr><td colspan="2" align="center">Machine Language
Program</td><td colspan="2" align="center">Corresponding
Assembly Language program
<code>e0301.a</code></td></tr>
</table>

```
0000000000000110           ld x      ; load ac with value at x
0010000000000111           add y     ; add value at y to ac
0001000000001000           st z      ; store value in ac at z
1111000000000010           dout      ; display value in ac in decimal
1111000000000001           nl        ; move cursor to next line
1111000000000000           halt      ; stop execution
0000000000000010     x:    .word 2   ; data
0000000000000011     y:    .word 3   ; data
0000000000000000     z:    .word 0   ; data
```

If a semicolon appears in a line of an "`.a`" file, everything from the semicolon to the end of that line is a comment. A *comment* is information simply for our edification—it does not contribute to the specification of the program.

Consider the first instruction—the `ld` instruction—in the two programs above. The assembly language program uses "`ld`" in place of the binary opcode 0000. We call the names like `ld` that we use in place of opcodes *mnemonics* because they are easy to remember ("mnemonic" means "aiding memory"). In place of the address in the `ld` machine language instruction, we use the label x. Think of x as a symbolic address. It represents the address of the line in the program that starts with the label x:

```
x:          .word 2
```

The directive `.word 2` indicates that 2 in binary should completely occupy the memory location corresponding to this line. That is, the corresponding word in the machine language program should contain 0000000000000010. We do not call `.word` a mnemonic because it is not the name of an opcode. Instead, we call it a *directive* because it directs us to do something when translating the program—namely, to replace the line with the specified data converted to binary.

In place of the address in the `add` instruction, we use the label y, which represents the address of the line that starts with the label y. That line has a `.word` directive that "fills" the memory location corresponding to that line with 3 in binary.

Rule: Mnemonics and directives but not labels are *case insensitive*. That is, they can be in either upper or lower case in an assembly language program. Thus, add and ADD are equivalent but the labels x and X are not.

Rule: A label must start in column 1 unless it is followed by a colon. Mnemonics and directives can start in any column except column 1. Comments can start in any column.

In a .word directive (or equivalently, a .fill directive), we can specify a number in decimal or hex, (hex constants start with "0x"), a character constant (a character within single quotes), or a label. A character constant is translated to its ASCII code. A label is translated to its corresponding 16-bit address. For example, if the following statements appear in a program, and the address of the line that starts with the label b is 0124 hex, then the memory location corresponding to the line that starts with the d label would contain 0000000100100100 (0124 hex).

```
a:          .word 3     ; translated to 0000000000000011 (3 in binary)
b:          .word 0xf1  ; translated to 0000000011110001 (f1 hex in binary)
c:          .word 'A'   ; translated to 0000000001000001 (ASCII code for 'A')
d:          .word b     ; translated to the addr of line that starts with b
```

One of the great benefits of using labels in place of addresses is that insertions and deletions do not require any changes in labels. For example, suppose we want the modify the programs in e0301.a so that it displays the computed sum in both decimal and hex. In the assembly language program, we simply insert

```
        hout        ; displays value in ac in hex
        nl          ; move cursor to next line
```

just before the halt instruction. No other changes are required. But in the machine language program, the insertion of the machine language instructions hout and nl *changes the addresses of the three data words* at the bottom of the program. Thus, the addresses in the ld, add, and st instructions have to be adjusted so that they correspond to the new addresses of the data. In a large program with many instructions that address the data, a *single insertion or deletion might require hundreds of additional modifications* to correct for the altered addresses of the data. Clearly, this would be a clerical nightmare.

Assembly language instructions that have label operands can be written with the actual addresses specified in decimal or hex in place of the label operands. For example, the ld instruction in e0301.a can be written this way:

```
    ld 6      ; load the value at address 6
```

instead of this way:

```
    ld x      ; load the value at the label x
```

These instructions are translated by the assembler to the same machine code. However, if we use addresses instead of labels, we incur the problem of having to adjust the addresses if we make insertions or deletions in the program, or if the load point of the program is not zero. For this reason, we will always use label operands rather than addresses.

Rule: A label must start with "_", "$", or "@", or a letter. After the first character, the digits 0 to 9 are allowed in addition to "_", "$", "@", and letters.

Assembly language is not machine language. It cannot be executed directly by the CPU. Before an assembly language program can be executed, it must be translated to machine language. It is tedious but not difficult to translate assembly language programs to machine language by hand. But an easier and more reliable approach is to use a program—called an *assembler*—to do the translation for us. The `basic` program (or equivalently, the `b` program) in the software package for this book is an assembler for the basic instruction set. To assemble the program in `e0301.a`, start the command line program (the `command prompt` program on Windows or the `Terminal` program on the Mac, Linux, and Raspberry Pi systems). Next position your system on the folder that contains the software package for this book (use the `cd` command to do this). Then enter on the command line

```
        basic e0301.a            (on Windows)
or
        ./basic e0301.a          (on OS X, Linux, or Raspberry Pi)
```

The assembly process consists of two passes over the program in the input file. During the second pass, the machine code is outputted to the file `e0301.e`. This file has the extension ".e" (which indicates the file holds an executable machine language program) and the same base name as the input file.

The `basic` program also produces a ".lst" file with the same base name as the input file. Thus, for the input file `e0301.a`, it produces the file `e0301.lst`. This file contains the *source program* (i.e., the program we start with—that is, the assembly language program) along with the corresponding machine code and addresses in hex format.

To run the executable program in `e0301.e` produced by the `basic` assembler, we use the `sim` program (in the software package for this book). To run `sim`, on the command line specify `sim` and the name of the executable file produced by the `basic` assembler:

```
sim e0301.e                 (on Windows)
   or
./sim e0301.e               (on OS X, Linux, or Raspberry Pi)
```

When `sim` is invoked, you will see on the display screen

```
sim Simulator Ver 3.0 Copyright (c) 2022 by Anthony J. Dos Reis
Opening machine code file e0301.e
Opening microcode file b.m
Opening log file e0301.log
======================================== output
5


==================================================
Machine code size                 =       9 (dec)
Machine instructions executed =       6 (dec)
Microcode size                    =      71 (dec)
Microinstructions executed     =      35 (dec)
Load point                        =       0 (hex)
```

The first few lines displayed by sim indicate the files it is using or creating. Notice that for this example, sim is using the microcode file b.m. This is the microcode file that defines the basic instruction set. Any executable file created by the basic assembler will trigger sim to use the microcode in b.m. sim determines the microcode to use from the first character in the executable file. This character is the *file signature* which identifies the type of the file. For executable files that contain machine code in the basic instruction set, the file signature is the letter "b" (62 hex). When sim inputs an executable file whose signature is "b", its uses the microcode file with the base name "b" and the extension ".m" (i.e., b.m), which contains the microcode for the basic instruction set. In subsequent chapters, we will study the stack, register, and optimal instruction sets. The file signatures for executable files that use these instruction sets are "s", "r", and "o", respectively, which trigger sim to use the microcode files s.m, r.m, and o.m , respectively, for those instruction sets.

sim also produces a ".log" file with the same base name as the input file but with the extension ".log" that contains a time-stamped record of what you see on the display when you run sim. In addition, the ".log" file contains a copy of the ".lst" file created by sim. Thus, it contains everything your instructor needs to evaluate your program. Here is the e0301.lst file produced by the basic assembler which is appended to the ".log" file created by sim when it executes e0301.e:

Note: Header, Addr, and Code numbers are in hex

```
basic Assembler Ver 3.0   Fri Feb 25 15:45:41 2022
DosReis Anthony J.


Header
b
A 0000
A 0001
A 0002
C


Addr   Code           Source Code


0000   0006               ld x     ; load ac with value at x
0001   2007               add y    ; add value at y to ac
0002   1008               st z     ; store sum in ac in z
0003   f002               dout     ; display value in ac in decimal
0004   f001               nl       ; move cursor to next line
0005   f000               halt     ; stop execution
0006   0002 x:            .word 2  ; data
0007   0003 y:            .word 3  ; data
0008   0000 z:            .word 0  ;
```

Load Immediate Instruction (ldi)

In an assembly language `ldi` instruction, the immediate operand can be a decimal, hex, or character constant, or a label. For example, consider the following program (*Note*: Numbers to the left are the hex addresses of each line, and they are not part of the program):

```
; e0302.a    ( addresses in hex )
0              ldi 15    ; immediate operand is 00f in hex
1              dout      ; displays 15
2              ldi 0xf   ; "0x" prefix so immed operand specified in hex
3              dout      ; displays 15
4              ldi 'A'   ; immediate operand is 041 hex (ASCII code for 'A')
5              hout      ; displays 41
6              dout      ; displays 65
7              aout      ; displays A
8              ldi x     ; immediate operand is 009 hex (address of x)
9              dout      ; displays 11 (the address of x)
a              halt
b x:           .word 5   ; address of this word in b hex, 11 decimal
```

In the first `ldi` instruction, the operand is a decimal constant. The assembler puts this constant in binary form into the immediate field (the 12 rightmost bits) of the `ldi` machine instruction. Because the immediate field is 12 bits wide, it can accommodate constants in the range of 0 to 4095 decimal (0 to fff hex).

In the second `ldi` instruction, the immediate operand is prefixed with "`0x`". This prefix indicates the operand is a hex number. Both the first and second `ldi` instructions are translated to the machine instruction 1000000000001111 (`800f` in hex)

In the third `ldi` instruction, the operand is a character constant. It is translated to its ASCII code. Thus, the immediate field of this instruction contains 000001000001 (041 hex), the ASCII code for the letter A. When executed, this `ldi` instruction loads the `ac` register with the value in its immediate field, zero-extended to 16 bits. Thus, it loads the `ac` register with 0000000001000001 (0041 hex), the ASCII code for A. The `hout` (hex out) and `dout` (decimal out) instructions at addresses 5 and 6 then display, respectively, 41 and 65 (65 is the decimal equivalent of 41 hex). The `aout` instruction at address 7 displays the character whose ASCII code is in the `ac` register. Thus, it displays the letter A.

In the fourth `ldi` instruction, the operand is a label. The assembler always translates labels to their corresponding addresses. Thus, x is translated to 00000000101b (00b hex), which is the address of x. Thus, this `ldi` instruction loads the address of x into the `ac` register.

.zero and .string Directives

In addition to the `.word` directive, two directives that we will use frequently are `.zero` (or equivalently, `.blkw`) and `.string` (or equivalently, `.stringz` or `.asciz`). The `.zero` directive reserves and initializes to zero a block of words in memory. For example, the following `.zero` directive reserves and initializes 100 words in memory:

```
buffer:     .zero 100          ; 100 is a decimal constant
   or
buffer:     .zero 0x64         ; 0x64 is a hex constant
```

Either one of these `.zero` directives is equivalent to

```
buffer:     .word 0  ⎫
            .word 0  ⎬  100 .word directives
              ⋮      ⎭
            .word 0
```

If a program inputs a string from the keyboard, it must have a memory area big enough to receive the string. We call a memory area in a program that receives data on an input operation or provides data on an output operation a *buffer*. If the maximum length of an inputted string is *n*, then the buffer should be at least *n*+1 words long (the "+1" is for the null character at the end of the string). Thus, the buffer defined above can accommodate strings with lengths up to 99 characters.

We use the `.string` directive to create a null-terminated string. For example, the `.string` directive

```
greeting: .string "Hello, world"
```

creates the sequence of ASCII codes corresponding to the characters in the string followed by the null character. Recall that the null character is a word that contains zero. The "z" (for zero) at the end of the directive `.asciz` (an often-used equivalent of `.string`) is an indication that this directive creates a string with a zero word (i.e., the null character) at the end. Recall that a character constant is delimited with *single* quotes (for example, `'A'`). Note that string constants are delimited with *double* quotes.

Let's now write an assembly language program that reads in a string from the keyboard and echoes it to the display. We will use the `sout` trap instruction (to display a prompt message and to echo the inputted string) and the `sin` trap instruction (to input the string). For both instructions, the `ac` register must have the appropriate address: For the `sout` instruction, the `ac` register must have the address of the string to be displayed; for the `sin` instruction, the `ac` register must have the address of the buffer that is to receive the string. We will use the `ldi` instruction to load the `ac` register with the required addresses.

```
 ; e0303.a    ⟨ addresses in hex ⟩
 0            ldi prompt         ; load ac with addr of prompt message
 1            sout               ; display prompt message
 2            ldi buffer         ; load ac with addr of buffer
 3            sin                ; read string from keyboard into buffer
 4            sout               ; echo string to display
 5            halt
 6 prompt:    .string "Enter string\n"
14 buffer:    .zero 100          ; 100 word buffer
```

The addresses on the left are not part of the program. The addresses are in hex so that last line is at address 14 hex (20 decimal). We list the address of each line in our program listings so we can easily refer to specific lines in the program. The assembler translates "prompt" in the `ldi` instruction to its corresponding address (006). Thus, 006 is the immediate value in the first `ldi` instruction. When the `ldi` instruction is then executed, its immediate value is zero-extended to 0006 and loaded into the `ac` register.

Thus, the `ac` register receives 0006, which is the address of the prompt message created by the `.string` directive.

The `sout` instruction displays the message whose address is in the `ac` register (0006), which prompts the user to enter a string. The `ldi` instruction at address 2 loads the `ac` register with the address of the 100-word buffer created with the `.zero` directive. The `sin` instruction then reads in a string entered on the keyboard into memory starting at that address. After the `sin` instruction is executed, the address of the buffer is still in the `ac` register. Thus, when the `sout` instruction at address 4 is executed, it echoes the string just inputted to the display. For example, if "hello" is entered on the keyboard when this program is run, the program will echo back the string entered. Thus, you will see on the screen two occurrences of "hello":

```
hello
hello
```

Branch Instructions and Loops

Instructions are normally executed in memory order. For example, after the instruction at address 0000 is executed, the instruction at address 0001 is executed, then the instruction at 0002, and so on. However, a branch instruction can alter this pattern of instruction execution. When executed, a branch instruction can load the `pc` register with an address, causing the CPU to "branch" to that address (recall the `pc` holds the address of the instruction to be executed next). For example, if the branch instruction at address 0000 loads the `pc` register with 0030, then the next instruction the CPU executes will be the instruction at the address 0030—not the instruction at 0001.

In assembly language, a branch instruction consists of the mnemonic that specifies the opcode and the label on the line of code to branch to. For example, the following branch instruction branches to the line of code that starts with the label "`sub`":

```
br sub
```

Recall that in addition to the unconditional branch instruction `br`, there are the conditional branch instructions: branch on negative (`brn`) and branch on zero (`brz`). The conditional branch instructions branch depending on the value in the `ac` register. For example, the `brz` instruction branches if the value in the `ac` register is zero. If the value in the `ac` register is not zero, then execution continues with the instruction in memory that physically follows the `brz` instruction.

Here is the looping program in `e0205.hex` in hex form from chapter 2 along with its assembly language equivalent in `e0304.a`:

```
address     e0205.hex                              e0304.a
   0   | 8003   ; ldi   |                 ldi 3       ; init ac with 3
   1   | e005   ; brz   |      loop:      brz done    ; branch when ac = 0
   2   | f002   ; dout  |                 dout        ; display value in ac
   3   | 3006   ; sub   |                 sub @1      ; subtract 1 from ac
   4   | c001   ; br    |                 br loop     ; branch back to loop
   5   | f000   ; halt  |      done:      halt        ; stop execution
   6   | 0001   ; 1     |      @1:        .word 1     ; constant 1
```

The `ldi` instruction initializes the `ac` register with 3. Each pass through the loop displays the value in the `ac` register and then decrements it by 1. At the beginning of the fourth pass through the loop, the `ac` register contains 0. Thus, on the fourth pass, the `brz` instruction at address 1 branches to the `halt` instruction at the label `done`. This program displays "321".

The label `@1` in `e0304.a` is a legal label (recall that labels can start with @, $, _, or a letter). Alternatively, we could have used the label `x` in place of `@1`. But `@1` is better because it indicates the constant at that label. When we see the label `@1` in an instruction, we know immediately that it labels a `.word` directive with the constant 1. We do not have to search for its `.word` directive (a time-consuming process in a big program) to determine its corresponding constant. Labels on `.word` directives with non-negative constants should be prefixed with "@". Labels on `.word` directives with negative constants should be prefixed with "@_". We cannot use a minus sign within a label. In its place, we use the underscore character. For example, the `.word` directive for −5 should be

```
@_5:        .word −5
```

Accessing the Stack

A *stack* is a linear data structure that is accessed from one side only. The side accessed is called the *top* of the stack. The operation that adds an item to the top of the stack is called a *push*; the operation that removes the item on top of the stack is called a *pop*.

In an assembly language program, the stack is located at the top of memory (i.e., starting at the address 65535 decimal). As items are pushed onto the stack, the stack grows in the downward direction (i.e., toward locations with smaller addresses). Thus, on a push, the address of the top of the stack decreases by one; on a pop the address increases by one. To keep track of the top of the stack, we use `sp` register. It always "points to" (i.e., contains the address of) the top of the stack.

When several items have been pushed onto the stack, we frequently want to access them without popping them. We do this with the relative instructions (`ldr`, `str`, `addr`, and `subr`). For example, suppose the stack and the `sp` register are configured as follows:

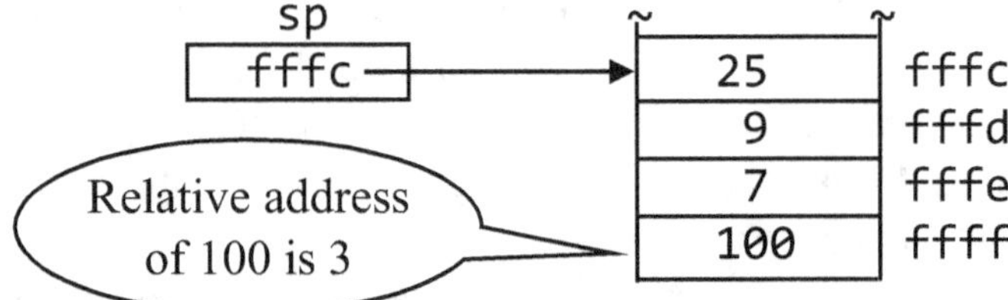

25 is in the location `sp` points to. Thus, its relative address (i.e., its address relative to the location `sp` points to) is 0. The value 9 has the relative 1 because it is one word higher in memory than the location `sp` points to. Similarly, 7 has the relative address 2, and 100 has the relative address 3. To load the `ac` register with the word at relative address 3, we use a `ldr` instruction in which specify the relative address 3:

```
ldr  3
```

To then add the value at relative address 2 (which is 7), we use

```
addr 2
```

To then subtract the value in at relative address 1 (which is 9), we use

```
subr 1
```

To then store the value in the `ac` register into the location corresponding to relative address 0, we use

```
str 0
```

This instruction stores $100 + 7 - 9 = 98$ into the location that `sp` points to, overlaying the 25 that is there.

Sometimes we want to reserve some slots on the stack into which we later store values. To do that, we simply decrement the value in `sp` using the `asp` instruction. For example, to reserve two slots on the stack, we use

```
asp -2
```

This instruction adds the value it specifies (−2 in this example) to the address in the `sp` register. Thus, its effect is to decrement the address in the `sp` register by 2, thereby reserving two slots on the stack. The stack then looks like this:

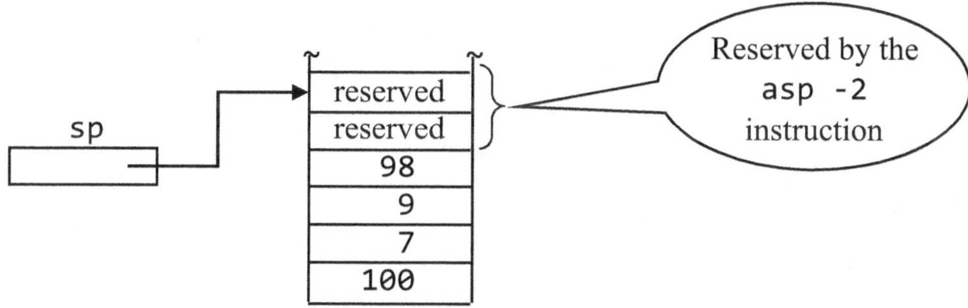

We now have two reserved locations on the stack that we can use later. We can now store values in them. For example, to store 11 in the lower reserved location (the one that `sp` points to), we use

```
ldi 11       ; load the ac register with 11
str 0        ; store it at relative address 0
```

Note that by reserving two slots on the stack, the relative addresses on each item on the stack increase by two. For example, the relative address of 100 is now 5. Before reserving the two slots, it was 3.

The CPU treats the 12-bit field in the `asp` instruction as a *signed* number. Thus, it can hold numbers from −2048 to +2047 decimal. We use a negative number in an `asp` instruction to reserve words on the stack; we use positive numbers to remove items on the stack. For example, to reserve 10 words, use

```
asp -10
```

To remove the top 10 items from a stack, use

```
asp 10
```

Calling Subroutines

A *subroutine* is a segment of code in a program that performs a specific task. It is executed when an instruction in the program *calls* it. When finished performing its task, a subroutine executes a *returning instruction* that loads the pc register with the address of the instruction in memory that follows the calling instruction, causing the CPU to return to the calling module and execute instructions from there:

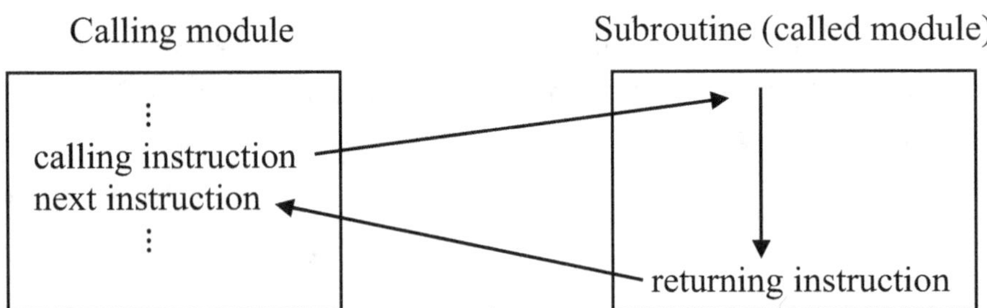

We refer to the module that contains the calling instruction the *caller* or the *calling module* and the subroutine as the *called module.*

The calling instruction causes the CPU to branch to the subroutine (by loading the pc register with the address of the beginning of the subroutine). But it also saves the address of the instruction that follows the calling instruction. This address—the *return address*—is needed by the returning instruction. When executed, the returning instruction loads the return address into the pc register, causing a return to the instruction that follows the calling instruction in the calling module.

The calling instruction in the basic instruction set is the `call` instruction. Here is the call instruction that calls a subroutine that starts with the label `sub`:

```
call sub
```

Recall from the preceding chapter that before the CPU executes an instruction, it increments the pc register. Thus, when a `call` instruction is executed, the pc register has the address of the next instruction. This address in the pc *is the return address*. The `call` instruction saves this address by pushing it onto the stack. After the `call` instruction saves the return address on the stack, it loads the pc register with the address of the subroutine (which is in the rightmost 12 bits of the `call` instruction), which causes the CPU to branch to the subroutine. When the subroutine subsequently executes the `ret` (return) instruction, the `ret` instruction pops the return address off the stack and into the pc register, causing a branch back to the caller—specifically to the instruction that follows the `call` instruction.

Let's look at a program that consists of a main module and a subroutine. The main module calls the subroutine twice. The subroutine displays "hello" and returns to the main module. Here is the program:

```
  ; e0305.a
0 main:      call sub        ; saves return addr (0001) and branches to sub
1           call sub         ; saves return addr (0002) and branches to sub
2           halt
3 ;================  comment does not occupy space in memory
3 sub:       ldi msg
4           sout
5           ret              ; pop return addr into pc
6 msg:       .string "hello\n"
```

Note that the return address for the first call of `sub` is the address of the second call. For the second call of `sub`, the return address is the address of the `halt` instruction. When executed, this program displays "hello" twice, once for each call of `sub`. Note that the label on the subroutine, `sub`, is also the mnemonic for the subtract instruction. However, this use of `sub` does not cause a problem. The assembler determines from the way `sub` is used that it is a label rather than the subtract instruction mnemonic.

The *entry point* of a program is the location in a program where execution should start. By default, the entry point of a program is the physical beginning of the program. If, however, the entry point is not the physical beginning of a program, we must specify it with a `.start` directive. For example, suppose we reverse the order of the `main` and `sub` modules in the preceding program. We get

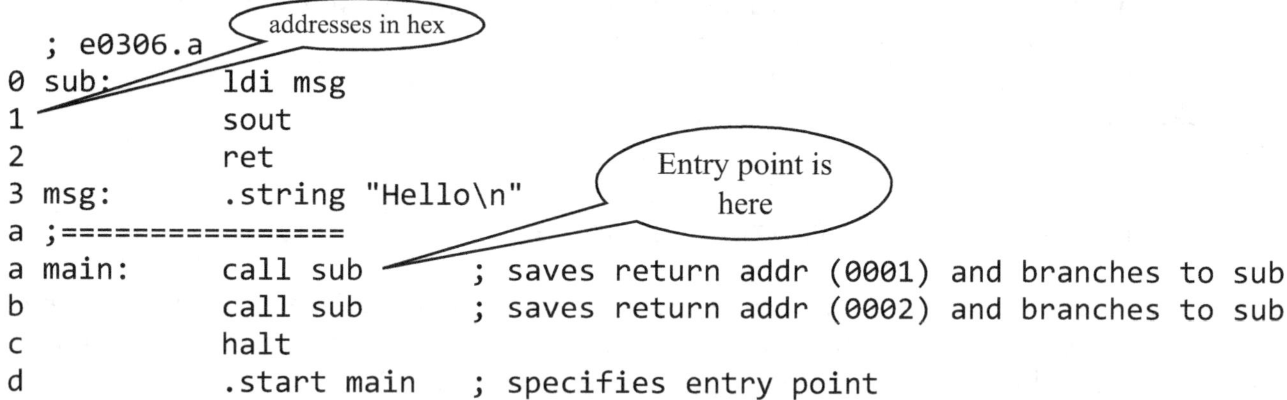


```
  ; e0306.a
0 sub:          ldi msg
1               sout
2               ret
3 msg:          .string "Hello\n"
a ;=================
a main:         call sub     ; saves return addr (0001) and branches to sub
b               call sub     ; saves return addr (0002) and branches to sub
c               halt
d               .start main  ; specifies entry point
```

Because the entry point is `main`, and `main` is not at the physical beginning of the program, we have to indicate the entry point with a `.start` directive. The `.start` directive at the end of the program,

```
        .start main
```

indicates that the entry point of the program is at the label `main`.

A `.start` directive can appear anywhere in the program. For example, it can appear between the two `call` instructions in the program above. A `.start` directive is not translated to machine code. Thus, if we place the `.start` directive in between the two `call` instructions in the program above, the two `call` instructions would still be right next to each other in memory.

Passing Arguments Via the Stack

Let's now write a program that consists of a `main` function and a subroutine. The `main` function passes two arguments, 9 and 8, to the subroutine via the stack. The subroutine accesses them on the stack, subtracts 8 from 9, leaving the difference in the `ac` register. On return to the main function, `main` removes the two arguments from the stack and then displays the difference returned in the `ac` register. Here is the program:

```
; e0307.a          ( addresses in hex )
0 main:         asp -1     ; 3 inst sequence that pushes 9 onto the stack
1               ldi 9
2               str 0
3               asp -1     ; 3 inst sequence that pushes 8 onto the stack
4               ldi 8
5               str 0
6               call sub   ; call sub (push return address and branch to sub)
7               asp 2      ; remove parameters from stack
8               dout       ; display value in ac returned by sub
9               nl         ; move cursor to the next line
a               halt
b ;====================
b sub:          ldr 2      ; load 9
c               subr 1     ; subract 8 from 9
d               ret        ; return with 1 in ac register
```

The three-instruction sequence that starts at address 0 pushes 9 onto the stack. The `asp` instruction reserves one word on the stack, the `ldi` instruction loads the `ac` register with 9, and the `str` instruction stores the value in the `ac` register into the reserved slot on the stack. At addresses 3, 4, and 5, we repeat to sequence but with the constant 8. The `call` instruction at address 6 pushes the return address (0007) in the `pc` register onto the stack and then branches to the subroutine. On entry into the subroutine, the stack looks like this:

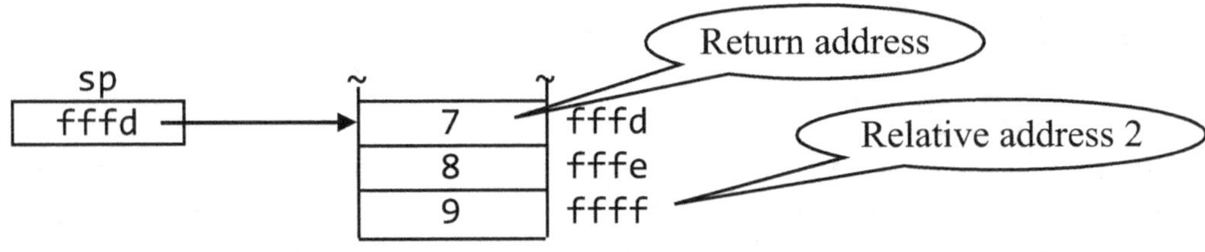

The relative address of 9 is 2; the relative address of 8 is 1. Thus, the instructions

```
ldr 2
subr 1
```

load the `ac` register with 9 and then subtracts 8 from it. Thus, when the `ret` instruction is executed, the difference 1 is in the `ac` register.

The `ret` instructions pops the return address off the stack into the `pc` register, causing a return to the `asp` instruction at the address 7. The `asp` instruction pops the two parameters previously pushed onto the stack by adding 2 to the `sp` register. `main` then displays the value in the `ac` register (1), moves the cursor to the beginning of the next line, and then terminates.

Note that the calling function (`main` in this program) creates the parameters passed to the subroutine by pushing 9 and 8 onto the stack. It is the responsibility of the calling function to ultimately remove these parameters. It does so immediately after the subroutine returns to the calling function.

Basic Instruction Set Summary

Opcode	Format		Description
0	ld	x	ac = mem[x];
1	st	x	mem[x] = ac;
2	add	x	ac = ac + mem[x];
3	sub	x	ac = ac - mem[x];
4	ldr	x	ac = mem[sp + x];
5	str	x	mem[sp + x] = ac;
6	addr	x	ac = ac + mem[sp + x];
7	subr	x	ac = ac - mem[sp + x];
8	ldi	x	ac = x;
9	asp	s	sp = sp + s;
a	call	x	mem[--sp] = pc; pc = x;
b	ret		pc = mem[sp++];
c	br	x	pc = x;
d	brn	x	if (ac == 0) pc = x;
e	brz	x	if (ac < 0) pc = x;
f	trap	y	see below

halt	or	trap 0	Terminate program
nl	or	trap 1	Output newline character
dout	or	trap 2	Output number in ac as signed decimal
udout	or	trap 3	Output number in ac as unsigned decimal
hout	or	trap 4	Output number in ac in hex
aout	or	trap 5	Output character in ac
sout	or	trap 6	Output string pointed to by ac
din	or	trap 7	Input decimal number into ac
hin	or	trap 8	Output hex number into ac
ain	or	trap 9	Input character into ac
sin	or	trap 10	Input string to address in ac
bp	or	trap 14	Breakpoint

x: bits 0 to 11 in machine instruction zero-extended to 16 bits
s: bits 0 to 11 in machine instruction sign-extended to 16 bits
y: bits 0 to 7 in machine instruction zero-extended to 16 bits
ac: accumulator register
pc: program counter register
sp: stack pointer register

Directives: .word/.fill, .zero/.blkw, .string/.stringz/.asciz, .start

This summary is also in Appendix B and in the file basicInstructionSet.pdf in the software package. You may find it helpful to print out this file and have it handy as you write programs using the basic instruction set. The summary gives the opcode in hex, the format, and a description of each instruction.

In the summary of the basic instruction set, we let x represent the unsigned number in the 12 rightmost bits in the instructions like ld and st, and we view memory as an array named mem. We can then describe the action of instructions using C-like statements. For example, the effect of the ld instruction is described with the following C-like assignment statement:

```
ac = mem[x];
```

which indicates that a ld instruction "assigns" the word at the address x in memory to the ac register. In these descriptions, x represents an unsigned number. But s represents a signed number—the signed number in the 12 rightmost bits of the asp instruction. Thus, s can be any number from −2048 to +2047. y represents the unsigned number in the eight rightmost bits of the trap instruction.

The call instruction pushes the address in the pc register onto the stack before it loads the pc register with a new address. This push operation can be succinctly captured using our C-like notation. In a push operation, the sp register is first decremented. It is then used to provide the address of the memory location into which the pc is stored. Here is the C-like notation that captures this sequence of operations:

```
mem[--sp] = pc;        // push pc
```

In this statement, the decrement operator "−−" precedes "sp." It indicates that the sp register is decremented *before* the address it contains is used in the memory store operation.

The ret instruction can similarly be described using our C-like notation:

```
pc = mem[sp++];        // pop into pc
```

The increment operator, "++", follow the sp register. It indicates that the sp register is incremented *after* the address it contains is used to access memory. The ret instructions performs a pop operation.

Little Endian Versus Big Endian

The *word size* of the LCC is 16 bits. That is, its computational circuits operate on 16-bit units of data. For example, its ALU in one operation can add two 16-bit numbers. It is possible to add longer numbers on the LCC, but that would require multiple add operations.

The size of the registers in a computer typically matches the word size of a computer. The LCC with a word size of 16 bits has registers that hold 16-bit numbers. A computer with a 32-bit word size would likely have registers that hold 32-bit numbers.

The word size of most computers today is 32 bits, or more recently, 64 bits. Moreover, unlike the LCC, they have *byte-addressable* main memories—that is, each byte has a distinct address. Thus, the first byte has the address 0, the second byte has the address 1, and so on. In contrast, on the LCC, the first word has the address 0, the second *word* has the address 1, and so on. The address 1 on the LCC corresponds to the second word—not the second byte.

For computers that have byte-addressable main memories, there is more than one way in which the contents of a register can be stored in main memory. For example, suppose on a computer with a 32-bit word size, a 32-bit binary number in a register is to be stored in its byte-addressable memory. To accommodate the four bytes in the register, four consecutive bytes in main memory are required. One way that is commonly used is to store the bytes in the register is from the "little end" (i.e., the rightmost byte) to the "big end" (i.e., the leftmost byte). The other common way of storing the four bytes in a register is to store them from the "big end" to the "little end." We call a computer that uses the former approach a *little-endian computer*; a computer that uses the latter approach, a *big-endian computer*. For example, suppose a register contains the 32-bit number 0001 0010 0011 0100 0101 0110 0111 1000 (12345678 hex). Here is how the number in the register is stored in main memory at the addresses 1001 to 1004 on the two types of computers:

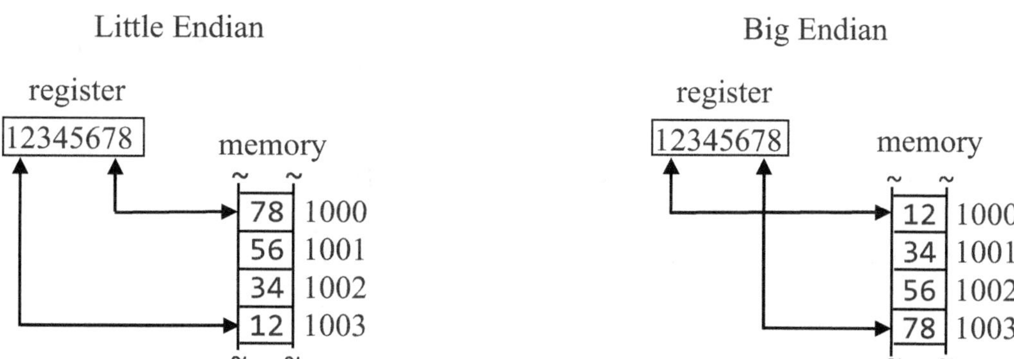

When the four-byte number that starts at address 1000 in the above diagram is written to a file, it is written in the order in which it is in memory. Thus, the four-byte number on a little-endian computer would appear as 78563412 in the file. Note that it is *in backwards order*. In contrast, on a big-endian computer, it would appear in its normal order: 12345678.

The backwards order on a little-endian computer, however, is no problem to the computer. When the computer reads the number back into memory and then loads it into a register, the bytes that make up the number in memory are loaded back into to the register in the correct order, as the arrows in the diagram above indicate. Thus, the bytes end up in the register where they should be. A problem occurs only if the computer that outputs a number and the computer that later reads it in have different endianness. For example, suppose a *little-endian* computer outputs the binary equivalent of 12345678 hex to a file. Then the number is in the file in 78, 56, 34, 12 order. If a *big-endian* computer then reads the number from that file and loads it into a register, it loads the register left to right with 78, 56, 34, 12. Thus, the register is loaded with 78563412—a number quite different from 12345678, the number that was outputted by the little-endian computer (see problems 17 and 18). To confirm this, enter on the command line

```
see endian.bin   (or ./see endian.bin)
```

The `see` program in the software package displays the bytes in the specified file in hex *in the order in which they appear in the file*. The file, `endian.bin`, was created on a *little-endian* computer by a program that outputted the binary equivalent of the number 12345678 hex. Thus, the `see` program will show that the bytes in `endian.bin` are in 78, 56, 34, 12 order. If you then compile and run `endian.c` which reads in and displays in hex the number in `endian.bin`, you will see 12345678 on a little-endian computer but 78563412 on a big-endian computer.

Incidentally, the little (i.e., rightmost) end of a number is so called because its weights are the littlest; the big (i.e., leftmost) end is so called because its weights are the biggest.

Debugger

The `sim` program has a debugging facility that can facilitate the debugging or examination of your programs as they execute. The debugger can work at either the machine instruction level or the microinstruction level. To run a program with the machine-level debugger active, specify the `-T` command line argument. *Be sure to use an uppercase "T" preceded by a hyphen (a lowercase "t" starts the* microlevel debugger). For example, to run the program in `e0301.a`, first assemble it with the `basic` assembler if you have not already done so to get the executable file `e0301.e`. Then enter on the command line

        sim e0301.e -T

`sim` responds by displaying a prompt message that lists all the debugger commands:

        Enter/g/<num>/m/ml/m<addr>/p<addr>/p-/p/r/t/q/h(elp):

Here is a brief description of each debugger command (for more information, see the file `sim.txt`):

Enter   Recall that the CPU repeatedly executes four steps:

                    1. fetch machine instruction pointed to by the `pc` register
                    2. increment the `pc` register
                    3. decode the machine instruction
                    4. execute the machine instruction.

                  Each time you hit the Enter key, `sim` executes the four steps above, at which point it pauses and waits for another command. `sim` displays the effect of each instruction. For example, if a `ld` instruction loads 2 into the `ac` register which currently holds 0, `sim` displays the before and after contents of the `ac` register separated by a slash:

                        ac =0000/0002

g   Causes `sim` to execute to the end of the program unless a breakpoint is set.

<num>   If you enter a positive number, thereafter that number of machines instructions is executed each time you hit the Enter key.

m   Displays memory. Successive `m` entries display successive blocks of memory.

ml   Displays memory starting at the load point. The *load point* is the memory address at which the loading of the program starts. Note that "1" in this command is the letter "L".

m<addr>   Displays memory starting at the specified address.

p<addr>   Sets a breakpoint at the specified address. Lower case p sets a microlevel breakpoint; uppercase P sets a machine-level breakpoint.

p-   Cancels breakpoint. Lowercase p is for the microlevel; uppercase P is for the machine level.

p   Displays current breakpoint address. Lowercase p is for the microlevel; uppercase P is for the machine level.

r   Displays all registers, or if r is followed by a register name (e.g., ac), or a register number in decimal (e.g., 22), only that register.

t   Toggles tracing off and on. Lowercase t is for the microlevel; uppercase T is for the machine level.

q   Quit the program.

h   Displays an explanation of each debugger command.

Here is a short example of the use of the debugger on the program in e0301.e. First assemble e0301.a if you have not already done to get the executable program e0301.e. Then enter on the command line

```
sim e0301.e -T
```

sim responds with the prompt

```
Enter/g/<num>/m/ml/m<addr>/p<addr>/p-/p/r/t/q/h(elp):
```

If you hit the Enter key, sim processes the first instruction and shows its effect:

```
read machine inst 0006 from addr 0
pc = 0000/0001
ir = 0000/0006
read 0002 from mem[6]
ac = 0000/0002
```

The trace shows that

- the ld machine instruction 0006 at the address 0 was fetched
- pc was incremented from 0 to 1
- ir was loaded with the fetched instruction (0006)
- 0002 was read from location 6.
- the execution of the ld instruction changed the ac register from 0000 to 0002.

To confirm that the ac register now contains 0002, enter rac and you will see:

```
ac = 0002
```

Each time you hit the Enter key without first entering a command, sim processes the next instruction. For example, if you hit the Enter key again, you will see

```
read machine inst 2007 from addr 1
pc = 0001/0002
ir = 0006/2007
read 0003 from mem[7]
ac = 0002/0005
```

This is the trace of the `add` instruction 2007. It shows the `add` instruction changes the `ac` register from 0002 to 0005 (by adding 0003 at the address 0007 to the `ac` register).

To see the program in memory, enter `m`. `sim` then displays 32 words of memory starting at the load point:

```
0000:   0006 2007 1008 f002 f001 f000 0002 0003
0008:   0000 0000 0000 0000 0000 0000 0000 0000
0010:   0000 0000 0000 0000 0000 0000 0000 0000
0018:   0000 0000 0000 0000 0000 0000 0000 0000
```

If you now enter g, the program executes to completion since no breakpoints are set. A `st, dout, nl` and finally a `halt` instruction are executed. `sim` produces the following trace for those instructions:

```
read machine inst 1008 from addr 2
pc = 0002/0003
ir = 2007/1008
mem[8] = 0000/0005

read machine inst f002 from addr 3
pc = 0003/0004

read machine inst f001 from addr 4
pc = 0004/0005

read machine inst f000 from addr 5
pc = 0005/0006
```


From the trace, you can see that the `st` instruction stored 5 into main memory at the address 8 (`mem[8]` represents the location in main memory at the address 8). The `dout` instruction outputs the number in the `ac` register (the sum of 2 and 3), the `nl` instruction moves the cursor to the next line, and the `halt` instruction terminates the program.

As illustrated in the example above, each time you hit the Enter key, `sim` processes one instruction. However, if you enter any positive number before hitting the Enter key, then `sim` will process that number of instructions each time you hit the Enter key. For example, to process 5 instructions each time you hit the Enter key, enter 5. Thereafter, each time you hit Enter without first entering a command, `sim` will process 5 instructions.

If you specify on the command line the `-f` argument when you invoke `sim`, then `sim` (whether or not `-T` is specified) will give you the opportunity to display registers and memory when the program terminates.

The debugger in `sim` allows only one machine-level breakpoint to be active at a time. If you specify a new breakpoint with the P command, the previous one is cancelled. However, you can have as many breakpoints in your program as you like by using the `bp` assembly language instruction. Whenever the `bp` instruction is executed, it forces `sim` to pause at which time the user can enter any debugger command.

A breakpoint can be very helpful when you are debugging a program with a loop. You can set a breakpoint at the beginning of a loop. That way, just before each iteration of the loop, the breakpoint occurs, pausing `sim`. You can then examine the state of your program with the various debugger commands. For example, the program in `e0304.a` has a loop that starts at the address 1. To set a breakpoint at this address, start `sim` on `e0304.e`, specifying the `-T` argument. In response to the prompt message `sim` displays when it starts, set a breakpoint at the address 1 by entering an uppercase P followed by the breakpoint address *in hex*:

```
P1
```

Be sure to use an uppercase "P". Next, enter `g`, which causes the program to execute until it terminates (by executing a `halt` instruction) unless it first reaches a breakpoint. Because of the breakpoint at the address 1, `sim` pauses each time it reaches this breakpoint (which is the start of the loop). If at each breakpoint, you display the `ac` register by entering

```
rac
```

you can observe how on each iteration of the loop (initiated by hitting Enter), `ac` is one less than on the preceding iteration. When `ac` reaches 0, a `brz` instruction branches out of the loop to a `halt` instruction.

To set a breakpoint on a line of code, you need the hex address of that line of code. The simplest way to determine the hex address of a line is to refer to the lst file that the `basic` assembler outputs. It lists the hex (and decimal) address for each line of code.

Breakpoints are also useful for testing and debugging a function in a multi-function program. When testing a function, you will probably want to turn off the trace until the function of interest starts executing. To do this, use the `T` debugger command which toggles the trace off and on. Here is the specific procedure to follow to trace one function and only that function:

- Invoke `sim` with the `-T` command line argument.
- Set a breakpoint at the starting address of the function (get the address from the lst file produced by the `basic` assembler).
- Enter `T` to turn off the trace function so `sim` does not trace the code leading up to the breakpoint.
- Enter `g` to execute to the breakpoint.
- At the breakpoint, enter `T` to turn the trace on.
- Enter `1` so `sim` pauses after each instruction.
- Step through the function by repeatedly hitting the Enter key.
- Examine the trace as you step though the function to determine if the function is working correctly. If necessary, use the `r` and `m` debugger commands to display the registers and memory.

A Entries

In the following program, the machine instruction for the `ld` instruction is 0006. The initial hex 0 (0000 in binary) represents the four-bit opcode of the `ld` instruction. The remaining three hex digits, 006 (0000 0000 0110 in binary), represents the 12-bit memory address from which the `ld` instruction loads the `ac` register. When this program is loaded into main memory starting at the address 0, the constant 2 is at the address 006. Thus, the `ld` instruction loads 2 into the `ac` register.

Recall that the *load point* of a program is the address at which its loading starts in main memory. What if the load point for the program is 100 instead of 0? Then the constant 2 would be at the address 106, not 006. For the `ld` to load 2, the address in the `ld` instruction address must adjusted. Specifically, the address in the `ld` instruction *must be increased by the load point*. If the load point is 100, then the address in the `ld` instruction must be increased by 100—to 106—because the constant 2 is now at the address 106. The addresses in the `add` and `st` instructions must be similarly adjusted.

Here is the `e0301.lst` file that the `basic` assembler creates when it assembles `e0301.a`:

```
basic Assembler Ver 3.0   Fri Feb 25 15:45:41 2022
DosReis Anthony J.

Header
b
A 0000
A 0001
A 0002
C

Addr    Code            Source Code

0000    0006            ld x     ; load ac with value at x
0001    2007            add y    ; add value at y to ac
0002    1008            st z     ; store sum in ac in z
0003    f002            dout     ; display value in ac in decimal
0004    f001            nl       ; move cursor to next line
0005    f000            halt     ; stop execution
0006    0002 x:         .word 2  ; data
0007    0003 y:         .word 3  ; data
0008    0000 z:         .word 0  ;
```

The adjustment of addresses in instructions is performed by the `sim` program as it loads a program into memory. But this function gives rise to an interesting question: How does `sim` know where the addresses are in the program? The `sim` program loads in the machine language form of a program. It is difficult or impossible to determine where addresses are in the program from *just the machine code.* For example, a constant such as 0002 in the program above could be a `ld` instruction because it starts with the opcode for that instruction. If 0002 is a constant, then 002 is not an address. But if 0002 is a `ld` instruction, then 002 is an address.

Executable files, such as `e0301.e` in the example above, start with a header. Following the header is the machine code:

`e0301.e`

Header
Machine code

The header for a program starts with a *file signature* (a letter that indicates the type of the file). For executable files created by the `basic` assembler, the file signature is the letter "b". Following the file signature are a list of A entries. Each *A entry* specifies the address of an instruction that contains an address. For example, the program in `e0301.e` has three instructions—the `ld`, `add`, and `st`—that contain addresses. These instructions are at the addresses 0, 1, and 2 respectively. Thus, the program's header contains the three A entries, one for each instruction, that specify the *addresses of these instructions* (0, 1, and 2) —*not the addresses they contain* (006, 007, and 008).

The header is terminated with the letter "C". Following the letter "C" is the machine code for the program. When the basic assembler outputs an executable file, it outputs the file signature, the A entries, and the letter "C" before outputting the machine code.

The lst file that the `basic` assembler outputs shows the header as well as the assembly and machine code for the program. Look at the beginning of the `e0301.lst` file produced by the `basic` assembler. You will see near the top the header displayed as follows:

```
Header
b
A 0000
A 0001
A 0002
C
```

We mentioned that by examining the *machine code* for a program, it is difficult or impossible to determine which words contains addresses. But it is easy for the `basic` assembler to find them in the *assembly language program* it translates. It simply looks for any instruction that uses a label. Remember a label is a symbolic address. For example, the `ld` instruction in `e0301.a` is

```
ld x
```

x is a label. Thus, the machine code version of this instruction contains an address. Because this instruction is at the address 0, the basic assembler outputs to the executable file the A entry that specifies the address 0000:

```
A 0000
```

which indicates that at address 0 in the program, there is an address that needs adjustment if the load point is not zero.

Examine the `e0301.e` executable file with the `see` program to see what is really there. `see` displays

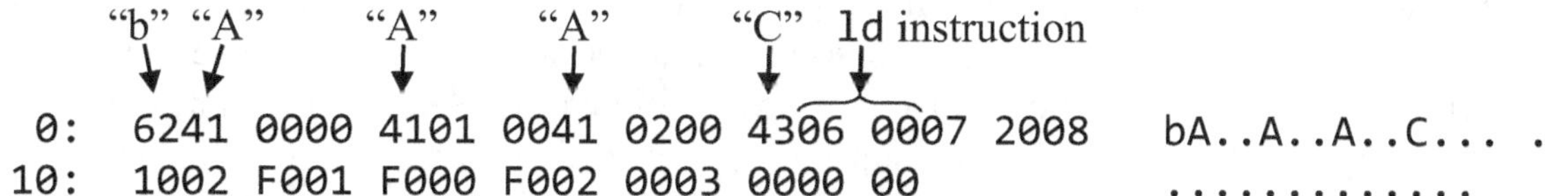

The file starts with **62**, the ASCII code for the letter "b". Following the "b" is the first A entry: **41**, the ASCII code for the letter "A", followed by the address **0000**. The second **41** is the start of the second A entry followed by the address **0100**. Recall that your computer is a little endian computer—the "little" end of the number is stored first. Thus, **0100** represents the address **0001**. The third A entry, **41 0200** is followed by **43**, the ASCII code for the letter "C". Following the **43** is the `ld` instruction **0600** (its bytes are in reverse order because your computer is a little-endian computer).

Each line that `see` outputs starts with the hex address of the first word on that line. Next are eight words in the file in hex notation. On the right are the characters that correspond to the eight words to the left. Because this is an executable file, most of the bytes contain numbers that are not ASCII codes. For these bytes, "." is displayed on the right. Thus, the characters in the right section start with bA because the first two bytes of the file are 62 and 41, the ASCII codes for "b" and "A". Following the 41 in the file are 00 and 00. Because there is no displayable character corresponding to 00, two periods are displayed for them in the section on the right. By examining the section on the right, it is easy to see that the file signature is "b", and the file contains three A entries.

A .start directive in an assembly language program indicates the entry point for the program. For example, the .start directive in e0306.a

```
.start main
```

indicates the execution should start at the location corresponding to the label main. The assembler creates an S entry for this directive and includes it in the header for the program. The S entry that the assembler creates for this .start directive is

S 000a   (000a is the address of main *relative to the beginning of the program*)

The entry point of the program after it is loaded into memory (i.e, where execution starts in memory) is given by

the load point (i.e., the address in memory at which the program begins)

+

000a (the address of main relative to the beginning of the program).

If a .start directive is not included in an assembly language program, no S entry is created. In that case, the program's execution starts at its load point.

Text and Binary Files

There are two categories of files: *text files* and *binary files*. An example of a text file is the assembly language file e0301.a; an example of a binary file is the executable file e0301.e. What is the difference between these two types of files? All computer files contain 0's and 1's. So all files, including text files, are binary. However, the term "text file" is used to denote those files created by entering textual information on a keyboard. For each key hit on the keyboard, the corresponding ASCII code goes into the file. Thus, each byte contains the ASCII code for some character on the keyboard. The term "binary file" denotes those files that are *not* text files. For example, the binary file e0301.e has a few ASCII codes (the file signature "b" and the letter "A" that starts its A entries). But most of its bytes are for machine instructions. Some of these bytes may coincidentally contain ASCII codes, but these bytes are not representing characters—they are simply parts of a machine instruction. For example, suppose an add instruction in some executable file is 2041. The 20 is the code for the space; the 41 is the code for "A". Thus, a space and the letter "A" would be displayed for them by a text editor. But these bytes are not functioning as representatives of those characters—they are simply parts of a machine instruction.

If you open a file with a text editor, it displays the character corresponding to each byte. A byte can contain a number from 0 to 255 decimal. The codes corresponding to the characters on the keyboard run only from 32 to 126 decimal. Thus, in a binary file like e0301.e, many of the bytes can be out of the 32--to-126 range for which corresponding characters exist. What is displayed for these out-of-range bytes is generally unpredictable—it depends on the text editor. For example, one text editor displays e0301.e as

```
bA   A☺ A   C♠ • ◘► ≡☺≡ ≡   ♥
```

The bytes with ASCII codes are displayed correctly. But the other bytes are displayed with unpredictable figures, such as the happy face, the heart, the arrowhead, and the triple-line equivalence symbol. Other text editors may display different figures for these bytes. That is why you need a special program like the `see` program—not a text editor—to see inside a binary file. A *hex editor* is a program that displays a file the same way the `see` program does. But it also allows the user to modify the file. Hex editors are useful for modifying an executable file for which you do not have the source code from which it was translated. They, of course, can also be used simply to look inside a file.

Problems

Note: Source programs should be properly indented and commented. Labels should have meaningful names when possible. Input should be prompted. Output should be labeled and well laid out with no spelling errors.

1) Write an assembly language program that displays your name.

2) Write an assembly language program that displays your name 20 times. Use a loop.

3) Write a program that repeatedly prompts for and reads in decimal numbers until a negative number is entered, at which point your program should display the sum of all the numbers previously entered. Test your program by entering 1, 2, 3, −1 (the sum displayed should be 6).

4) Write a program that prompts for and reads in a positive decimal number and then displays the sum of all the integers from 1 to the number entered. Test your program by entering 10.

5) Write an assembly language program that reserves a slot on the stack (by decrementing the `sp` register), pushes 1 and 2 onto the stack, and then calls a subroutine. Your subroutine should add the two numbers it is passed, *store the sum in the reserved slot on the stack*, and then return to the caller. The caller should then remove the two parameters from the stack, display the sum that is now on top of the stack, and finally remove the sum from the stack and terminate.

6) Write an assembly language program that displays a table of ASCII codes from 32 to 127 and their corresponding characters.

7) Write a program that works like the program in `e0206.hex` but prompts the user and labels the output.

8) Write an assembly language program in which the main module reserves one word on the stack (by decrementing `sp`) and calls a subroutine. Your subroutine should prompt for and read in a decimal number and store in the reserved word on the stack and then return to the caller. The caller should then display the number in the reserved word on the stack and then remove it from the stack. Test your program by entering −5.

9) Write an assembly language program that reads in 10 decimal numbers and displays the largest. Test your program by entering 3, 100, −30, −50, 101, 99, 0, −1, 5, 77. *Hint*: To determine if `x` is less than `y`, subtract `y` from `x` and examine the result. If the result is negative, `x` is less than `y`.

10) Write an assembly language program that prompts for and reads in a string. It should then display all and only the decimal digits in the string. Test your program with "A1b2C34". *Hint*: Each time through a loop, modify the machine instruction that loads a character from the inputted string.

11) Write an assembly language program that reads in a string and displays it with its characters in reverse order. Test your program by entering "hello". Use the stack.

12) Write an assembly language program that reads in a hex number and displays it in binary. Test your program by entering AB5D.

13) When the following program is executed, does it loop infinitely? If so, explain why. If not, explain why not. Assume the program is loaded into location 0.

```
            ld x
s:          asp -1
            str 0
            br s
x:          .word 0xf000
```

14) Write an assembly language program that reads in a four-bit binary number (with spaces separating the bits) and displays its equivalent hex digit. Test your program by entering 1 1 0 1 for which your program should display "d".

15) The .start directive is not translated to machine code. How then does the operating system know where the entry point is?

16) Hand assemble the program in e0305.a. Show in hex both the header and the machine code.

17) Write a Java program that reads the file endian.bin and displays in hex the four-byte integer number it contains. Why does your Java program display the number incorrectly? Fix your Java program so that it displays the number correctly.

18) Compile and run the C program in endian.c. It reads and displays in hex the 32-bit integer in the file endian.bin. What does it display? Does the number displayed depend on the type of computer?

19) Display the e0301.e file with the see program. In the output see produces, circle the words that contain the constant 2 and the constant 3.

20) Assemble and run the program in e0304.a. Set a machine-level breakpoint at the address corresponding to the label loop (get the address from the lst file e0304.lst that the basic assembler outputs). Display the contents of the ac register at each breakpoint.

21) Change the ld, add, and st in e0301.a to ld 6, add 7, st 8. Assemble and run with a load point of 0. Repeat with a load point of 100. Why does the program fail when the loadpoint is non-zero? *Hint*: Examine the A entries for the two versions of the program.

4 Simple Digital Circuits

Introduction

In this chapter, we will study the simple digital circuits that are the basic building blocks of the LCC. We will study the two categories of digital logic: combinational (a circuit whose output depends only on its present inputs) and sequential (a circuit that has memory, and therefore its output can depend on its past as well as its present inputs).

Transistors

A *transistor* is an electrical switch. It can be *off*, in which case it does not conduct electricity, or *on*, in which case it does conduct electricity:

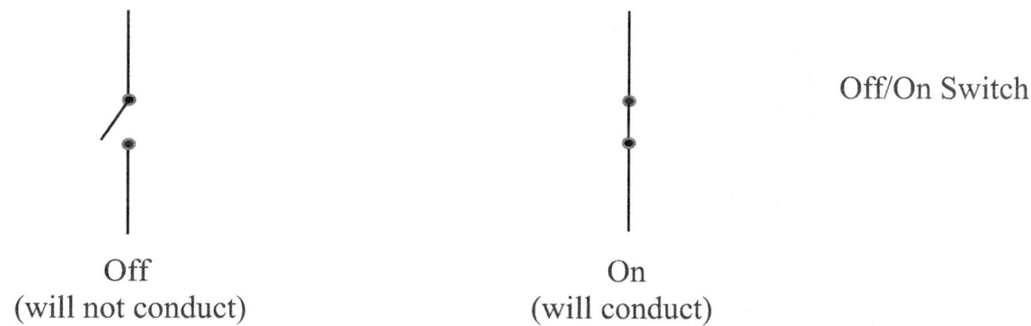

A transistor is similar to a switch on a wall that operates an overhead light. There is, however, one major difference. A light switch is mechanical. Because it has moving parts, its switching speed is very slow. A transistor, on the other hand, is electrical. Because it has no moving parts, its switching speed is very fast.

Transistors are made from silicon. Silicon is an element that is in abundant supply on the Earth (silicon is the principal component of sand). We call silicon a *semiconductor* because its electrical properties place it between conductors and insulators.

Among the several types of transistors, metal-oxide semiconductor (MOS) transistors are the most commonly used type in modern computers. MOS transistors come in two types: PMOS (positive metal-oxide semiconductor) and NMOS (negative metal oxide semiconductor). Most computer circuits with MOS transistors use complementary metal-oxide semiconductor (CMOS) technology. In this technology, both NMOS and PMOS transistors are used. By combining both types in a circuit, the power required by the circuit is minimized. MOS transistors have several properties that make them appropriate for computer circuits: low power consumption, high noise immunity, and high fanout (the *fanout* of a circuit is the number of circuits that its output can drive). MOS transistors, however, are generally slower that other types of transistors.

MOS transistors have three leads—the *source, gate,* and *drain.* An off/on switch exists between the source and drain. The status of this switch—on or off—is determined by the voltage applied to the gate. For example, here are schematic pictures of two NMOS transistors, one with 0 volts on its gate and one with 3 volts on its gate, along with their equivalent circuits:

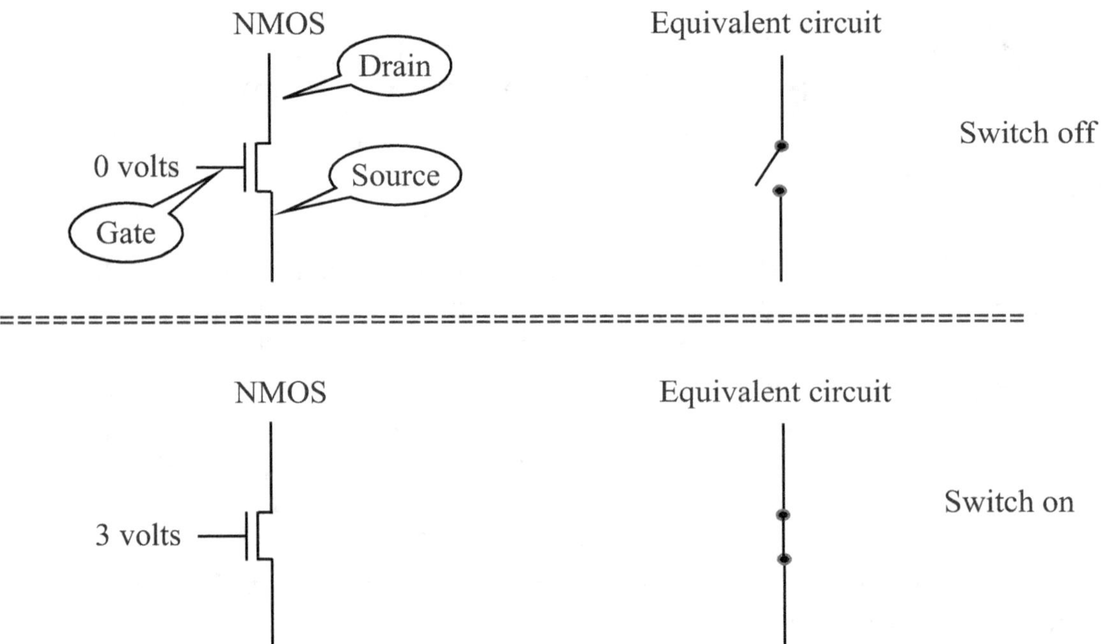

When 0 volts is applied to the gate of an NMOS transistor, the switch is turned off. When 3 volts is applied, the switch is turned on. A PMOS transistor works in the opposite way: When 0 volts is applied to the gate of a PMOS transistor, the switch is turned on. When 3 volts is applied, the switch is turned off:

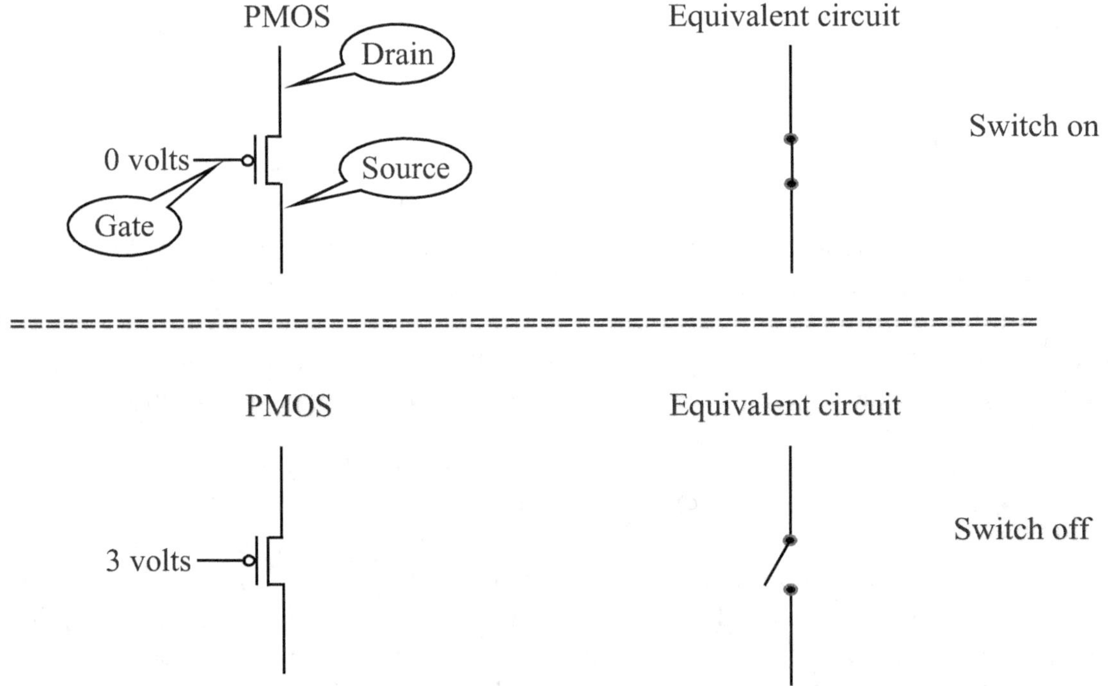

Note that the schematic representation for a PMOS transistor has a small "bubble" on the gate input. This bubble distinguishes it from a NMOS transistor, and it indicates that the transistor is activated (i.e., turned on) when a zero voltage is applied.

Two voltage levels are used on MOS transistors in a computer: typically, 0 volts and a low positive voltage (such as 3 volts). The two levels are used to represent the two values of a bit. For example, 0 volts can represent the bit 0, and 3 volts can represent the bit 1.

NOT Gate

A *NOT gate* (also called an inverter) is a digital circuit that inverts the input voltage. That is, if the input voltage is 3, the output voltage is 0; if the input voltage is 0, the output voltage is 3. Here is a NOT gate constructed with both a PMOS and a NMOS transistor (the equivalent circuit is for the NOT gate when 3 volts are applied to its input):

Equivalent circuit if input = 3 volts

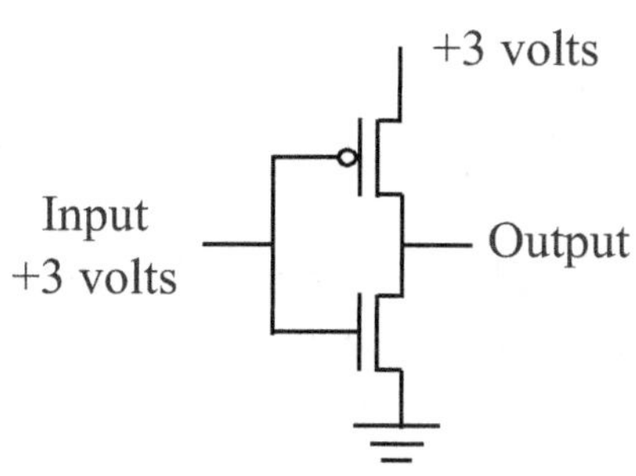

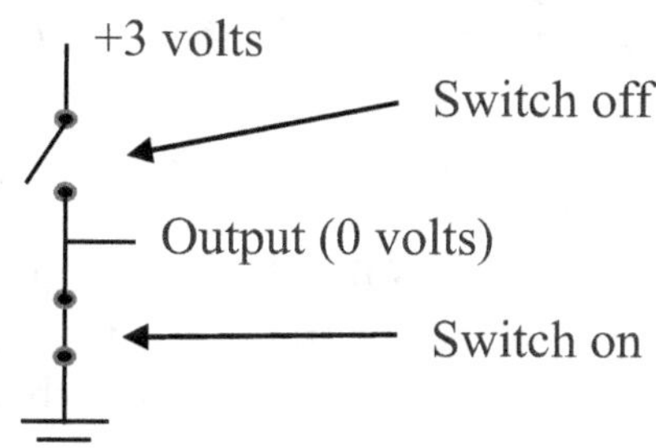

The symbol at the bottom of the circuit consisting of three, successively smaller horizontal lines represents ground (i.e., 0 volts). The top of the circuit is connected to +3 volts. If we apply 3 volts to the input of the circuit, the top transistor turns off (because it is PMOS) and the bottom transistor turns on (because it is NMOS). The effect is to connect the output directly to ground, setting it to 0 volts.

If, on the other hand, we apply 0 volts to the input, then the top transistor turns on and the bottom one turns off, connecting the output to +3 volts:

Equivalent circuit if input = 0 volts

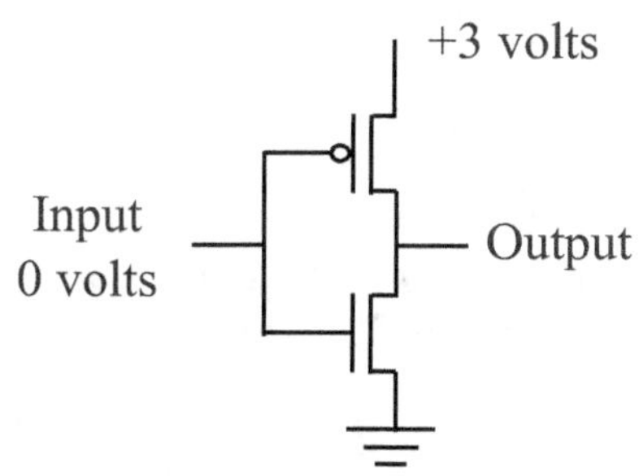

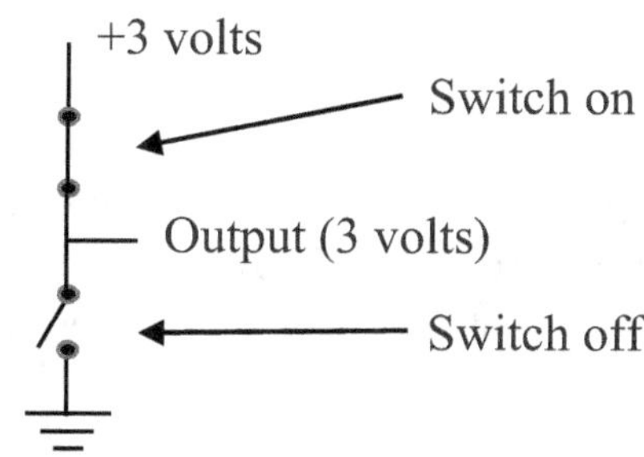

Here is a table that represents the input/output relationship of a NOT gate:

input	output	
0 volts	3 volts	NOT Gate
3 volts	0 volts	

If we represent a 1 bit with 3 volts and a 0 bit with 0 volts, we get the following table:

input	output	
0	1	NOT Gate
1	0	

We call these tables that show the input/output relationship of a digital circuit *truth tables*.

In a circuit diagram that consists of multiple gates, we typically represent each gate with a simple symbol that indicates its type. The symbol for a NOT gate is

Input — Output

XOR, OR, NOR, AND, and NAND Gates

In this section we investigate several more gates. Like the NOT gate, these gates can be implemented with MOS transistors.

An *XOR* (exclusive OR) *gate* is a digital circuit that has two inputs and one output. It is a difference-detecting gate. That is, it outputs 1 if the values on its two input lines differ (i.e., one is 0 and the other is 1), and 0 otherwise. Here is the symbol that represents an XOR gate:

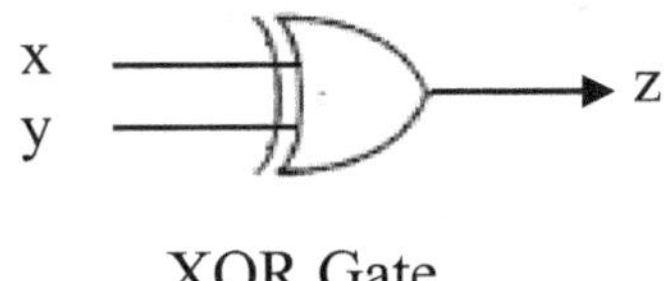

XOR Gate

The following table specifies the input-output relationship of an XOR gate:

x	y	z
0	0	0
0	1	1
1	0	1
1	1	0

The table shows that z is 1 if x and y have different values. Otherwise, z is 0.

One application of an XOR gate is to selectively complement (i.e., flip) a data bit. Consider the following configuration in which one input to an XOR gate is a control line, and the other input is a data line:

control

data — equal to data if control = 0
equal to data flipped if control = 1

Case 1: the control line is 0.
If the data line is 0, then the two inputs are 0, in which case the gate outputs 0. If the data line is 1, then the two inputs differ (0 on the control line, 1 on the data line), in which case the gate outputs 1. Thus, if the control line is 0, the input data appears unchanged on the output line.

Case 2: the control line is 1.
If the data line is 0, then the two inputs differ in which case the gate outputs 1. If the data line is 1, then the two inputs are the same, in which case the gate outputs 0. Thus, if the control line is 1, the complement of the input data appears on the output line.

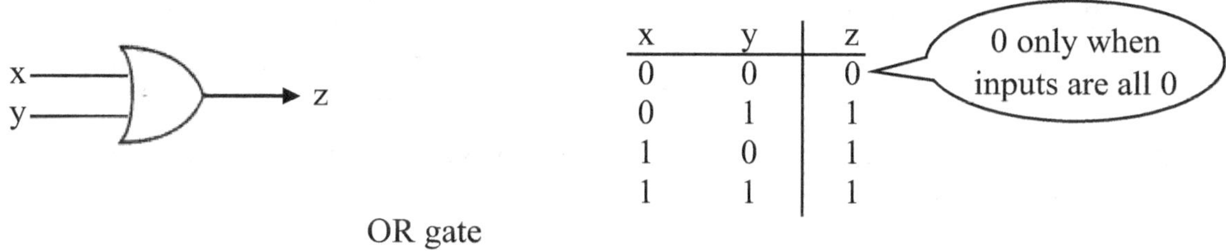

Rule: If the control line of an XOR is 0, the data passes through the gate unchanged. If the control line is 1, the data is complemented (i.e., flipped).

An *OR gate* is a digital circuit that has two or more inputs and one output. It is a not-zero-detecting gate. That is, it outputs 1 if its inputs are not all zero, and 0 otherwise. Here is the symbol that represents a two-input OR gate and its input/output relationship:

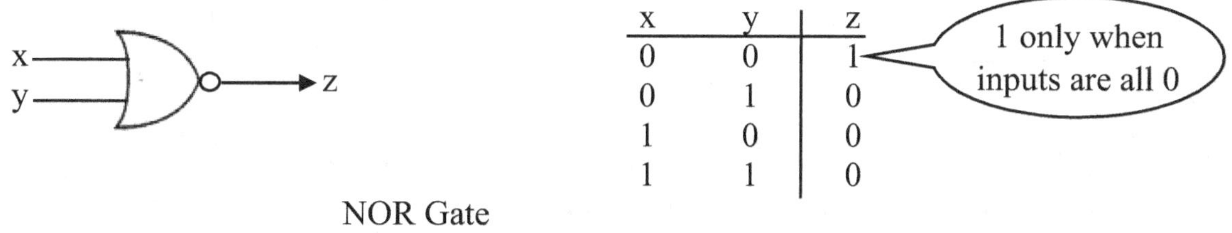

A *NOR gate* is a digital circuit that has two or more inputs and one output. It is equivalent to an OR gate followed by a NOT gate ("NOR" is a contraction of "NOT OR"). A NOR gate is an all-zeros-detecting gate. That is, it outputs 1 if all its inputs are 0, and it outputs 0 otherwise. Here is the symbol that represents a two-input NOR gate and its input/output relationship:

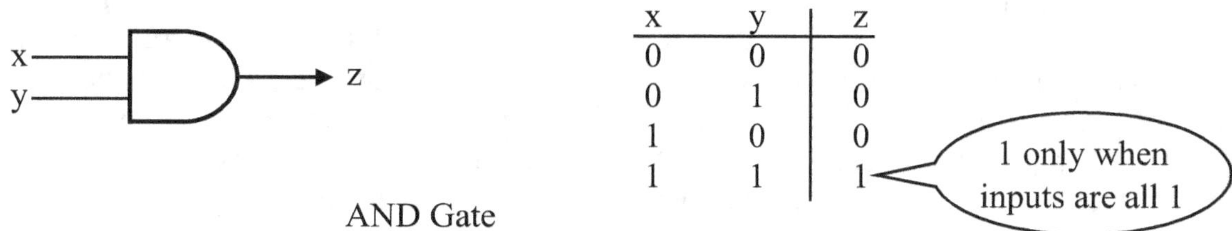

An *AND gate* is a digital circuit that has two or more inputs and one output. It is an all-ones-detecting gate. That is, it outputs 1 if all its inputs are 1, and 0 otherwise. Here is the symbol that represents a two-input AND gate and its input/output relationship:

One application of an AND gate is to selectively block or propagate data. Consider the following configuration in which one input to an AND gate is a control line, and the other input is a data line:

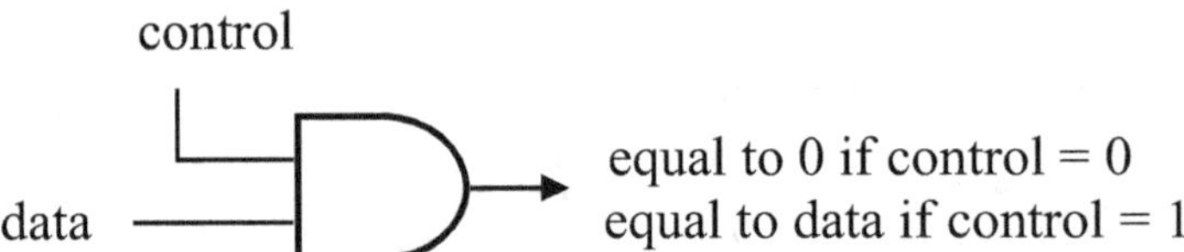

If the control input is 1, the data on the data input flows unchanged through the gate to the output. Think of the gate as being "open" so data can pass through. If, however, the control is 0, then the gate is "closed" so data cannot pass through. Specifically, the output is held at 0 regardless of the data on the data input.

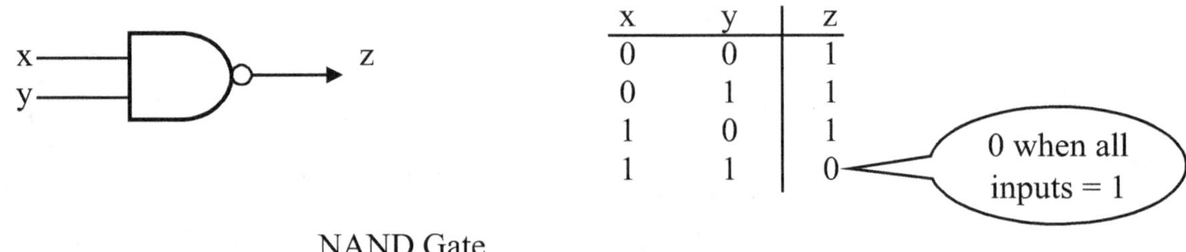

Control	Data	Output of AND
0	0	0
0	1	0
1	0	0
1	1	1

Rule: If the control line of an AND is 1, the data passes through the gate unchanged. If the control line is 0, the output is held at 0.

A *NAND gate* is a digital circuit that has two or more inputs and one output. It is equivalent to an AND gate followed by a NOT gate ("NAND" is a contraction of "NOT AND"). It is a not-all-ones-detecting gate. That is, it outputs 1 if at least one of its inputs is 0, and 0 otherwise. Here is the symbol that represents a two-input NAND gate and its input/output relationship:

<table>
<tr><td>x
y
</td><td>z</td><td>

x	y	z
0	0	1
0	1	1
1	0	1
1	1	0

</td></tr>
</table>

NAND Gate

Tri-State Buffer

As the MOS diagrams in the preceding section indicate, the output of a NOT gate is either +3 volts (which represents the bit 1) or to 0 volts (which represents the bit 0). This is true of most gates. That is, their outputs can be in one of two states (3 volts or 0 volts). However, a *tri-state buffer* is an exception: Its output can be in any one of three states: 3 volts, 0 volts, or not connected to anything.

The term impedance refers to the opposition to electrical current flow. If a wire is not connected to anything, then there obviously is a high impedance between it and anything else. For this reason, we call the not-connected state that the output of a tri-state buffer can assume the *high-impedance* or *high-Z state* (Z is the abbreviation for "impedance"). Here is the symbol for a tri-state buffer and its truth table:

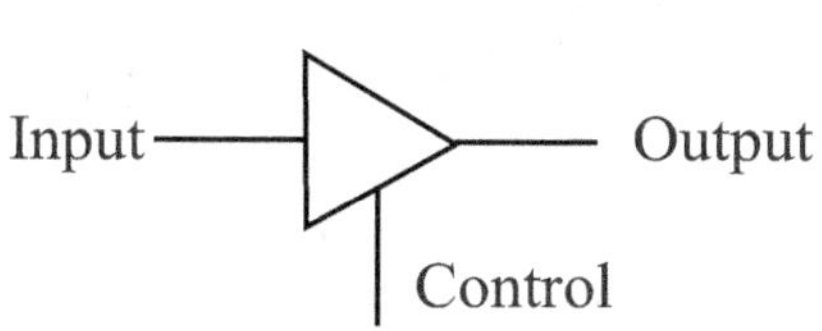

Input	Control	Output
0	0	High-Z
1	0	High-Z
0	1	0
1	1	1

Tri-State Buffer

When the control line is 1, the input data passes unchanged through to the output. If, however, the control line is 0, then the output line is in the high-Z state. When the output line is in the high-Z state, it acts as if you had taken a scissors and cut the output line so it is no longer connected to anything.

Computers often use shared buses. A bus is a bundle of wires that connects one circuit in a computer to another. To avoid interference when one device is driving a shared bus (i.e., putting data on the bus), the other devices physically connected to the bus must be electrically disconnected from it. This is the job of tri-state buffers. For example, suppose two circuits are connected to the same one-wire bus. Circuit A uses the bus to send data to circuit 2. Circuit B uses the same bus to send data to circuit A. We call this kind a bus a *bidirectional bus* because data can flow in both directions. Only one circuit at a time can use the bus. Moreover, when one circuit is using the bus, the other circuit must be disconnected from the bus to avoid interference. Here is the circuit we need:

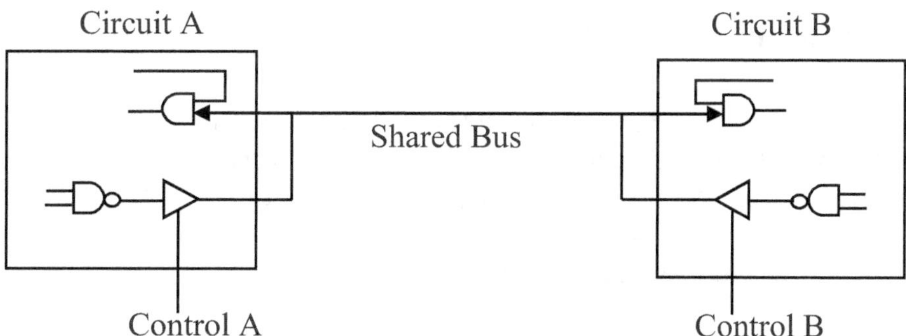

When circuit A needs to send data to circuit B, control A is set to 1 and control B to 0. Similarly, when circuit B needs to send data to circuit A, control B is set to 1 and control A to 0. There is no interference because when one circuit is using the bus, the NAND gate in the other circuit is disconnected from the bus by a tri-state buffer. If, however, the NAND gates were connected directly to the shared bus (i.e., no tri-state buffers), then each would attempt to drive the bus at the same time. For example, the NAND gate in circuit A might output a 1 while at the same time the NAND gate in circuit B might output a 0.

Here is an implementation of a tri-state buffer that uses a PMOS/NMOS pair:

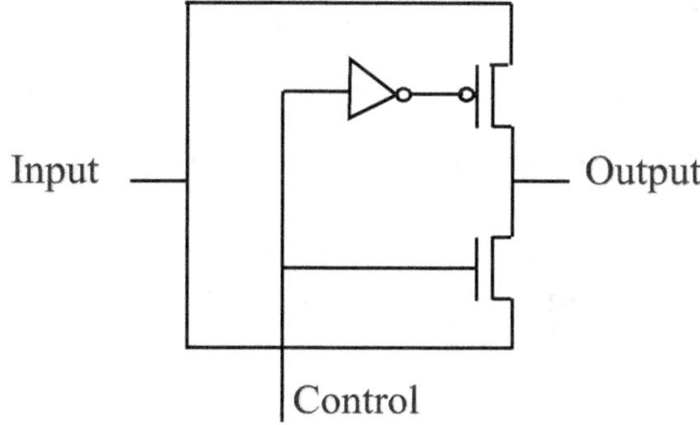

When the control input is 1, the two transistor switches are on. Thus, there is a direct connection from the input to the output. When the control input is 0, both switches are off, which isolates the output from the input. Here is the equivalent circuit when the control input is 0

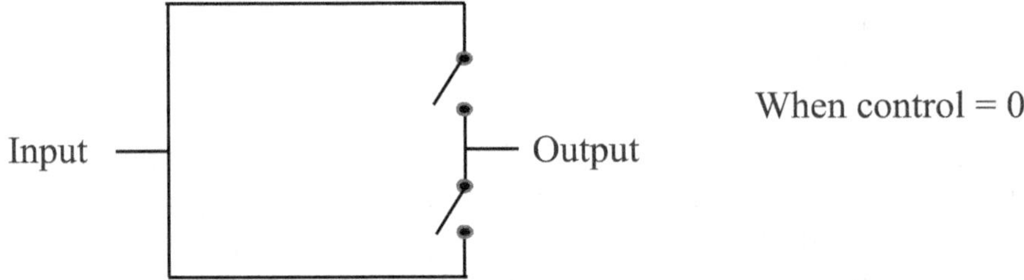

You can see that the output is not connected to anything.

The implementation of a tri-state buffer shown above uses CMOS (complementary MOS) technology. In CMOS technology, circuits consist of PMOS/NMOS pairs. Note that if we replace the PMOS transistor with an NMOS transistor in our implementation of a tri-state buffer, we can eliminate the NOT gate. But CMOS technology has some important advantages over using NMOS transistors exclusively. Thus, the CMOS implementation is superior.

Realizing Boolean Functions with Digital Logic

Truth tables represent Boolean functions. A Boolean function is a function whose inputs and outputs are all two-valued. Typically, the values of Boolean functions are either true/false or 1/0. Given any Boolean function in truth table form, we can easily implement a circuit consisting of AND, OR, and NOT gates that realizes that function.

Let's implement a circuit that realizes the XOR Boolean function:

x	y	z
0	0	0
0	1	1	← Select this row
1	0	1	← Select this row
1	1	0

To implement this function, we select only those rows whose output column contains a 1. Thus, for this function we select only the second and third rows. For each of these rows, we create a circuit using one AND gate that will output 1 only when the inputs are as specified in that row. For example, for the second row we create the following circuit:

x —▷o— ⟩ —— Outputs 1 only if x = 0 and y = 1
y ————

This circuit will output a 1 if and only if its x input is 0 and its y input is 1 (the inputs for the second row). For the third row, we create a similar circuit:

x ———— ⟩ —— Outputs 1 only if x = 1 and y = 0
y —▷o—

Finally, we feed the output of each of these circuits to a common OR gate and tie all the common inputs together to get

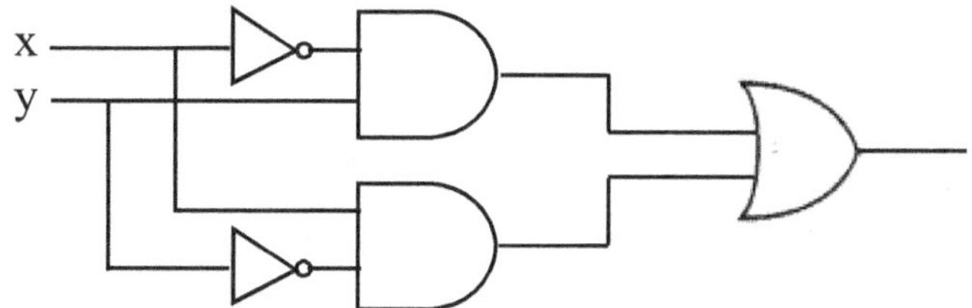

Let's analyze this composite circuit. If we input 0 and 1 for x and y, respectively, the top AND gate outputs a 1, causing the OR gate to also output a 1. Similarly, if we input 1 and 0 for x and y, respectively, then the bottom AND gate outputs a 1, again causing the OR gate to output a 1. However, all other input combinations cause both AND gates to output a 0, causing the OR gate to also output a 0. Thus, this circuit implements the truth table for the XOR function.

Since the XOR circuit is so important, we have a special symbol for it:

Half and Full Adders

A half adder is a digital circuit that add two bits. It outputs both a sum bit and a carry bit. Here are the four cases when adding two bits:

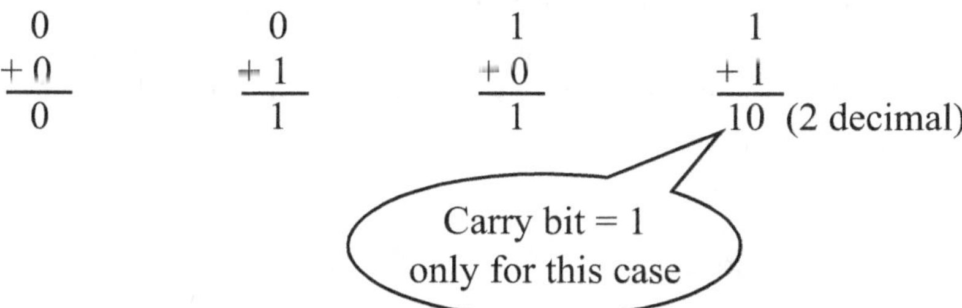

Note that the carry bit is 1 if and only both bits that are added are 1. Thus, the carry is equal to the AND of the two bits that are added. The sum bit is 1 if and only if the two bits that are added differ (i.e., 0 and 1 or 1 and 0). Thus, the sum bit is equal to the XOR of the two bits that are added. Using these observations on a half adder, we can easily implement it. We need an XOR gate (to compute the sum) and a AND gate (to compute the carry). Here is the circuit:

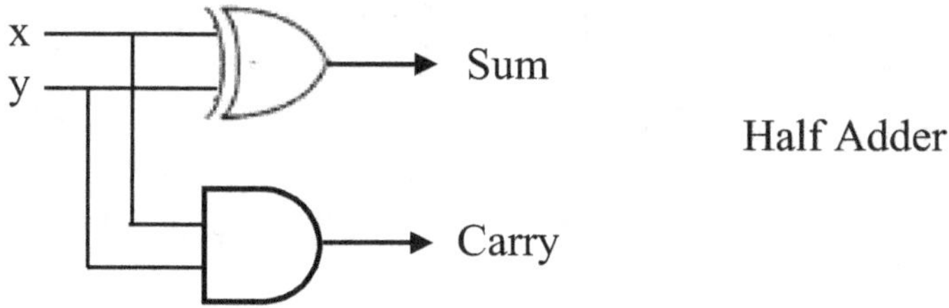

Half Adder

When we add two multi-bit binary numbers, for each column (except the rightmost column), we have to add three bits: the two bits in that column from the two binary numbers and the carry (0 or 1) from the addition of the column to the right:

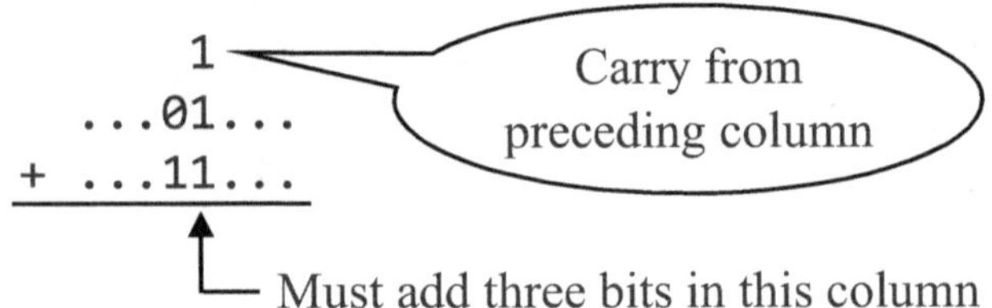

The circuit that adds three bits and outputs a sum bit and a carry bit is called a *full adder*. Here is the truth table for a full adder:

x	y	carry in	sum	carry out
0	0	0	0	0
0	0	1	1	0
0	1	0	1	0
0	1	1	0	1
1	0	0	1	0
1	0	1	0	1
1	1	0	0	1
1	1	1	1	1

In the preceding section, we learned how to implement a circuit that realizes a Boolean function. The resulting circuit consists of AND, NOT, and OR gates. We can do that for both the sum bit in a full adder and the carry out bit. However, a simpler way to implement a full adder is to use two half adders. The first half adder adds two bits and outputs a sum. Then the second half adder adds this sum and the third bit and outputs the three-bit sum. If either half adder produces a carry out, then the full adder should also produce a carry out. Thus, the full-adder carry out is the OR of the carry outs from the two half adders. Here is the circuit:

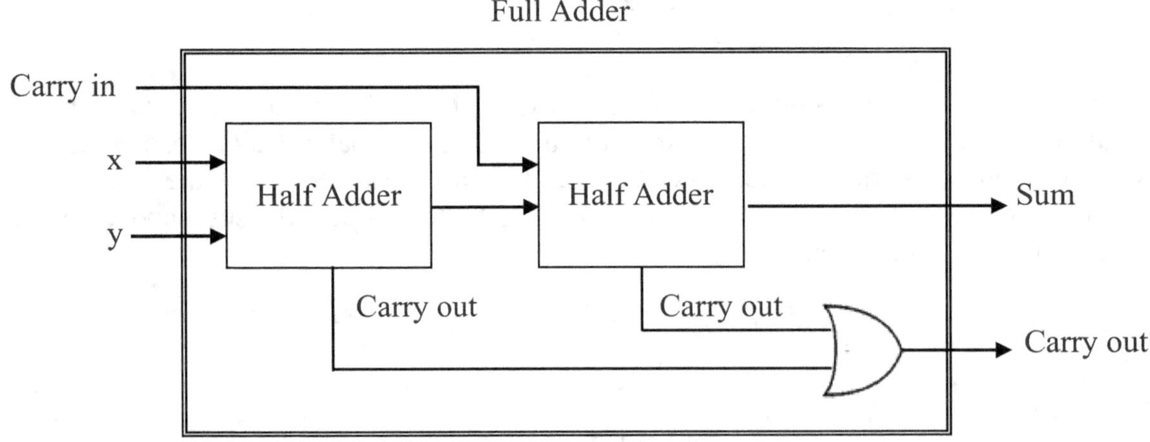

Sequential Circuits

A *sequential* circuit is a circuit that has memory. Because it has memory, its output can depend on the *sequence* of inputs leading up to and including the present input (hence the name "sequential").

Our first sequential circuit is the SR latch. An SR latch has two inputs labeled S and R It also has two outputs. These two outputs have values that are usually (but not always) the complements of each other (i.e., when one is 1, the other is 0). Accordingly, the outputs are labeled Q and Q' (Q' is the complement of Q). "S" stands for "set"; "R" stands for "reset". The SR latch consists of two NOR gates. The output of each NOR gate is fed back to the input of the other NOR gate:

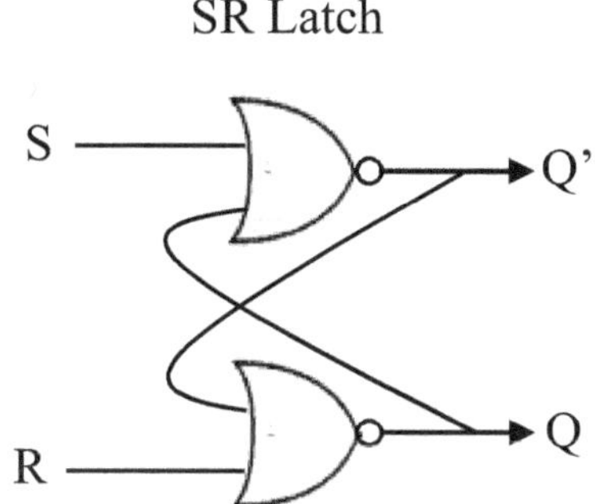

The truth table for an SR latch is unusual in that it includes *two* rows with the *same* inputs (S = R = 0) but with *different* outputs.

S	R	Q	Q'	
0	1	0	1	
0	0	0	1	
1	0	1	0	Two rows for S = R = 0
0	0	1	0	
1	1	0	0	

Let's examine the circuit and confirm that this table does, indeed, describe its operation. Let's start with the first row of the truth table (S = 0, R = 1). The 1 on the R input propagates through the bottom gate but is inverted before it exits. Thus, Q, the output of this gate is 0. The top gate has 0 on its S input and 0 (from the bottom gate) on its other input. The two 0's are ORed and inverted by the NOR gate. Thus, Q' is 1. A similar analysis can be done for the third row of the table. For the fifth row (S = R = 1), both gates necessarily output 0 because both have one input equal to 1.

Now here's the interesting part. Let's assume S = 0 and R = 1. Then the output of the top gate is 1. This 1 is fed back into the bottom gate, making both inputs to the bottom gate equal to 1. If we now change R from 1 to 0, the bottom gate still has one input equal to 1 (from the output of the top gate) which holds the output of the bottom gate at 0. The inputs of the upper gate do not change. Thus, its output also does not change. Changing R from 1 to 0 does not change the outputs of the circuit. The circuit is in a stable state (i.e., a state which will not change unless new inputs are applied). In this state, S = R = 0, Q = 0 and Q' = 1 (the second row of the table). We say the latch is *reset*.

Now let's start with the inputs S = 1 and R = 0. For this case, both inputs to the top gate are 1. If we now change S from 1 to 0, the top gate still has one input equal to 1 (from the output of the bottom gate) which holds the output of the top gate at 0. The inputs of the bottom gate do not change. Thus, its output also does not change. The circuit, therefore, is in another stable state (described by the fourth row of the table). In this state, S = R = 0, Q = 1, and Q' = 0. We say the latch is *set*. We have two possible outputs for the input S = R = 0, corresponding to the second and fourth rows of the truth table. Typically, we use the set state to represent the bit 1 and the reset state to represent the bit 0.

A *clock* in a computer is a circuit that outputs an alternating sequence of 1's and 0's. We often need a latch in a computer that can be set or reset only when a synchronizing signal (like the clock signal) is 1, and which can be set or reset with a single data input. A latch with these properties is the clocked D latch:

Clocked D Latch

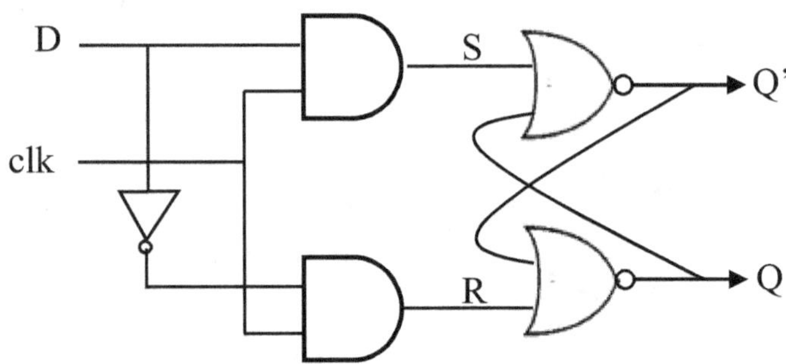

The back end of a clocked D latch is a SR latch. The two AND gates determine if the D data and the complement of D (provided by the NOT gate) get through to the SR latch. If clk = 1, then the AND gates are "open.". Thus, if clk = 1, the D data is passes through the upper AND gate to the S input of the SR latch; the complement of D passes through the lower AND gate to the R input of the SR latch. Thus, if D is 1, the SR latch is set (because the S input is 1 and the R input is 0). Similarly, if clk = 1 and D = 0 the SR latch is reset (because the S input is 0 and the R input is 1). The set state of an SR latch represents the bit 1; the reset state represents the bit 0. Thus, when clk = 1 in a clocked D latch, its SR latch in effect stores the bit on the D input: if D = 1, the latch is set; if D is 0, the latch is reset. If, however, clk = 0, then the AND gates are "closed." Thus, the SR latch does not respond to the D input.

Typically, we use a clocked D latch in this way. To set the latch, we place a 1 on the D input, and then apply a 1 to the clk input. This combination provides the S = 1, R = 0 input to the internal SR latch, causing it to set. Similarly, to reset the latch, we place a 0 on the D input and apply a 1 to the clk input.

Here is the how we represent a clocked D latch in a circuit diagram:

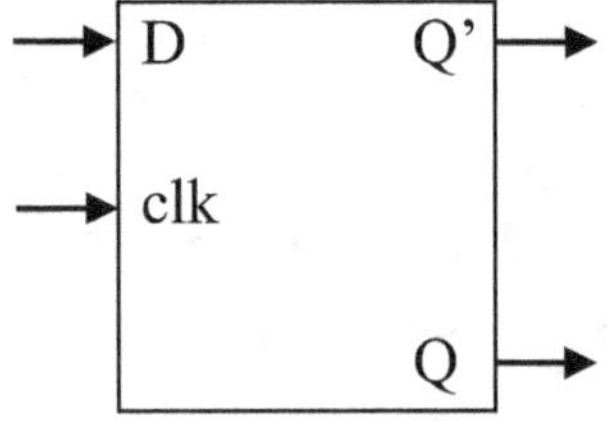

The clocked D latch sets or resets according to its D input *whenever* there is a 1 on its clk input. However, it is often the case that we need a one-bit storage device that sets or resets only during the brief period when the clk input is changing from 0 to 1 (or from 1 to 0). We call such a circuit a *flip-flop*.

The following is a graph of the clk signal versus time:

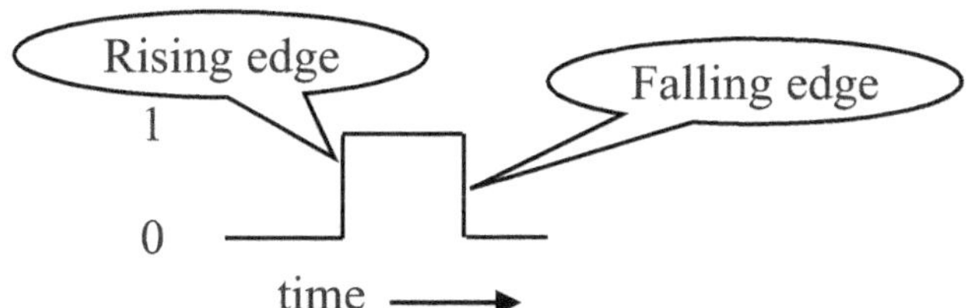

The edge of the graph corresponding to the transition from 0 to 1 is called the *rising* (or *positive*) *edge*; the edge corresponding to the transition from 1 to 0 is called the *falling* (or *negative*) *edge*. If a flop-flop sets or resets only during the rising edge of the clk signal, we say it is *positive edge triggered*. If it sets or resets only during the falling edge, we say it is *negative edge triggered*.

Here are the representations for positive and negative edge triggered D flip-flops:

Positive edge triggered D flip-flop 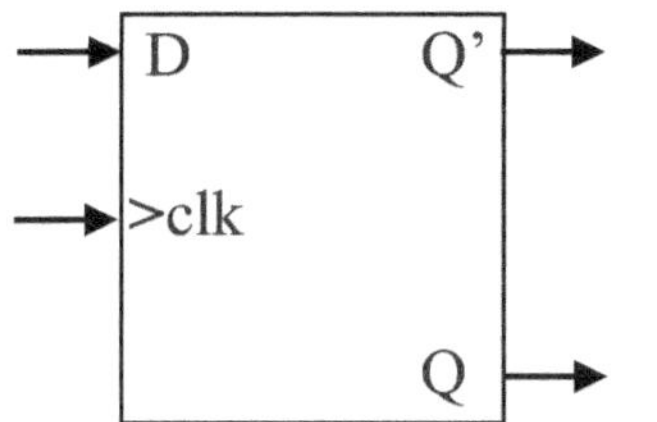 Negative edge triggered D flip-flop 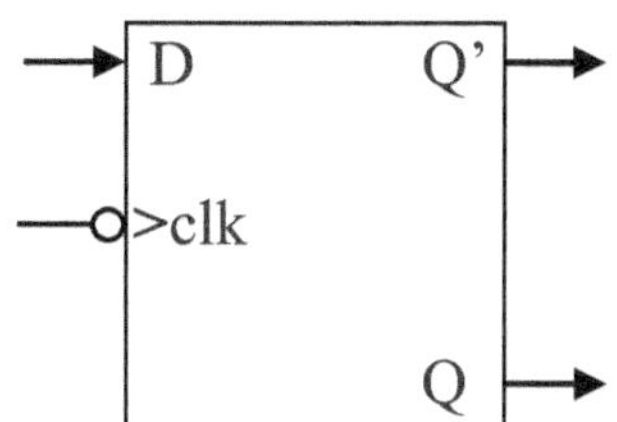

The greater-than sign but no buble on the clk input indicates the device is positive edge triggered. A bubble and a greater-than sign indicate the device is negative edge triggered.

Two other flip-flops that are important are the SR flip-flop, which is the edge triggered version of the SR latch, and the JK flip-flop. A JK flip-flop functions just like the SR flip-flop (the J input acts like the S input in an SR flip-flop, and the K input acts like the R input) except when $J = K = 1$. For this input, the JK flip-flop changes state each time a clock pulse is applied to the clk input. That is, if the flip-flop is set, it resets; if the flip-flop is reset, it sets.

SR flip-flop 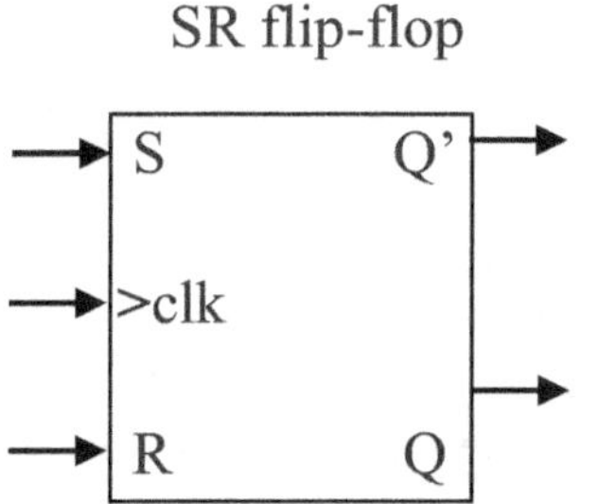 JK flip-flop 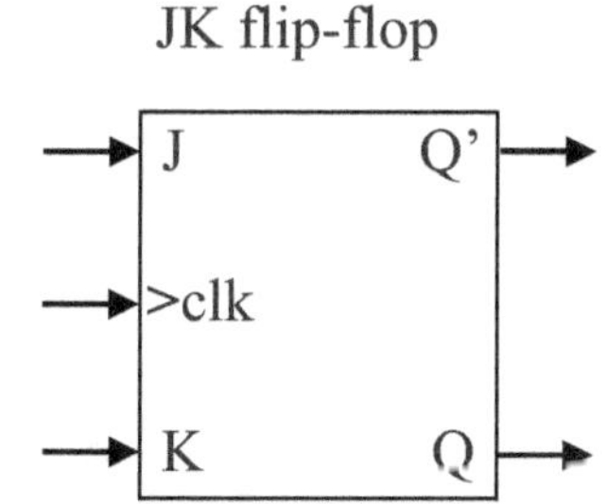

Problems

1) Using four MOS transistors, construct a NOR gate. *Hint*: Connect two PMOS in series (i.e., end to end) and two NMOS in parallel.

2) Using two AND gates, one OR gate, and one NOT gate, implement the following function:

x	y	output
0	0	0
0	1	0
1	0	1
1	1	1

3) Implement the function in problem 2 using no gates.

4) Using AND, OR, and NOT gates, implement the following function:

x	y	z	output
0	0	0	0
0	0	1	0
0	1	0	0
0	1	1	0
1	0	0	0
1	0	1	1
1	1	0	1
1	1	1	1

5) What happens if the output of a NOT gate is fed back to its input?

6) What happens if the output of a tri-state buffer is fed back to its input when the control input is 1?

7) Suppose the four two-input gates in a clocked D latch are replaced with NAND gates. Does the resulting circuit work the same way as the original circuit? Explain.

8) Construct a circuit that outputs 1 if and only if its three inputs are all 0. Use only two-input gates.

9) Construct a circuit that outputs 1 if and only if its four inputs are all 1. Use only two-input gates.

10) Construct the circuit that corresponds to the truth table for a full adder. Use an AND gate for each row in the truth table with a 1 output.

11) The *number of levels* in a circuit is the maximum number of simple gates in a path from an input to an output. Why is the number of levels important? What is the number of levels in the XOR gate? In a half adder implemented with an XOR gate and an AND gate? In a full adder implemented with two half adders?

12) What is the difference in function between an OR gate and an XOR gate? Why is an XOR gate called an *exclusive* OR gate.

13) What happens when an SR latch goes from the $S = R = 1$ state to the $S = R = 0$ state?

14) Modify the circuit for a clocked D latch so that it has two additional inputs: *clear* and *preset*. Both are *active high* (i.e., they have an effect only when set to 1). The clear input resets the latch regardless of the clk input. Similarly, the preset input sets the latch regardless of the clk input.

15) Same as problem 14 but for the latch in problem 7. The clear and preset inputs should be *active low*. That is, they have an effect only when set to 0.

16) Construct a two-bit register using two positive edge triggered flip-flops. The clk signal to the register should cause the two flip-flops to be loaded from two data lines.

17) Construct a NOT gate using NAND gates exclusively.

18) Construct an AND gate using NAND gates exclusively.

19) Construct an OR gate using NAND gates exclusively.

20) Why is the NAND gate called a *universal gate*? *Hint*: See problems 17, 18, and 19.

5 Complex Digital Circuits

Introduction

In this chapter, we investigate complex digital circuits whose component parts are gates and flip-flops. For most of them, we will not investigate how they are implemented. However, you may find that you can easily implement them on your own using only what you learned about digital circuits from chapter 4.

16-bit AND, OR, XOR, and NOT Circuits

A bitwise operation on a binary number is an operation that operates on each bit independently of the other bits in the number. For example, a *16-bit AND circuit* performs a bitwise AND operation on two 16-bit operands. A bitwise AND operation ANDs corresponding bits in the two operands. The result for each pair of bits depends *only* on those two bits. For example, consider the following bitwise AND operations:

```
1010101010101010        operand 1
1100110011001100        operand 2
1000100010001000        result of bitwise AND
```

The two operand bits in each column are ANDed, each producing a one-bit result. If the two operand bits in a column are both 1, the result for that column is 1. Otherwise, it is 0.

A 16-bit AND circuit uses 16 AND gates. The 16 bits of one operand are applied to the left inputs of the 16 AND gates; the 16 bits of the other operand are applied to the right inputs of the 16 AND gates. Here is the representation for a 16-bit AND circuit:

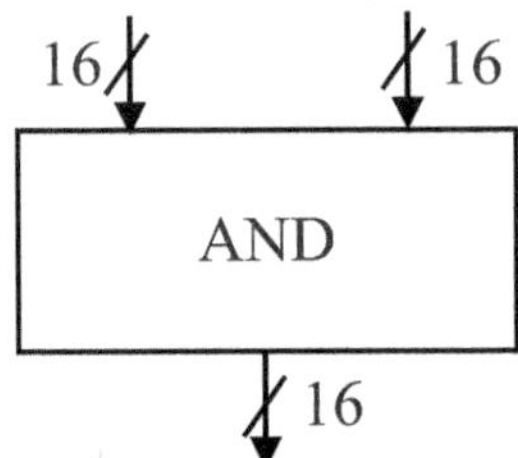

The cross-hatch labeled with 16 on each input indicates that each input is a 16-line bus (a *bus* is a bundle of wires that carries multi-bit data).

A *16-bit OR circuit* and a *16-bit XOR circuit* are configured just like an AND circuit but with 16 OR gates and 16 XOR gates, respectively, in place of the 16 AND gates. A *16-bit NOT* circuit is even simpler. It consists of 16 NOT gates, each one between an input line and its corresponding output line. Like the AND circuit, the OR, XOR, and NOT circuits perform bitwise operations.

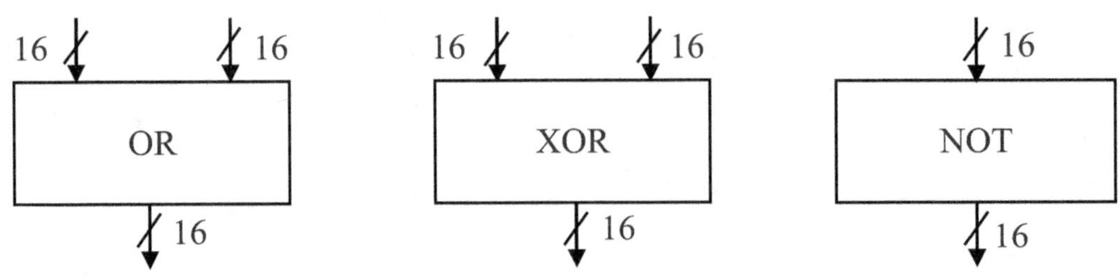

SEXT Circuit

A *SEXT* (sign extension) *circuit* has two inputs:

- a 16-bit operand with a right-justified signed number
- a 16-bit mask that indicates (with 1 bits) which bits in the first operand are occupied by the signed number. Suppose the signed number in the first operand occupies bit positions 0 to i. Then the mask should have 1 bits in positions 0 to i, and 0 bits in positions $i+1$ to 15.

For example, suppose the first operand is 1010101010101011 and its three rightmost bits (011) is the signed number it contains. Then the mask operand should have its three rightmost bits equal to 1 and the other bits equal to 0. Thus, the correct mask is 0000000000000111. The output of the SEXT circuit is the three-bit signed number in the first operand sign extended to 16 bits. In our example, the signed number in the first operand is 011. Because its sign bit is 0, it is extended to 16 bits with 0's. Thus, the SEXT circuit outputs 0000000000000011.

Now suppose the first operand to the SEXT circuit is again 1010101010101011 but its signed number is in its four rightmost bits. Then the correct mask is 0000000000001111. Because the rightmost *four* bits of the mask are 1's, the signed number in the first operand is its *four* rightmost bits: 1011. Because its sign bit is 1, it is extended to 16 bits with 1's. Thus, for this case the SEXT circuit outputs 1111111111111011. Here is the representation of the SEXT circuit:

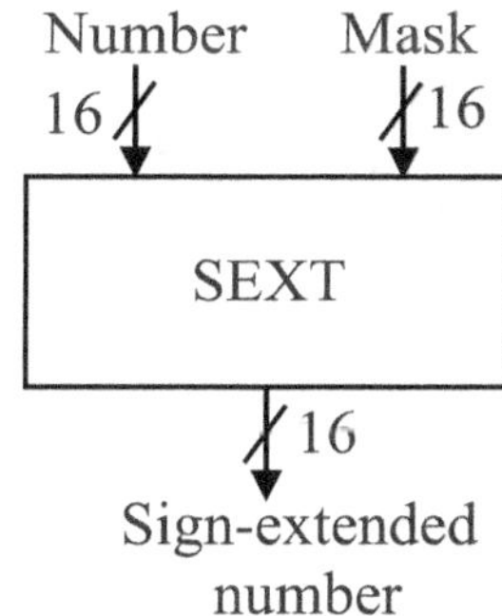

Multiplexer

A *multiplexer* is a combinational circuit that has multiple data inputs and one output. It also has control inputs. The control inputs determine which one of the multiple data inputs drives the output. In diagrams, multiplexers are usually represented with a trapezoidal figure. Here is the representation of a multiplexer with four data inputs:

Four-input multiplexer

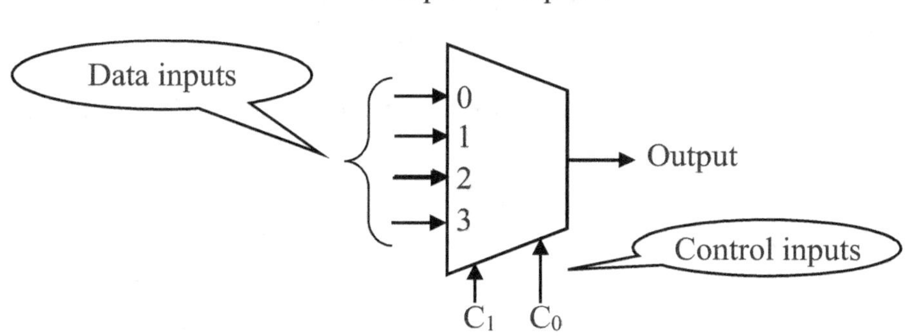

In this multiplexer, the two control inputs determine which data input drives the output. For example, if the control inputs are 10 (i.e., $C_1 = 1$ and $C_0 = 0$), which is 2 in decimal, then data input 2 is selected for output. Because this multiplexer has four data inputs (0, 1, 2, and 3), it needs two control inputs to specify the numbers 0 to 3. A multiplexer with eight data inputs needs three control inputs to specify the numbers 0 to 7 (000 to 111 in binary). In general, a multiplexer with 2^n data input needs n control lines.

In the multiplexer above, the data inputs are single lines. However, multiplexers can also have inputs which are buses. For example, here is a two-bus multiplexer:

Two-Bus Multiplexer

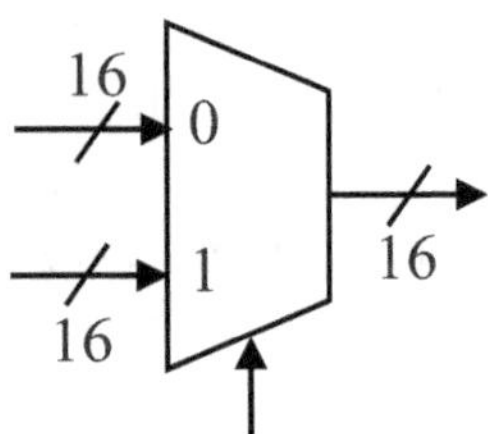

Note that the control input has no cross hatch. Thus, it is a single wire. If it is 0, then bus 0 drives the output bus; if it is 1, then bus 1 drives the output bus.

Decoder

1100 is the binary encoding of the number 12 decimal. A decoder "decodes" an unsigned binary number. That is, it is a circuit that indicates the number represented when given the binary encoding of that number. Here is the representation of a two-bit decoder:

Two-bit decoder

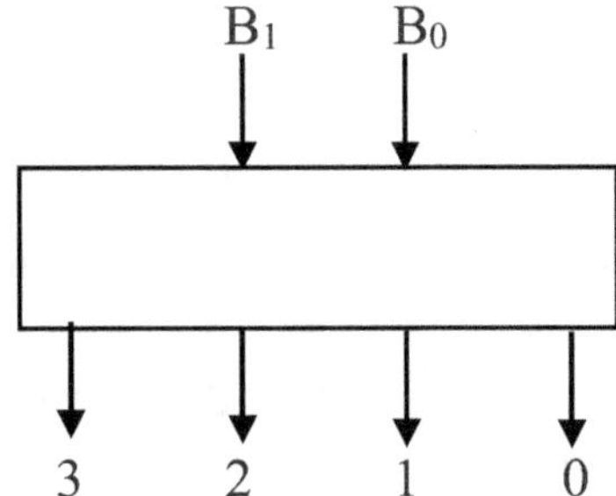

A two-bit binary number in applied to the B_1, B_0 inputs. The decoder responds by placing a 1 on the output line that corresponds to the inputted number. For example, suppose $B_1 = 1$ and $B_0 = 0$. Thus, 10 binary (2 decimal) is the inputted number. The decoder responds by placing a 1 on output line 2. It puts 0 on the three other lines.

Two-bit unsigned binary numbers can range from 0 to 3. Thus, a two-bit decoder has four output lines. An n-bit decoder has 2^n output lines labeled from $2^n - 1$ to 0.

Multi-Bit Addition and Subtraction

When we add two binary numbers by hand, we work from the rightmost column to the leftmost column. In each column except the rightmost, we have to add three bits: the two bits in that column plus a possible carry in from the column to the right. In each column, we have to determine two results: the sum of the bits added for that column and the carry out into the next column to the left. A computer adds binary numbers in exactly the same way. It has a sub-circuit—called a *full adder*—for each column that performs the computation for that column. Thus, an adder that adds two 16-bit numbers has 16 full adders.

A full adder has three inputs: carry in, top bit in, and bottom bit in. It has two outputs: sum out and carry out. If the addition of the bits on the three input lines produces a carry, the full adder outputs a 1 on the carry out line. Otherwise, it outputs a 0.

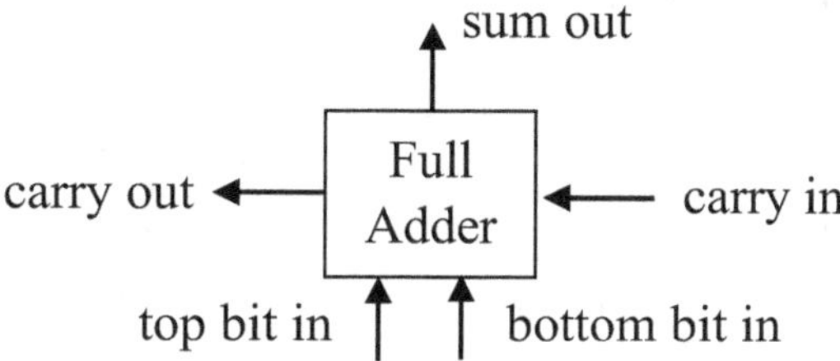

An *adder/subtractor circuit* consists of a full adder for each column to be added or subtracted, connected together in a serial fashion. For example, the following diagram shows the configuration of a three-bit adder/subtractor.

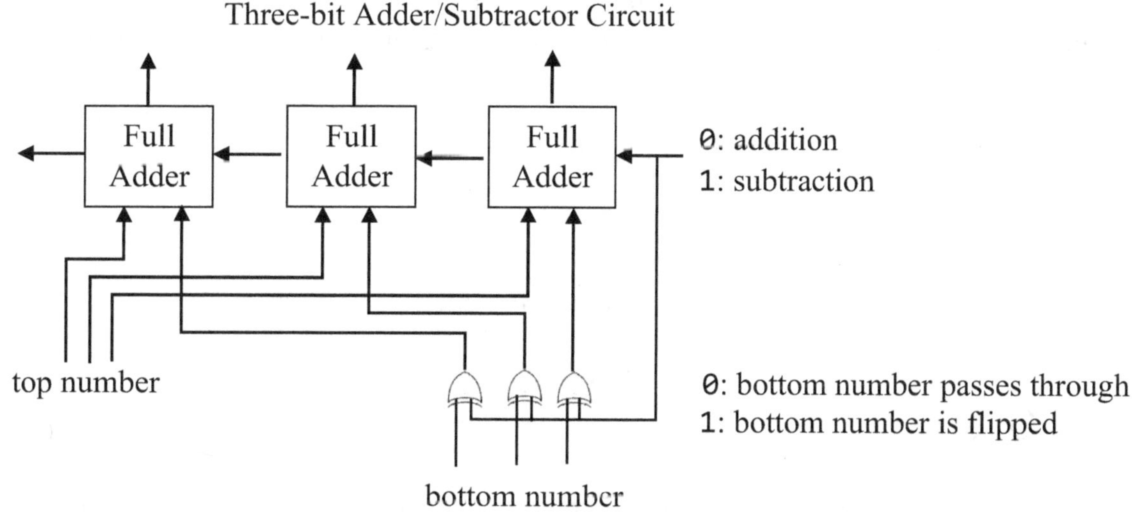

This one circuit does both addition and subtraction. We do not need separate circuits for addition and subtraction. A 16-bit version of this circuit is part of the arithmetic/logic unit in the CPU of the LCC.

On an addition, there is never a carry into the rightmost column. Thus, the carry-in line of the rightmost full adder in the adder circuit above is set to 0 on an addition. This input is also applied to the XOR gates so the bottom number passes unchanged into the full adders. On a subtraction, the carry-in line of the rightmost full adder is set to 1. This input is also applied to the XOR gates through which the bottom number passes, causing the bottom number to be flipped. The bottom number flipped plus the 1 applied to the carry-in input of the rightmost full adder *yields the two's complement of the bottom number*. Thus, the circuit in this case adds the two's complement of the bottom number to the top number, which is equivalent to subtracting the bottom number from the top number. Let's summarize what happens on a subtraction: The circuit above computes the result of the following subtraction

```
    N
 -  M
 ___
```

where N and M are two's complement numbers by performing the following addition:

```
    N
   ~M      bottom number with its bits flipped
 + 1       carry into the rightmost full adder
 ___
```

For example, to subtract 2 from 5 (assuming four-bit numbers), the computer adds 5, 2 with its bits flipped, and 1:

```
0101 = +5
1101 = +2  with its bits flipped
   1
____
0011 = 3
```

Note that the computer does *not* first takes the two's complement of the bottom number and then add it to the top number. This approach would require *two* add operations: one to add 1 to get the two's complement of the bottom number, and a second to add the complemented bottom number to the top number. Instead, the computer complements the bottom number and adds it to the top number *all in one operation*. For example, to subtract 0 for 0, the computer adds 0, 0 with its bits flipped, and 1 in one operation:

```
0000 = 0
1111 = 0  with its bits flipped
   1
____
0000 = 0
```

Note that this computation produces a carry out of the leftmost column.

Signed Overflow

In a computer, the result of an addition or subtraction is usually stored in an area of fixed size. Thus, the range of values that can be stored is limited. For example, if the result of an addition or subtraction is stored in a 16-bit register, then the range of signed numbers that can be accommodated is -32768 to $+32767$ (a *register* is a one-word storage area within the central processing unit of a computer). If the result of an addition or a subtraction is outside this range, we say *overflow* has occurred. If two positive numbers are added, the sum may be too big to fit into a fixed size storage area. Similarly, if two negative numbers are added, the result may be too negative to fit.

When a positive number and a negative number are added, overflow never occurs. The sum has to be less than the positive number because a negative number is added to the positive number. The sum also has to be greater than the negative number because a positive number is added to the negative number. Thus, the sum must lie between the negative number and the positive number. For example, suppose P is a positive number and N is a negative number. Then their sum lies between N and P:

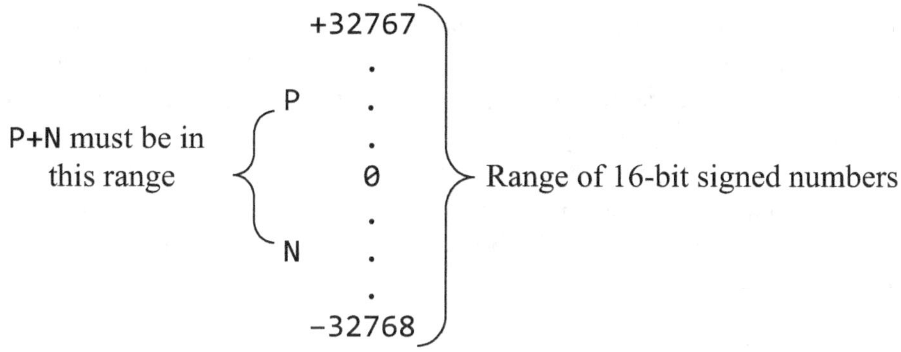

The sum cannot be more positive than the positive number or more negative that the negative number. Thus, overflow cannot occur.

A computer subtracts by adding the two's complement of the bottom number. Thus, the computer subtracts two numbers with the same sign by adding two numbers with different signs, in which case overflow cannot occur.

Rule: If two signed numbers *with different signs* are added or two signed numbers *with the same sign* are subtracted, overflow cannot occur.

If two signed numbers are added and overflow occurs, the sign of the result does not match the sign of the numbers added. Here are the two possible scenarios for overflow:

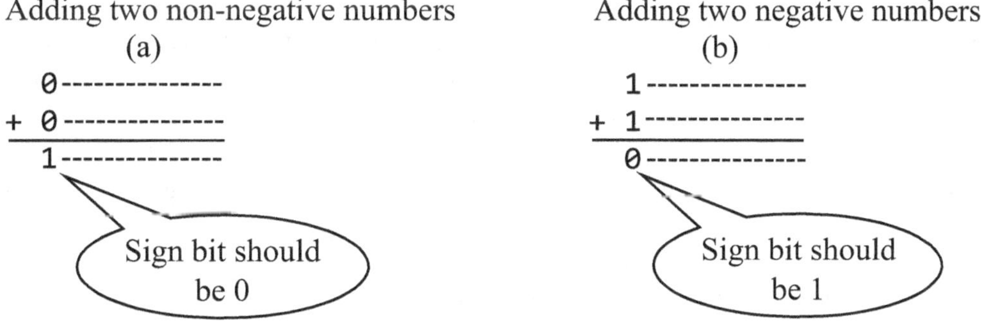

Here are all the possible scenarios for no overflow:

For case (a), there must have been a carry into the leftmost position because the bit in the result in that position is 1, but no carry out of the leftmost position. In case (b), there must have been no carry into the leftmost position because the result in that position is 0 (if there were a carry in, then the result bit would be 1). But there is a carry out of the leftmost position. Thus, for both overflow scenarios *the carry into the leftmost position does not match the carry out*. However, in all the non-overflow cases, the carry into the leftmost position matches the carry out. That is, if a carry in occurs then a carry out also occurs; if a carry in does not occur, then a carry out also does not occur. In case (c), neither a carry in nor a carry out of the leftmost position occurs. In case (d), both a carry in and a carry out occur. In case (e), both a carry in and a carry out occur. In case (f), neither a carry in nor a carry out occur.

Because the symptom of signed overflow is a mismatch between the carry into the leftmost position and the carry out, the computer hardware can easily test for signed overflow using a single XOR gate (recall that an XOR gate is a difference-detecting gate). In a computer, the full adder circuit that operates on the leftmost bits has a carry-in line and a carry-out line. A 1 on these lines indicates a carry; a 0 indicates no carry. Thus, if the values on the carry-in and carry-out lines differ, then signed overflow has occurred. If the carry-in and carry-out lines are applied to an XOR gate, its output is 1 if its input values differ (in which case signed overflow has occurred) or 0 if the input values are the same (in which case signed overflow has not occurred):

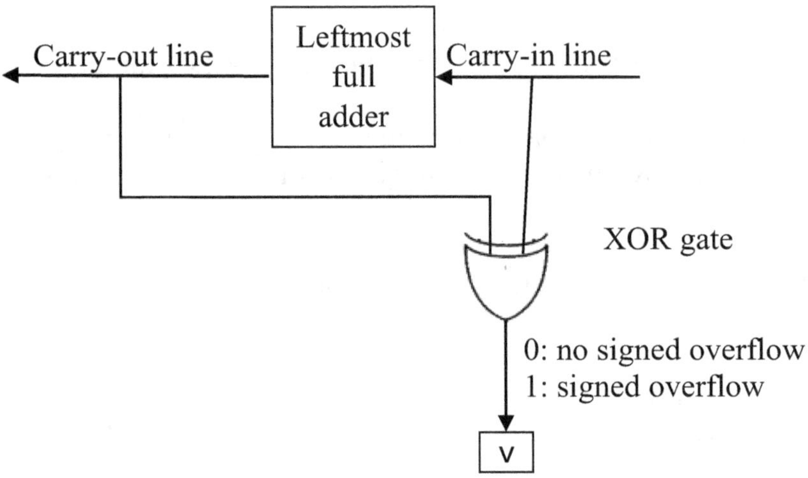

The output of the XOR gate is saved in a one-bit register named v (for o**V**erflow). Thus, if v is 1 after an addition or subtraction of signed numbers, then overflow has occurred. v is called a *flag* because it flags a condition that results from an arithmetic/logic unit operation.

Rule: In an addition or subtraction of signed numbers, overflow has occurred if the carry into the leftmost position does not match the carry out.

Rule: If overflow occurs during the addition of two signed numbers, the sign bit of the computed result is wrong. If the sign bit of the computed result is 0, then the sign bit of the *true* result is 1 (thus, the true result is negative). If the sign bit of the computed result is 1, then the sign bit of the true result is 0 (thus, the true result is greater than or equal to zero). The same is true for a subtraction of signed numbers.

Unsigned Overflow

The symptom of overflow when two *unsigned numbers* are added is a *carry out of the leftmost position*. This carry indicates another bit is needed to hold the result:

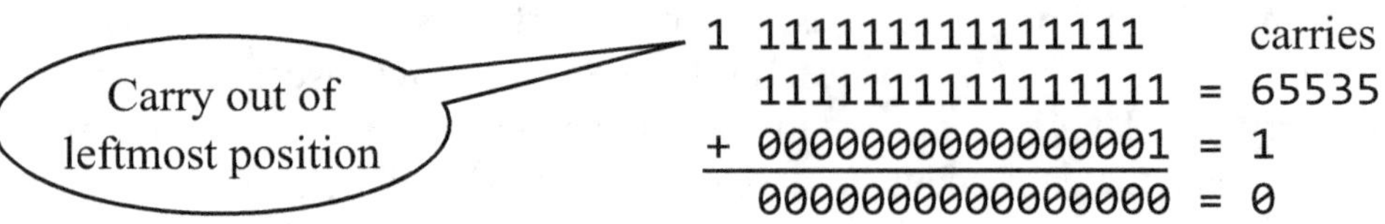


```
  1 111111111111111        carries
    1111111111111111  = 65535
  + 0000000000000001  = 1
    0000000000000000  = 0
```

On a subtraction of unsigned numbers, if the bottom number is larger than the top number, the result is negative. But the smallest *unsigned* number is 0. Thus, any negative result on a subtraction indicates unsigned overflow. If we subtract two unsigned numbers using the *borrow technique* (i.e., the subtraction technique you learned in grade school), a borrow into the leftmost position indicates that the top number is smaller than the bottom number. Thus, a *borrow into* the leftmost position indicates unsigned overflow on a subtraction. But a computer *does not subtract using the borrow technique*—it subtracts by adding the two's complement of the bottom number to the top number. It turns out that in a subtraction, if a *borrow in occurs* with the borrow technique, then a carry out *will not occur* with the two's complement technique. If a *borrow in does not occur* with the borrow technique, then a carry out *will occur* with the two's complement technique. Thus, in a subtraction of unsigned numbers, the computer hardware can determine if overflow has occurred from the carry out of the leftmost position: 1 indicates a borrow in would *not* have occurred if the borrow technique were used—thus, no unsigned overflow; 0 indicates a borrow in would have occurred if the borrow technique were used—thus, unsigned overflow. In an addition of unsigned numbers, *the test for overflow is the reverse*: on an addition, a carry out of 1 indicates signed overflow; a carry out of 0 indicates no unsigned overflow.

On an addition, the carry out of the leftmost position is stored in a one-bit register called the c flag. To make the tests for signed and unsigned overflow the same, the LCC *on a subtraction* (but not on an addition) flips the carry out with an XOR gate before storing it in the c flag. This modification of the carry out bit makes the overflow tests for the addition and subtraction of unsigned numbers the same: 1 in the c flag indicates unsigned overflow; 0 indicates no unsigned overflow.

In the circuit that follows, on a subtraction, the bits of the bottom number are flipped and a 1 is applied to the carry-in line of the rightmost full adder (which has the effect of two's complementing the bottom number). The 1 applied to the carry in of the rightmost full adder is also applied to the b input of the XOR gate that outputs to the c flag. Thus, on a subtraction (but not an addition), the carry out of the leftmost position is flipped by the XOR gate before it is stored in the c flag. Thus, for this circuit, on a subtraction, the c flag acts like a borrow flag. On a subtraction, 1 in the c flag indicates that a borrow into the leftmost position would have occurred if the subtraction were performed with the borrow technique. For this reason, the c flag is sometimes called the c/b flag (c for "carry", b for "borrow").

In addition to the v and c flags, the LCC also has an n flag and a z flag. The n flag is set to the leftmost bit of the computed result in an addition or subtraction (see the following diagram). Thus, the n flag is set to 1 if the result is negative (because the leftmost bit of a negative value is 1), and to 0 otherwise. The z flag is set to the output of a NOR gate whose inputs are all the bits in the result of an addition or a subtraction. Recall that a NOR gate is a zero-detecting gate. That is, if all its inputs are 0, it outputs 1. Otherwise, it outputs 0. Thus, the z flag is set to 1 if the result of an addition or subtraction is 0, and to 0 otherwise.

Rule: In an addition of unsigned numbers, a carry out of the leftmost position indicates overflow. In a subtraction, no carry out of the leftmost position (or a borrow in if the borrow technique is used) indicates unsigned overflow. Because the carry out of the leftmost position is flipped on a subtraction (but not on an addition) before it is loaded into the c flag, for both addition and subtraction, a 1 in the c flag indicates unsigned overflow.

Three-bit Adder/Subtractor Circuit with n, z, c, and v Flags

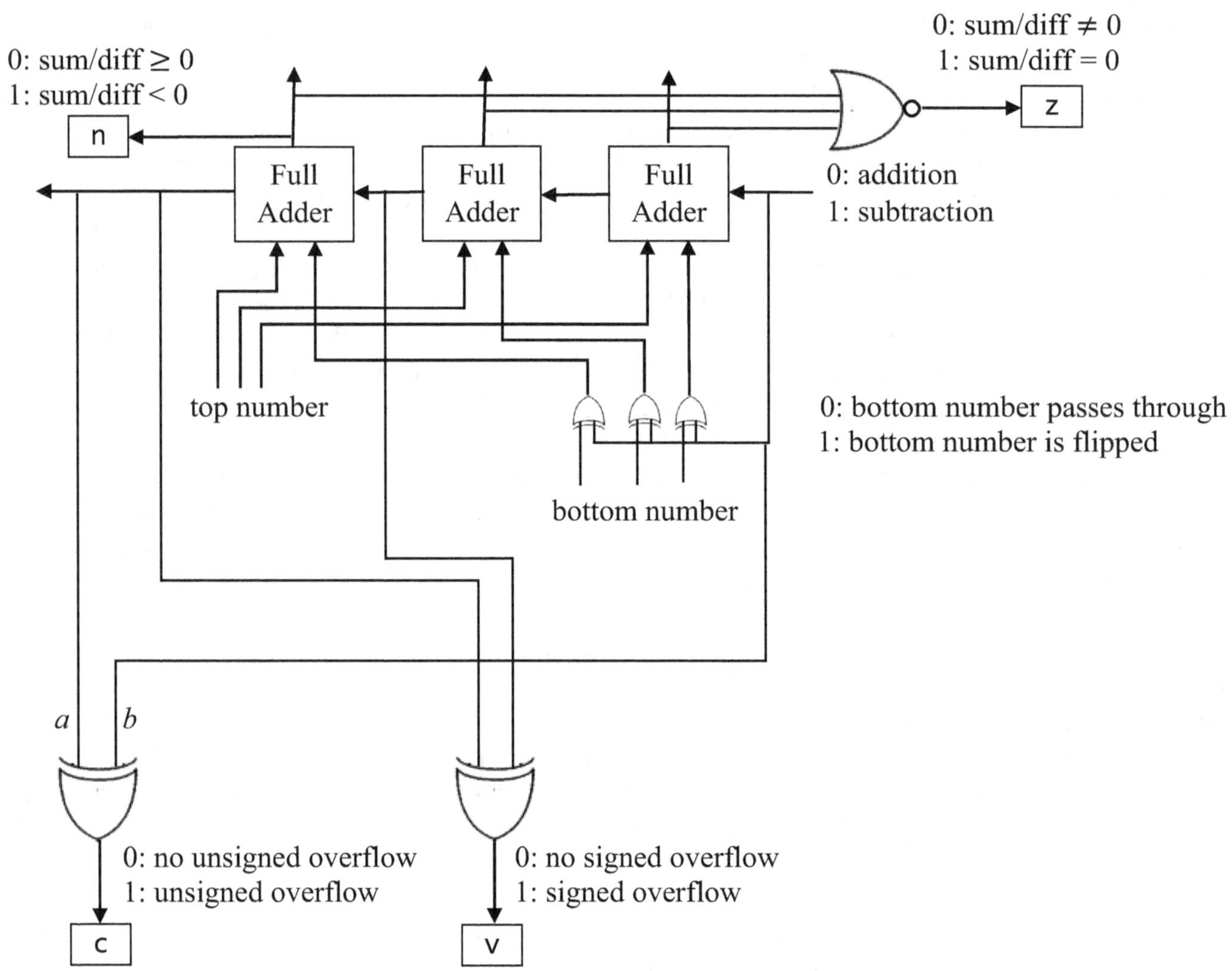

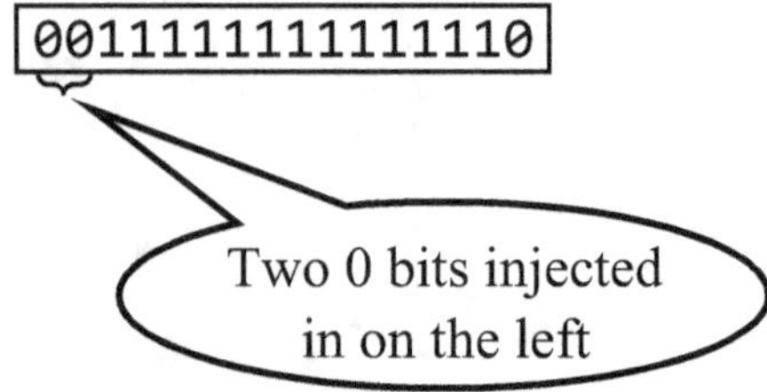

Barrel Shifter

Suppose a CPU register contains the following number (−7 decimal):

`1111111111111001`

If the register is *shifted right logically* two positions, all the bits in the register move two positions to the right. Two 0's are injected into the left side of the register to occupy the positions vacated by the shift. The two rightmost bits are shifted out of the register. The register would then contain

`0011111111111110`

If the register is *shifted left logically*, the bits move to the left the specified number of positions and 0 bits are injected into the right side of the register. Thus, a shift left logical works the same way a shift right logical works except in the opposite direction.

A *shift right arithmetic* works like a shift right logical except copies of the sign bit—which could be 0 or 1—are used to occupy the positions vacated by shift. For example, suppose the following register is shifted right arithmetically two positions:

1111111111111001

The register would then contain

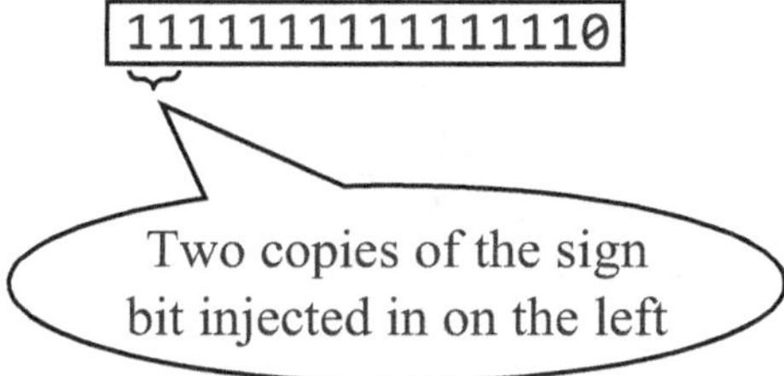

Another type of shift operation is a *rotate*. A rotate is analogous to the game of musical chairs: The bits shifted out of one side of a register and injected back into the other side of the register. For example, suppose the following register is rotated right two positions:

1111111111111001

The register would then contain

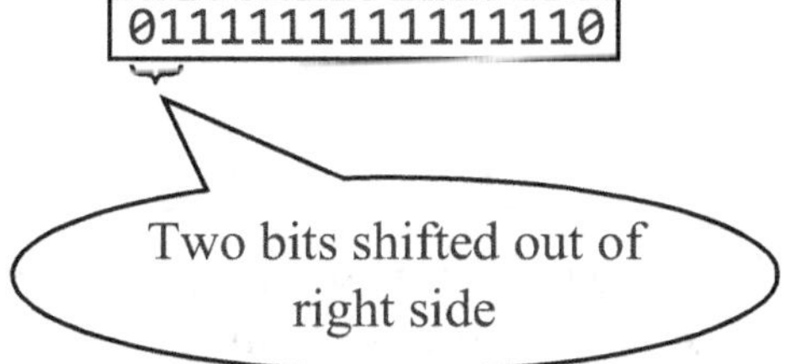

A *barrel shifter* is a combinational circuit that shifts a data word a specified number of positions. Here is the representation of a 16-bit barrel shifter that performs a logical right shift:

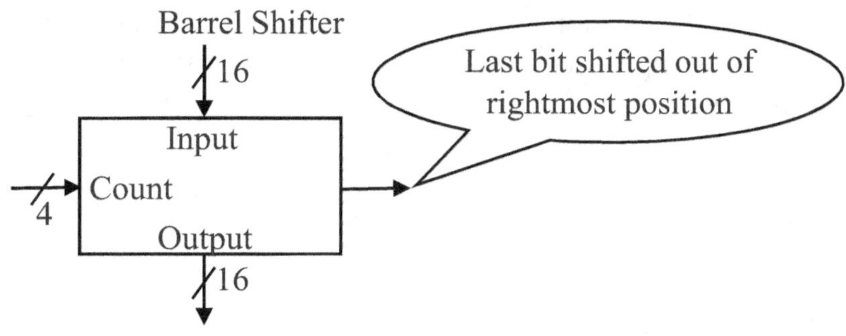

The data on the input lines are shifted right logically the number of positions specified by the count input. The shifted data appears on the output lines. The count input consists of four lines. Thus, it can specify a count in the range of 0000 to 1111 (0 to 15 decimal). The shifter also outputs the last bit shifted out of the rightmost position. This bit is routed to the c (carry) flag in the CPU.

To shift a register's contents, the register's contents and the shift count have to be routed to the barrel shifter. The output of the barrel shifter then has to be routed back to the register.

We abbreviate the names of the shift left logical, shift right logical, shift right arithmetic, rotate left, and rotate right operations sll, srl, sra, rol, and ror, respectively.

Multiplier and Divider/Remainder Circuits

The LCC has a multiplier circuit and a divider/remainder circuit (a remainder circuit provides the remainder that results when two integers are divided). These circuits have two 16-bit inputs (for the two numbers to be operated on) and a 16-bit output. Here are their representations:

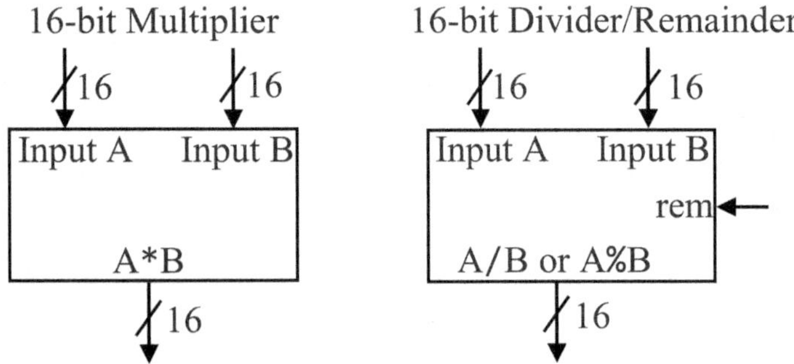

Random-Access and Read-Only Memory

Random-access memory (RAM) is memory that is both readable and writeable. It is "random" in the sense that any word can be read or written without having to access the words that precede it. Read-only memory (ROM) also has this random-access property. However, by convention, "random-access memory" refers only to readable/writeable memory.

RAM can be implemented using rows of D flip-flops, with one row for each word in memory. For example, we can implement the memory on the LCC with 65536 rows, each containing 16 D flip-flops. A decoder is used to determine which row is used in a read or write operation. Two control inputs, rd and wr, determine if a read or write operation occurs. Data is transferred between RAM and the memory data register (mdr) in the CPU via a bidirectional data bus. The address to read from (on a read operation) or the address to write to (on a write operation) is transferred from the memory address register (mar) in the CPU to RAM via a unidirectional address bus:

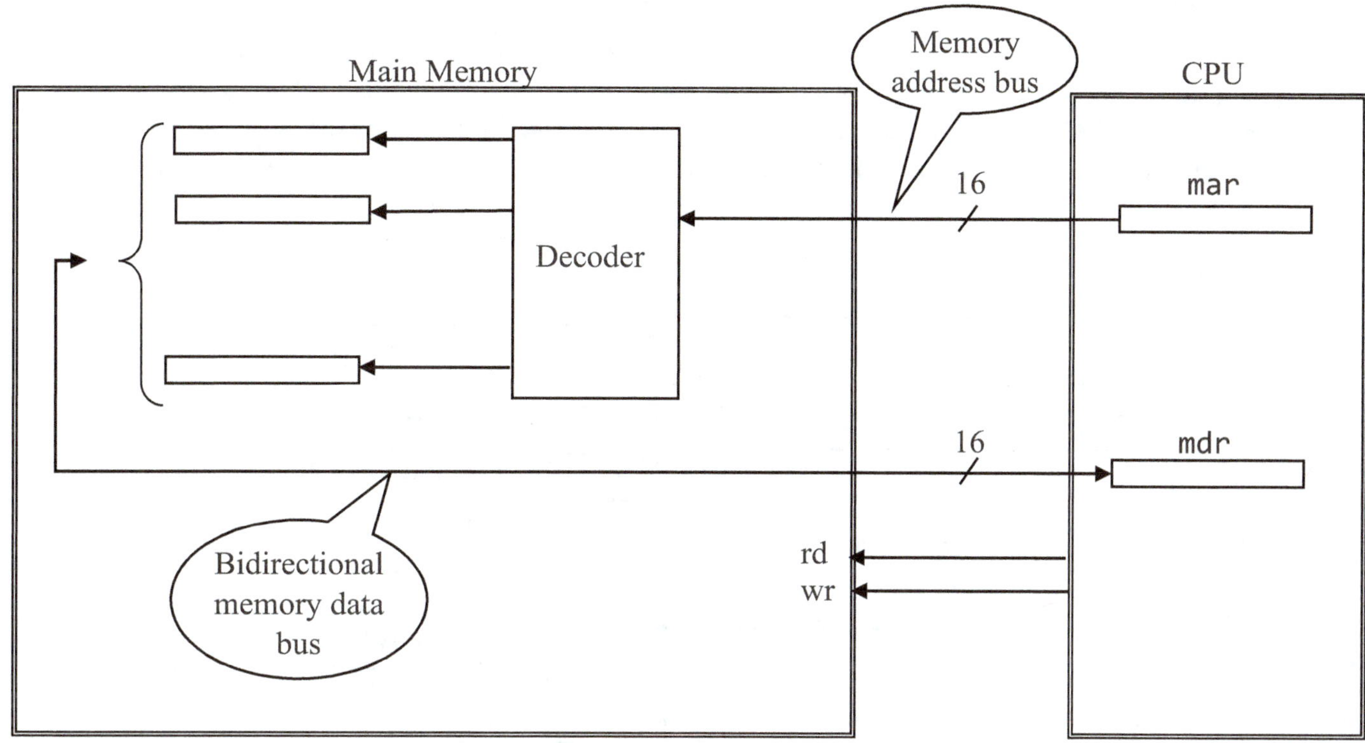

RAM is volatile. That is, its contents are lost when power is turned off. ROM (read-only memory), on the other hand, is non-volatile. That is, its contents are maintained whether or not power is on.

In the LCC, a ROM is used for the microstore (recall that microstore is the memory that holds the microprogram). Its interface is simpler than that of a RAM: It does not have the rd and wr control inputs. In addition, it is not connected to a bidirectional data bus, but to a strictly outgoing data bus. An incoming bus provides the address, and the outgoing data bus the provides the microinstruction at that address:

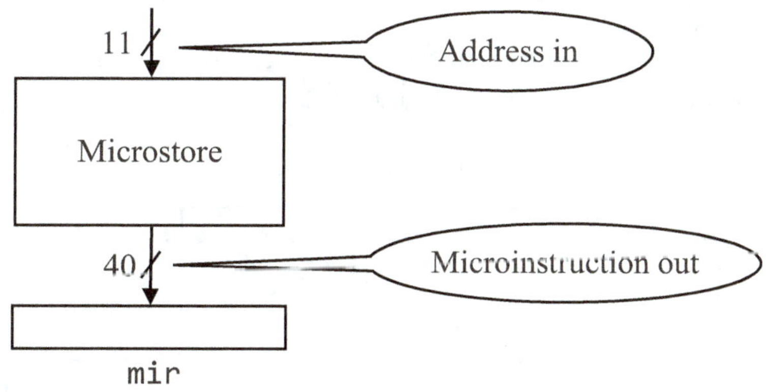

The ROM that contains the microprogram has 2048 locations whose addresses therefore, run from 0 to 2047. Eleven-bit unsigned numbers range from 0 to 2047. Thus, we need 11 bits to address the locations in microstore.

Registers

A register is a special memory area that holds one word of information. The CPU of the LCC has 32 16-bit registers named r0, r1, …, r31. Each register can drive the A bus and/or the B bus or neither. Here is the representation of r0 and its associated circuitry:

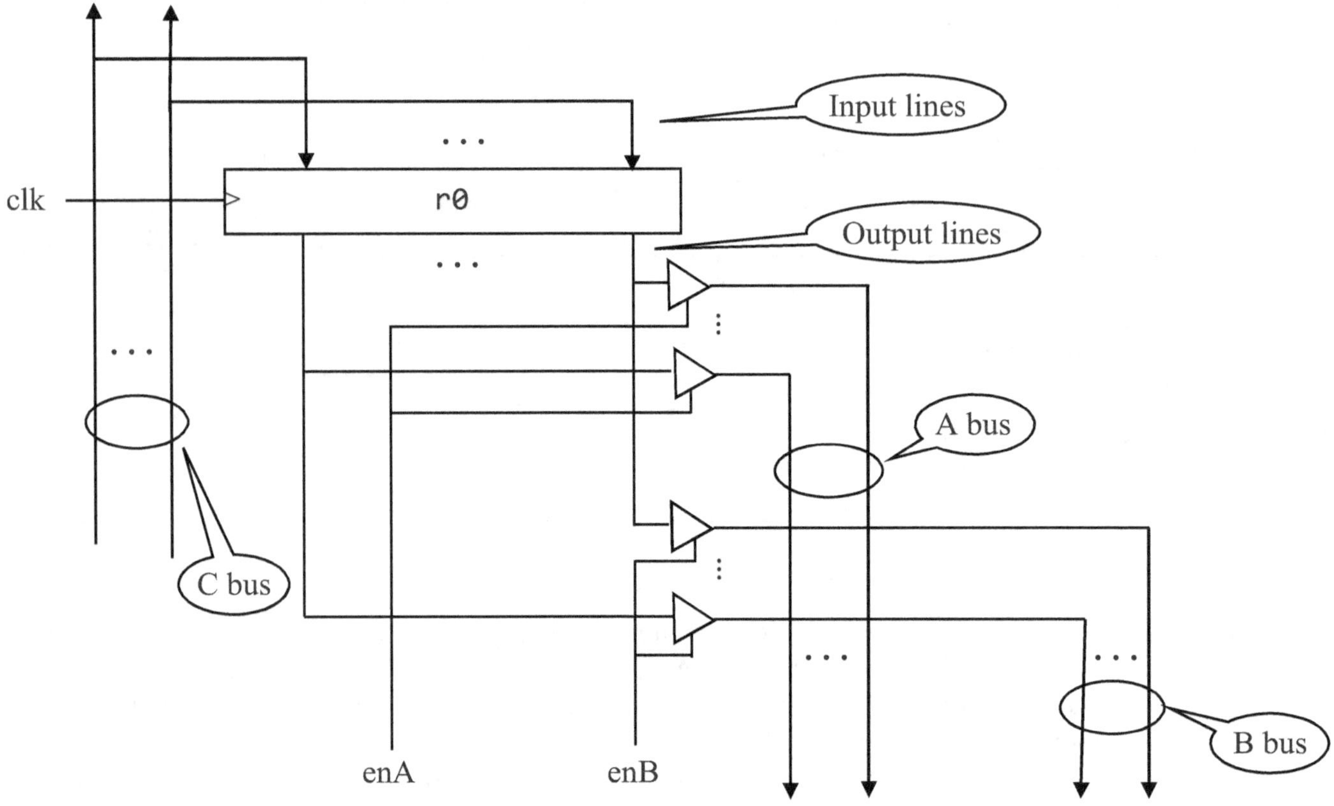

If enA = 1, the register drives the A bus. If enB = 1, the register drives the B bus. If clk goes positive, the register is loaded from the C bus.

When we represent a register in a circuit diagram, we will not include in its representation the tri-state circuitry. For example, here is our representation of r0:

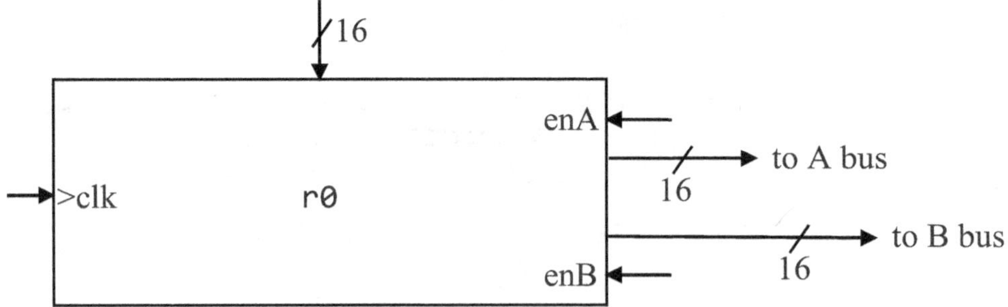

Arithmetic/Logic Unit

One typically first hears about an ALU (arithmetic/logic unit) in an introductory computer science course. We learn that an ALU is the unit within a computer that performs computations at incredible speeds. Surely, the ALU, the heart of a computer, must be awesomely complex. But this, in fact, is not necessarily the case. The ALU for LCC is actually quite simple, consisting of a straightforward combination of mostly simple circuits.

Let's examine the operation of the ALU in the LCC from an external point of view:

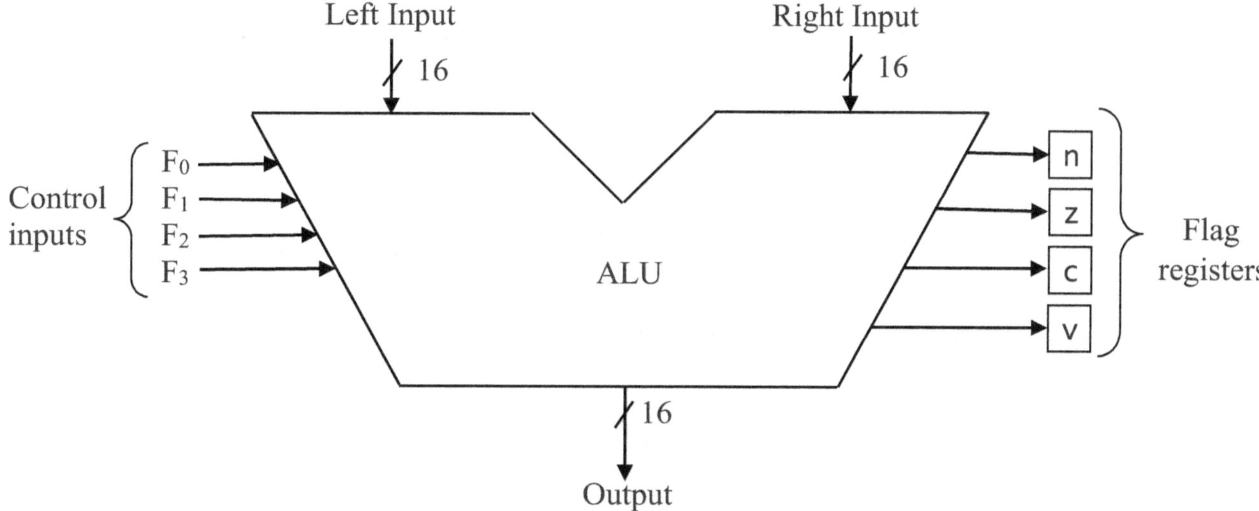

The ALU has two 16-bit input ports (left and right) and a 16-bit output port. Four control inputs, F_0, F_1, F_2, and F_3, determine the operation performed by the ALU. These four control inputs can specify a number from 0000 to 1111 (0 to 15 decimal), each of which triggers a different ALU operation as indicated by the following table:

F_3	F_2	F_1	F_0		Operation	Output	Flags Set
0	0	0	0	(0)	nop	left	
0	0	0	1	(1)	not	~left	nz
0	0	1	0	(2)	and	left & right	nz
0	0	1	1	(3)	sext	left sign-extended, (right is mask)	nz
0	1	0	0	(4)	add	left + right	nzcv
0	1	0	1	(5)	sub	left − right	nzcv
0	1	1	0	(6)	mul	left * right	nz
0	1	1	1	(7)	div	left / right	nz
1	0	0	0	(8)	rem	left % right	nz
1	0	0	1	(9)	or	left | right	nz
1	0	1	0	(10)	xor	left ^ right	nz
1	0	1	1	(11)	sll	left << right (logical)	nzc
1	1	0	0	(12)	srl	left >> right (logical)	nzc
1	1	0	1	(13)	sra	left >> right (arithmetic)	nzc
1	1	1	0	(14)	rol	left << right (rotate)	nzc
1	1	1	1	(15)	ror	left >> right (rotate)	nzc

The first two operations in this table operate on the left input only. For these operations, the ALU ignores the right input. The first operation (when $F_0 = F_1 = F_2 = F_3 = 0$) is a no-operation. That is, it allows the data from the left input to pass unchanged through the ALU. For this operation, the flag registers are not set.

It is easy to construct the ALU given the circuits for each operation it is to perform. We simply use a bus multiplexer that selects which circuit determines the ALU's output:

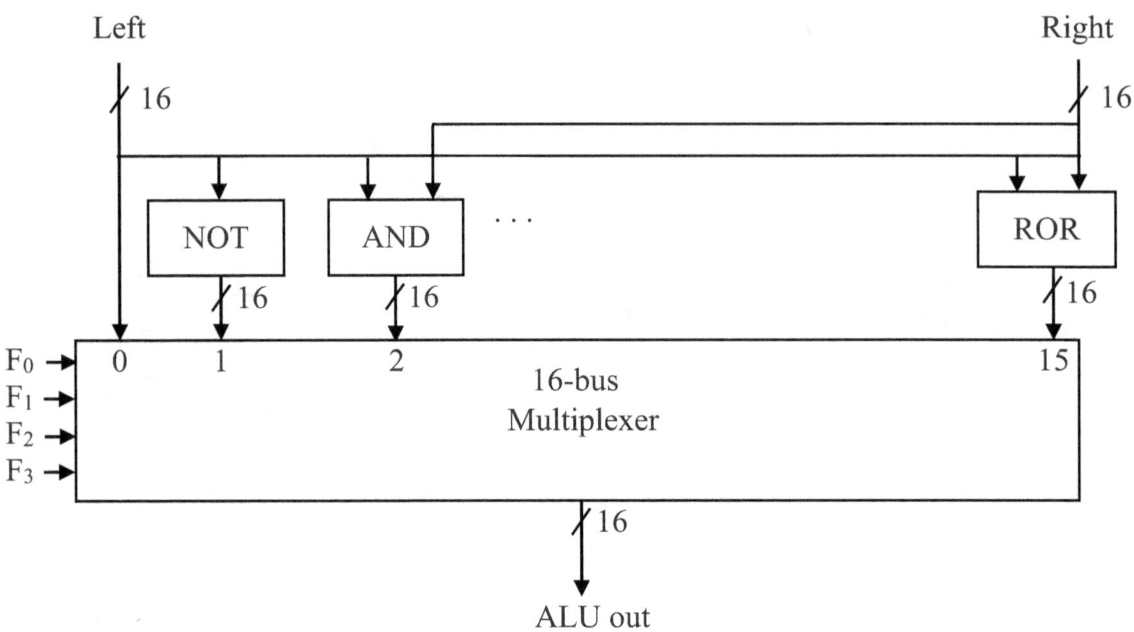

Loadable Binary Counter

A binary counter is a register that can hold a binary number. However, unlike a regular register, each time it receives an external clock pulse, the number it holds increases by one. When it contains all ones and then receives a clock pulse, it wraps around to all zeros.

The *microprogram program counter* (mpc) in the LCC is a binary counter. The function of the mpc at the microlevel is like the function of the pc register at the machine level. The pc register at the machine level holds the main memory address of the machine instruction to be executed next. Similarly, the mpc register at the microlevel holds the microstore address of the next microinstruction to be executed.

Because microstore has only 2048 slots, to address it requires only an 11-bit address (11-bit unsigned numbers range from 0 to 2047). For this reason, the mpc is an 11-bit counter. The address in the mpc is inputted to microstore. Microstore responds by outputting the microinstruction at that address to the microinstruction register (mir). As soon as the microinstruction is loaded into the mir, its bits are outputted to the various control inputs of the computational circuits in the LCC. For example, four of the output lines on the mir go to the F_0, F_1, F_2, and F_3 control inputs of the ALU. We refer to the process of loading a microinstruction into the mir and letting its bits drive the various control inputs in the CPU as *executing the microinstruction.*

Microstore has 2048 slots each of which is 40 bits wide. For this reason, in the diagram below, we label it with "2048 x 40."

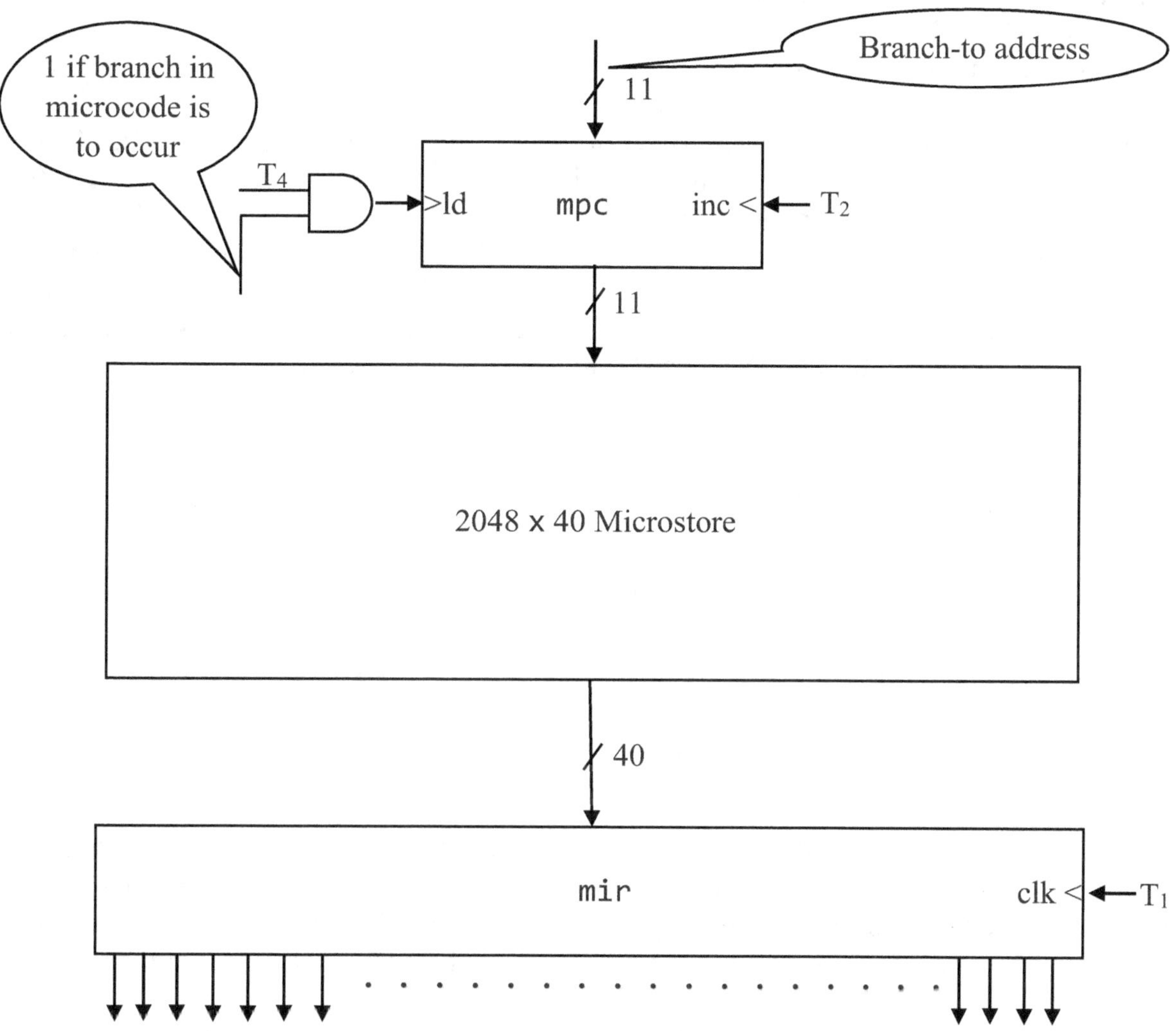

To the control inputs of the computational circuits

To execute the next microinstruction, a clock pulse is applied to the inc input of the `mpc`, causing it to be incremented. The new address in the `mpc` causes microstore to output the next microinstruction to the `mir`. Thus, this mechanism causes microinstructions in microstore to be executed in memory order. For example, after the microinstruction at address 0 is executed, the microinstruction at address 1 is executed, then at address 2, and so on. However, occasionally a branch in microcode has to occur. For example, suppose the `mpc` currently contains 5, but the next microinstruction to be executed is at the address 9, not 6. To effect a branch to location 9, the branch-to address—9—is applied to the 11 input lines on the `mpc`, and a 1 is applied to its ld input. This causes the branch-to address to be loaded into the `mpc`, which in turn causes the microinstruction at that address to be outputted by microstore and loaded into the `mir`. The result is that the microinstruction at location 9 is executed next.

Clock Sequencer

The various operations that a CPU performs often require a specific sequence of suboperations. For example, to add 1 to the `pc` register, the CPU must

1) Route the `pc` register contents and the number 1 to the adder circuit in the ALU.
2) Instruct the ALU to add.
3) Route the sum back to the `pc` register.

Obviously, the CPU cannot route the sum back to the `pc` register before the ALU has produced the sum. The ALU cannot produce the sum until it has the `pc` register contents and the number 1. Thus, the three steps above must be performed in the order given.

To enforce a particular order of operations to be performed, the LCC uses a sequencer circuit that outputs four clock signals: T_1, T_2, T_3 and T_4. When T_1 is 1, T_2, T_3, and T_4 are 0. When T_1 returns to 0, T_2 becomes 1. When T_2 returns to 0, T_3 becomes 1. When T_3 returns to 0, T_4 becomes 1. When T_4 returns to 0, the cycle repeats with T_1 again becoming 1. Here is a timing graph that shows the T_1, T_2, T_3 , and T_4 signals versus time:

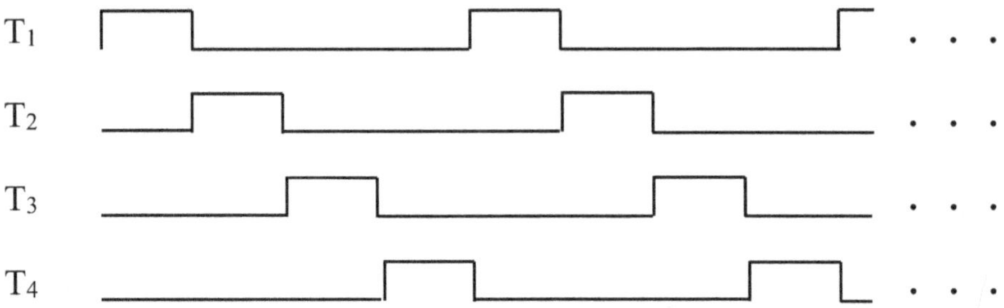

T_1 drives the clock input on the `mir`. Thus, every time T_1 goes to 1, a new microinstruction is loaded into the `mir`. T_2 is applied to the inc input of the `mpc`, causing the `mpc` to be incremented at T_2. The microinstruction at the new address immediately appears on the output lines of microstore. However, this microinstruction is not immediately loaded into the `mir` because the `mir` is loaded from microstore only at T_1.

If the two inputs to the AND gate that is driving the ld input on the `mpc` are 1, the AND gate outputs a 1 to the ld input, which causes the `mpc` to be loaded with the branch-to address. Because one of the inputs to this AND gate is T_4, the loading of the branch-to address into the `mpc` occurs only at T_4 and only if the other input to the AND gate is 1. Then on the next T_1, the next microinstruction—either at the incremented address (if no branch) or at the branch-to address—is loaded into the `mir` and executed.

Let's summarize: A microinstruction is executed simply by loading it into the `mir`. Once loaded into the `mir`, the bits in the microinstruction immediately flow out of the `mir` to the control inputs of the computational circuits in the CPU via wires that connect the bits in the `mir` to these control inputs. The computational circuits respond by performing those operations specified by the microinstruction.

At T_1, the `mir` is loaded from microstore with the microinstruction at the address in the `mpc`. At T_2, the `mpc` is incremented. At T_3 the flag registers are updated (unless the ALU is performing a no-operation). At T_4, if a branch in microcode is to occur, the branch-to address is loaded into `mpc`, replacing the address there, and some register is loaded from the C bus (unless the specified register is the read-only register `r31`). Every T_1-T_2-T_3-T_4 cycle, one microinstruction is executed.

Microinstructions are executed in memory order unless a branch occurs. The microinstructions determine what operations are performed. The T_1, T_2, T_3, and T_4 clock signals determine the order in which the suboperations for a microinstructions occur. In the next chapter, we will see what determines if a branch in microcode occurs and where the branch-to address comes from.

Because the `mpc`, microstore, and the `mir` together provide the control signals for the CPU, they are collectively called the *control unit*.

The operations that are triggered by a microinstruction and the clock signals are called *micro-operations*. The execution of one machine language instruction requires the execution of a sequence of microoperations. For example, consider the **add** machine instruction, 2007, in the basic instruction set. When executed, it adds the word at address 007 in main memory to the **ac** register. It requires the following sequence of microoperations:

1. Send the address 007 to main memory.
2. Initiate a main memory read operation.
3. Route the operand read from main memory and the contents of the **ac** register to the left and right inputs of the ALU, respectively.
4. Instruct the ALU to add its left and right inputs.
5. Route the output of the ALU to the **ac** register.

Problems

1) The **mir** is loaded at T_1, the **mpc** is incremented at T_2, and the **mpc** is loaded at T_4 with the branch-to address if a branch is to occur. Why is this order necessary?

2) Are four clock subcycles necessary? Would three (T_1, T_2, and T_3) be sufficient? Explain.

3) At what point in the T_1-T_2-T_3-T_4 clock cycle does the ALU start performing its calculation?

4) Can the clock input to the **mpc** be driven by T_3 instead of T_2? Explain.

5) The standard registers in the LCC can drive either the A bus or the B bus. Can a register drive both buses simultaneously?

6) Implement a two-input multiplexer using AND, OR, and NOT gates.

7) Implement a two-input multiplexer using tri-state buffers and one NOT gate.

8) Implement a two-bus multiplexer in which each bus has three wires.

9) Implement a four-bit bitwise AND circuit.

10) Implement a four-bit bitwise NOT circuit.

11) Implement a two-bit decoder.

12) What items have to be provided to main memory for a read operation.

13) What items have to be provided to main memory for a write operation.

14) The LCC has a bank of registers consisting of 31 standard read/write registers and one read-only register. How many control inputs does the entire bank of registers have?

15) There are more control inputs in the LCC than there are bits in a microinstruction. So how can a single microinstruction drive all the control inputs? *Hint*: A decoder has n inputs and 2^n outputs.

16) How do the `pc` and `mpc` registers differ? Are they implemented in the same way? Are they incremented in the same way? Are they the same size? To where are there outputs directed?

17) If microstore had 8192 slots, what would be the size of the `mpc` register?

18) Using the schematic representations of the sub-circuits that make up the ALU of the LCC, implement the ALU. In particular, show how the add, subtract, divide, and remainder operations are activated. Recall that the adder/subtractor circuit has a control input that determines which operation it performs. In your implementation show what drives this control input. Do the same for the divide/remainder circuit.

19) Design a two-input decoder that has an additional control input X. When X = 1, the decoder should work normally. However, when X = 0, the decoder outputs should all be forced to 0.

20) Design a 2-bit ALU that has one control input C. When C = 0, the output should be the NAND of its inputs; when C = 1, the output should be the AND of its inputs. Use as few gates as possible.

21) Design a circuit with 8 data inputs and one output P. P should be set equal to 0 if the parity of the eight data bits is even, and to 1, otherwise. Parity is even if the number of 1 bits is even; parity is odd if the number of 1 bits is odd.

22) When the adder/subtractor subtracts a number from itself, does a carry out of the leftmost position always occur? Consider 0 subtracted from 0, and 5 subtracted from 5.

23) Construct a two-bit counter. *Hint*: Use JK flip-flops.

24) Give the truth table for a full subtractor circuit. A full subtractor has two data inputs, a borrow-in, a difference-out, and a borrow-out.

6 Microlevel of the LCC

Introduction

In this chapter, we construct the LCC using the digital circuits we studied in the preceding two chapters. Our LCC, however, will still not be a working computer. The one item that will be lacking is the microcode that implements the basic instruction set that we learned in chapters 2 and 3. In the next chapter, however, we will learn how to write the microcode for the basic instruction set and incorporate it into the LCC.

Data Path

The *data path* of the LCC consists of a bank of 32 16-bit registers (named r0 to r31), the ALU, the A and B buses that connect the register bank to the left and right inputs of the ALU, and a C bus that connects the output of the ALU to the register bank:

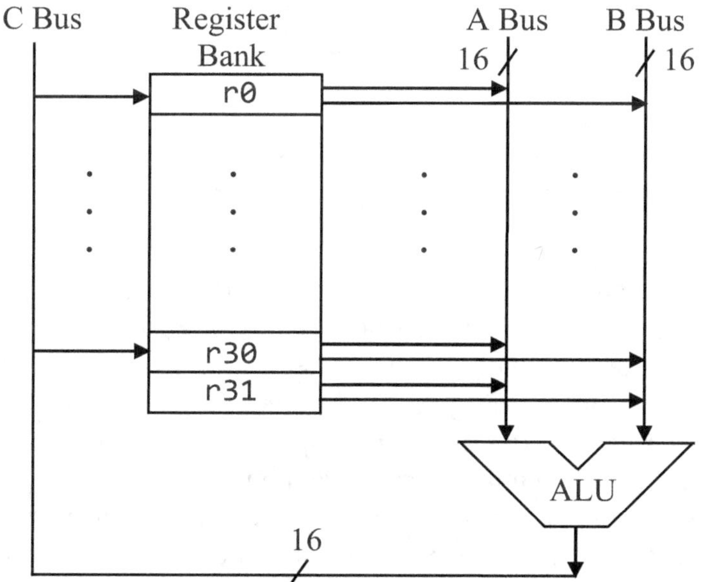

Registers r0 through r30 are read/write registers. Register r31 is read-only—it permanently contains 0. Each register can drive the A and/or B buses through a bank of tri-state buffers. Each register, except the read-only register r31, can be loaded from the C bus.

The data path in the LCC forms a circuit. Data in the registers flows through the A and B buses into the ALU. The result computed by the ALU then flows through the C bus back into one of the registers.

One of the operations that the ALU can perform (when $F_0 = F_1 = F_2 = F_3 = 0$) is to simply let its left input pass unchanged to its output. This operation is performed by the ALU when a microinstruction is executed that copies one register to another. For example, to copy r2 to r1, a microinstruction is executed that makes the data in r2 take the circular route from r2 straight through the ALU to r1.

Main Memory Interface

The data path forms a circuit. For it to do any useful work, data from main memory has to get into the circuit. Then when the computed results are available, the results have to get out of the circuit back into main memory. This data flow between the data path and main memory is accomplished with two buses (the *memory data bus* and the *memory address bus*), two registers in the register bank (the `mar` and the `mdr`), and two control signals (rd and wr) that emanate from the microinstruction in the `mir`:

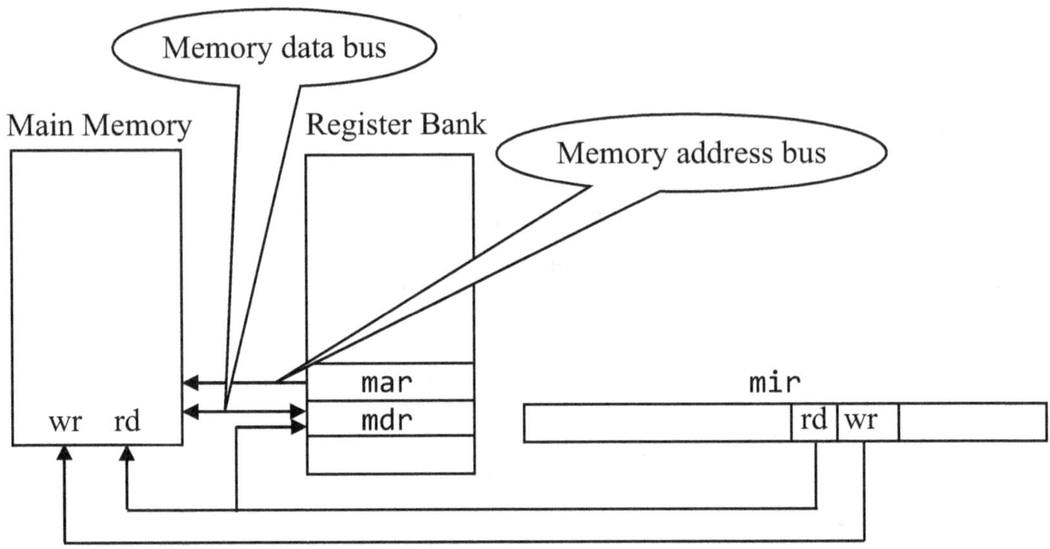

To read from main memory, a microinstruction first has to load the `mar` (the memory address register), which is `r29` in the register bank, with the address to read from. When the read-from address is in the `mar`, a second microinstruction has to be executed with 1 in its rd field. This 1 drives the rd input on the main memory unit, causing it to read the word at the given address and provide it to the `mdr` via the memory data bus. The rd signal from the microinstruction is also applied to the circuitry surrounding the `mdr`. The rd signal causes the `mdr` to be loaded from the memory data bus.

 To write to main memory, microinstructions first have to be executed that load the `mar` with the write-to address and the `mdr`, which is `r30` in the register bank, with the data to be written. When both the `mar` and `mdr` have been properly initialized, another microinstruction has to be executed with 1 in its wr field. This 1 then drives the wr input on the main memory unit, causing it to write the word in the `mdr` to the address given by the `mar`.

Decoding the Register Fields in a Microinstruction

Recall that each register in the register bank is connected to the A bus via a bank of tri-state buffers. The enA (enable A) control line for a register is connected to the control inputs of all the tri-state buffers that connect that register to the A Bus. Thus, if 1 is on the enA control line for a register, then that register drives the A bus. That is, the tri-state buffers let the contents of the register pass through to the A bus. If, on the other hand, the enA control input is 0, then the tri-state buffers electrically disconnect the register from the A bus. If you are fuzzy at this point on how registers work, you should review the section on registers in the preceding chapter.

Each register has an enA control input. Thus, there are a total of 32 enA control inputs. The A field in a microinstruction specifies which register should drive the A bus. But the A field has only five bits. How can five bits correctly drive all 32 enA control inputs? The answer is via a decoder. The A field in a microinstruction contains the 5-bit number of the register that is to drive the A bus. This number is inputted to a decoder. A five-input decoder has 32 outputs, one for each enA control input:

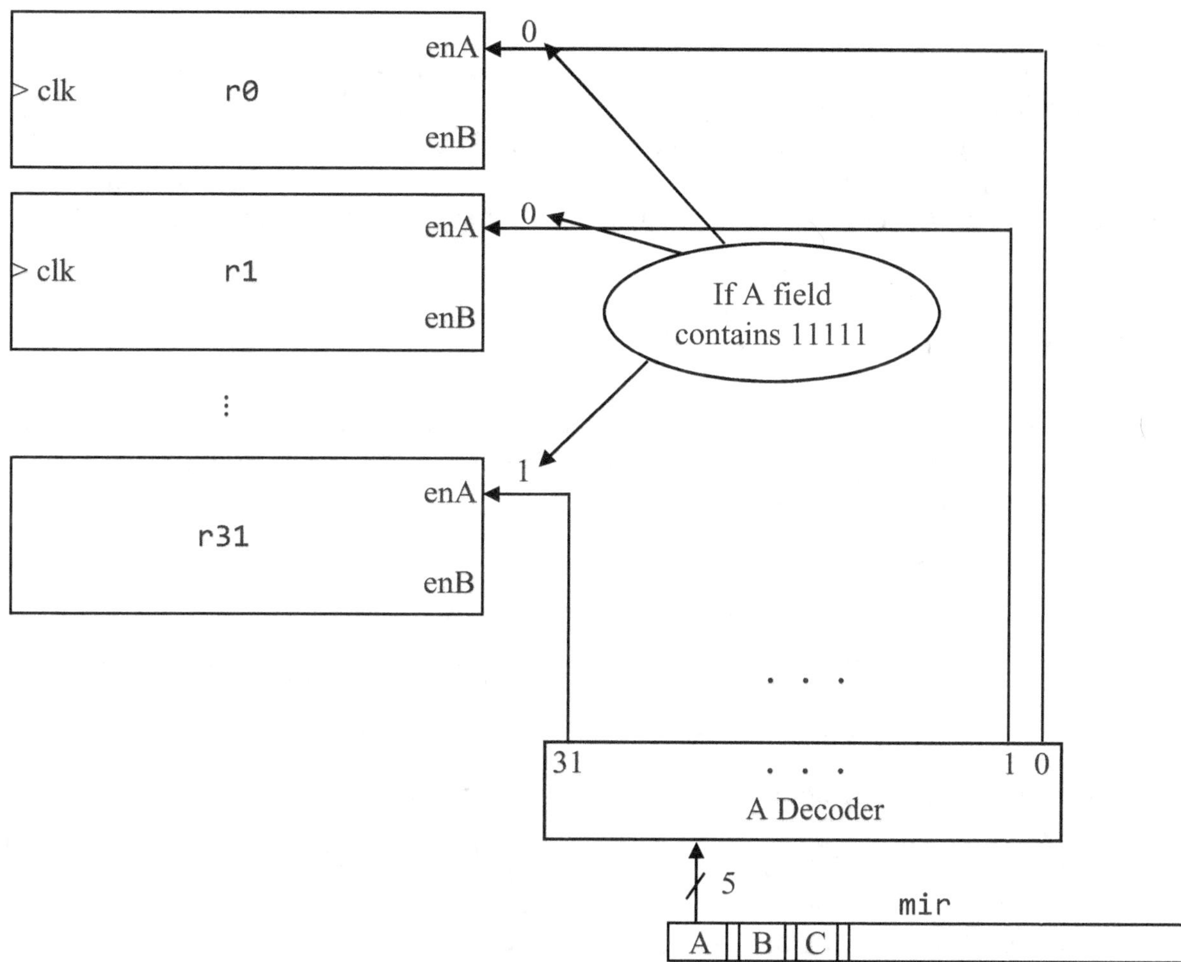

For example, suppose the A field in the microinstruction in the `mir` contains 11111 (31 decimal). Then the decoder outputs 1 on its output 31 and 0 on all its other output lines. Thus, only `r31` drives the A bus. Note that to make the diagram above easy to read, we have omitted in the connections between the registers and the A and B buses.

The B field similarly drives a B decoder whose outputs drives the enB control inputs of the registers. Thus, the B field in the microinstruction determines which register drives the B bus.

The C field drives a C decoder whose outputs drive AND gates that in turn drive the clk inputs on registers `r0` through `r30`. For example, here is the configuration at the clk input for `r30`:

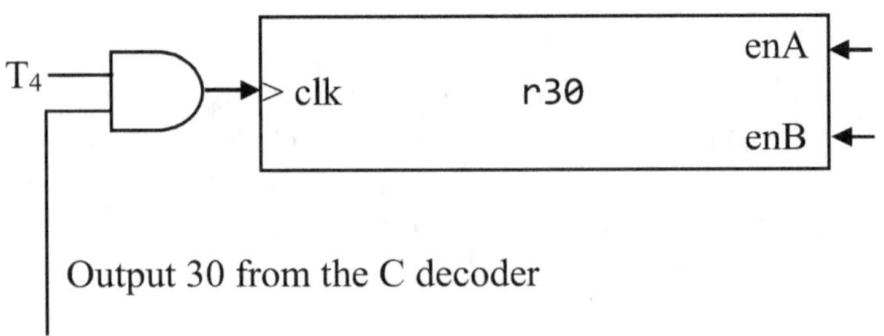

The second input to the AND gates that drive the clk inputs is T_4. Thus, if a register is to be loaded, it is loaded only at T_4. r31 is a read-only register so output 31 of the C decoder is not used. The C field in the microinstruction in the mir determines which register is loaded from the C bus.

Our description here of the circuitry that performs register decoding is somewhat simplified. For now, it is adequate for our purposes. In chapter 9, we will see the actual decoding circuitry in the LCC.

Specifying the ALU Operation

The alu field of the microinstruction in the mir determines the ALU operation. The alu field is a four-bit field. A four-bit field can hold unsigned numbers from 0000 to 1111 (0 to 15 decimal). Thus, the alu field can specify any one of 16 operations.

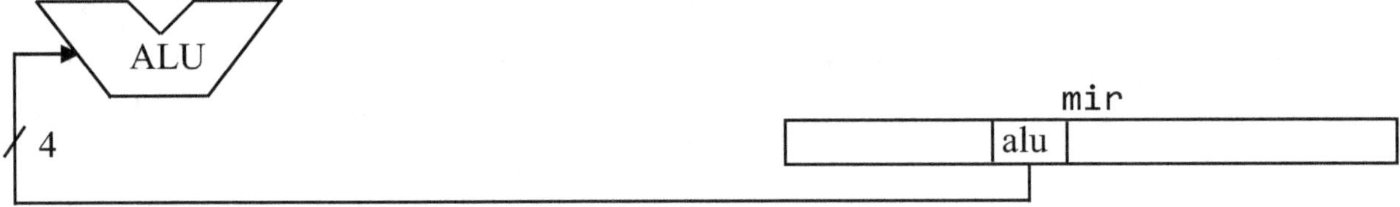

Here is a summary of the operations that the ALU can perform:

F_3	F_2	F_1	F_0		Mnemonic	Output	Flags Set
0	0	0	0	(0)	nop	left	
0	0	0	1	(1)	not	~left	nz
0	0	1	0	(2)	and	left & right	nz
0	0	1	1	(3)	sext	left sign-extended, (right is mask)	nz
0	1	0	0	(4)	add	left + right	nzcv
0	1	0	1	(5)	sub	left − right	nzcv
0	1	1	0	(6)	mul	left * right	nz
0	1	1	1	(7)	div	left / right	nz
1	0	0	0	(8)	rem	left % right	nz
1	0	0	1	(9)	or	left | right	nz
1	0	1	0	(10)	xor	left ^ right	nz
1	0	1	1	(11)	sll	left << right (logical)	nzc
1	1	0	0	(12)	srl	left >> right (logical)	nzc
1	1	0	1	(13)	sra	left >> right (arithmetic)	nzc
1	1	1	0	(14)	rol	left << right (rotate)	nzc
1	1	1	1	(15)	ror	left >> right (rotate)	nzc

Branch-Control Logic

As we previously discussed, after the `mpc` is incremented at T₂, a new address can be loaded into the `mpc` at T₄, triggering a branch in the microcode. This new address comes from the addr field of the current microinstruction (i.e., the microinstruction in the `mir`):

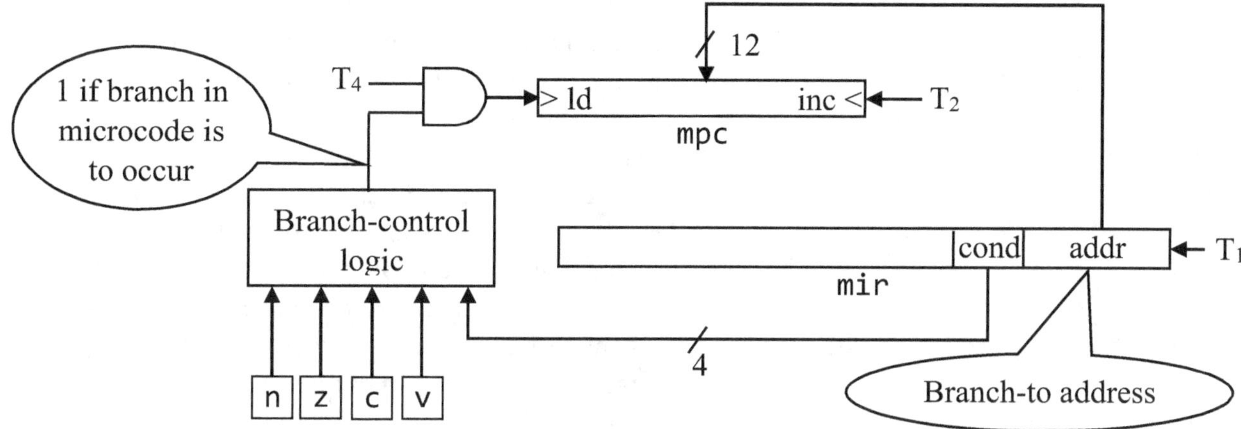

The output of the branch-control logic drives one of the inputs of the AND gate on the `mpc`. Thus, if the branch-control logic outputs a 1, then at T₄, a 1 is applied to the ld input of the `mpc`, causing the branch-to address to be loaded into the `mpc`. This, in turn, causes a branch in microcode to the branch-to address. The output of the branch-control logic depends on eight inputs: the four flag registers (n, z, c, and v) and the four-bit cond field in the microinstruction in the `mir`. If the cond field is 0000, then the branch-control logics output a 0 regardless of the contents of the flag registers, in which case a branch does not occur. If the cond field is 1111 (15 decimal), then the branch-control logic outputs a 1 regardless of the flag registers, in which case a branch occurs. The other 14 cond field values cause a branch only if the flag registers have specific values. For example, if the cond field is 0100 (4 decimal), then the branch-control logic outputs 1 if the n flag register contains 0 (which indicates the result of the most recent ALU operation was not negative). Thus, the cond field value 0100 in a microinstruction indicates that the microinstruction is a "branch on not negative" instruction. Similarly, the cond field value 0010 in a microinstruction indicates that the microinstruction is a "branch on not zero" instruction.

In the next chapter, the only cond values we use in the implementation of the basic instruction set are 0 (no branch), 2 (branch on not zero), 4 (branch on not negative), and 15 (unconditional branch). We will discuss the other cond values in later chapters when we need to use them.

Here is list of all the cond field values, what they test, and their effect:

cond	Mnemonic	Branch if	Branch on
0	nobr		never
1	zer	$z = 1$	zero
2	!zer	$z = 0$	not zero
3	neg	$n = 1$	negative
4	!neg	$n = 0$	not negative
5	cy or <	$c = 1$	less than (unsigned compare/overflow)
6	!cy or >=	$c = 0$	greater than or eq (unsigned compare)
7	v	$v = 1$	signed overflow
8	pos	$n = z$	positive
9	lt	$n \mathrel{!=} v$	less than (signed compare)
10	le	$n \mathrel{!=} v$ or $z = 1$	less than or equal (signed compare)
11	gt	$n = v$ and $z = 0$	greater than (signed compare)
12	ge	$n = v$	greater than or equal (signed compare)
13	<=	$c = 1$ or $z = 1$	less than or equal (unsigned compare)
14	>	$c = 0$ and $z = 0$	greater than (unsigned compare)
15	br		always

Complete Microlevel of the LCC

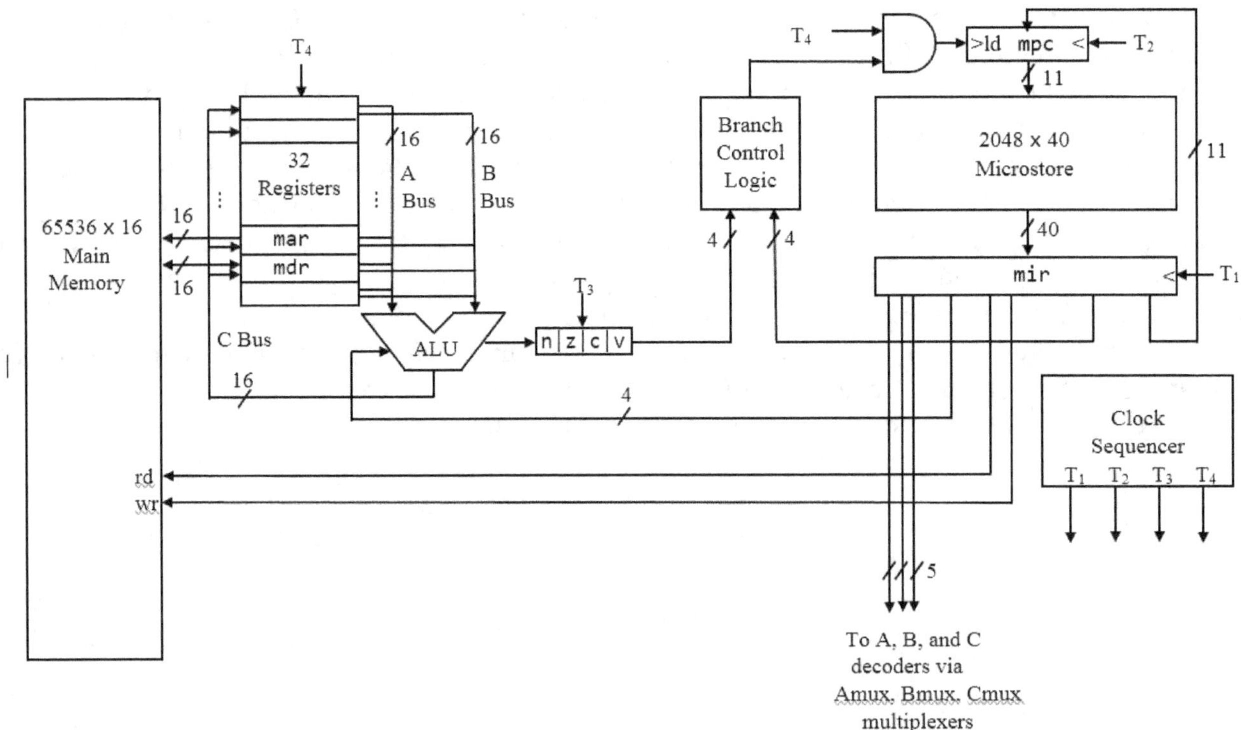

Problems

1) Implement the clock sequencer circuit. Use three D flip-flops. Assume that the left flip-flop is preset with 1 and the middle and right flip-flops are preset with 0. *Hint*: Drive each D input with the Q' output of the preceding flip-flop. Assume you have available a clock circuit that outputs an alternating sequence of 1's and 0's, each 1 and 0 lasting 1 microsecond. Drive you clock sequencer with the output of the clock circuit.

2) Would there be any advantage if the mar were a register separate from the register bank? From where would it be loaded? What would determine if it is to be loaded with a new address?

3) Design the circuitry associated with the mdr. Recall that the mdr drives the bidirectional memory data bus and can be loaded from either the C bus (if rd = 0) or from the memory data bus (if rd = 1). *Hint*: You will need tri-state buffers and a multiplexer.

4) Assume the cond field in the microinstruction contained only two bits that specified the following four actions: no branch (00), branch on negative (01), branch on zero (10), and unconditional branch (11). Design the branch-control logic for such a cond field.

5) If the n flag is not equal to the v flag after a subtraction of signed numbers, how do the numbers used in the subtraction compare?

6) If the c flag is equal to 1 after a subtraction of unsigned numbers, how do the numbers used in the subtraction compare?

7) If the n flag equals the z flag after a subtraction of signed numbers, is the result of the subtraction negative, zero, or positive?

8) How many more bits would a microinstruction have to have if the A, B, and C decoders were not used.

9) Why does the ALU have to have a no-operation function (when $F_0 = F_1 = F_2 = F_3 = 0$)?

10) Is it possible to do a bitwise OR operation without using the OR operation in the ALU?

11) With the LCC configured as described, is it possible for two registers to drive the A bus at the same time? Would you ever want two registers to drive the A bus at the same time?

12) With the LCC configured as described, is it possible for two registers to be loaded from the C bus at the same time? Would you ever want two registers to be loaded from the C bus at the same time?

13) Why is the rd signal applied to the mdr?

14) Which circuit or circuits in the LCC most likely limit how short the clock cycles can be?

15) Implement a SEXT circuit that inputs a five-bit signed number and outputs its eight-bit equivalent.

7 Microprogramming the Basic Instruction Set

Introduction

In this chapter, we create the microcode that implements the basic instruction set that we learned in chapters 2 and 3. You should print out a copy of the file `microlevel.pdf` that is in the software package for this book. This file provides all the information you will need to create and use microcode on the LCC. It is a reference that you will frequently want to refer to when you are writing microcode.

Microinstruction Format

Here is the name of each field of a microinstruction along with its width in bits:

A	Amux	B	Bmux	C	Cmux	alu	u	rd	wr	cond	addr	
5	1	5	1	5	1	4	1	1	1	4	11	width

To implement the basic instruction set, we do not need to use all the fields in a microinstruction. In this chapter we will study only those fields we need for the basic instruction set (A, B, C, alu, rd, wr, cond, and addr). We will study the remaining fields (Amux, Bmux, Cmux, and u) when we implement a more complex instruction set (the register instruction set) that requires them.

Alternate Register Names

The 32 registers in the register bank in the LCC are named "r0", "r1", …, "r31". Most, however, have alternate names that are easy to remember (and, therefore, are more convenient to use when writing microcode). For example, "ac" is the alternate name for the r0; "pc" is the alternate name for r25. Some of the registers have specific initial values. These registers are given alternate names that indicate their contents. For example, the alternate name for r31 is "0". This register contains the constant 0. The names "1", "3", "4", and "5" are alternate names for the registers that contain the corresponding constants.

The alternate name for r20 is "m8". This name indicates the register contains the constant consisting of all 0's except for its eight rightmost bits, which are all 1's. Thus, in hex it contains 00ff. Similarly, the register whose alternate name is "m12" contains the constant 0fff (four 0 bits followed by twelve 1 bits).

Some of the registers contain a 16-bit value that has only a single 1 bit. The alternate names for these registers consist of the prefix "bit" followed by the position of the 1 bit. For example, the register whose alternate name is "bit5" (r13) contains a 1 bit in position 5 and 0 bits elsewhere. Thus, in hex it contains 0020 (recall that bits are numbered right to left, starting with 0 so bit 5 is the sixth bit from the right).

When we write microcode, we sometimes need a register to hold some value temporarily. For this purpose, we use r26, whose alternate name is "temp".

Here is a listing of the registers with their alternate names and initial contents:

Register Number	Name	Initial Contents	Function
0	r0 or ac		accumulator register
1	r1		
2	r2		
3	r3		
4	r4		
5	r5 or fp		frame pointer register
6	r6 or sp		stack pointer register
7	r7 or lr		link register
8	r8 or 3	0x0003	
9	r9 or 4	0x0004	
10	r10 or 5	0x0005	
11	r11 or omask	0xf000	opcode mask
12	r12 or cmask	0x01e0	count mask (for shifts)
13	r13 or bit5	0x0020	
14	r14 or bit11	0x0800	
15	r15 or bit15	0x8000	
16	r16 or m3	0x0007	
17	r17 or m4	0x000f	
18	r18 or m5	0x001f	
19	r19 or m6	0x003f	
20	r20 or m8	0x00ff	
21	r21 or m9	0x01ff	
22	r22 or m11	0x07ff	
23	r23 or m12	0x0fff	
24	r24 or ir		machine instruction register
25	r25 or pc		program counter register
26	r26 or temp		
27	r27 or dc		decoding register
28	r28 or 1	0x0001	constant 1
29	r29 or mar		memory address register
30	r30 or mdr		memory data register
31	r31 or 0	0x0000	constant 0 (read-only register

In microcode, if we want to access the constant 1, we simply specify the register that contains the constant 1, which conveniently has the alternate name "1". We can similarly access the constants 0, 3, 4, and 5 using the names "0", "3", "4", and "5", respectively. But note that there is no register with the name "2" that contains the constant 2. Thus, in microcode we cannot access the constant 2 simply by specifying the name "2". To get 2, we have to use a microinstruction that adds 1 (which is available in a register) to 1. Be sure to understand that the register bank contains only a very small subset of constants. These are the only constants which we can access directly.

Symbolic Microcode

A microinstruction on the LCC consists of 40 bits. We can write microcode directly in binary. But doing that would be a very tedious and error-prone process. A much better way to write microcode is to use an easy-to-use symbolic form and then use an assembler to translate the symbolic form to the required 40-bit binary form. In other words, we can do at the microlevel exactly what we did at the machine level: Write code in symbolic form and then assemble it to the required binary form.

Let's look at a microinstruction in binary form that increments the pc register by 1 and initiates a read operation. To increment the pc, we need a microinstruction that will add the current contents of the pc register and the constant 1 and store the sum back into the pc register. Here is the microinstruction that will do this (the unspecified fields are all 0's) in addition to initiating a main memory read operation:

```
11001   11100   11001 0100   1
  A       B       C    alu    rd
```

The A field of the microinstruction contains 11001 (25 decimal), which is the number of the pc register. The B field contains 11100 (28 decimal), which is the number of the register than contains the constant 1. Thus, the contents of the pc register are placed on the A bus, and the constant 1 is placed on the B bus. The alu field contains 0100 (4 decimal) which specifies the add operation. Thus, the pc register contents and 1 are added, and the sum is outputted to the C bus. The C field, like the A field, contains the register number of the pc register. Thus, the sum is loaded into the pc register, thereby incrementing the pc by 1.

The order in which these operations occur is controlled by the clock sequencer. At the start of T_1, this microinstruction is loaded into the mir. During T_1, the A and B decoders enable the pc register and the register with 1 to drive the A and B buses. During T_2, the ALU performs the addition operation. At T_3, the flag registers are set. Finally, at the start of T_4, the pc register is loaded with the incremented value.

Now let's write this microinstruction in symbolic form:

```
a.pc add b.1 c.pc rd     ; increment pc register, start read
```

The add component of this instruction indicates that the ALU should perform an add operation (so the alu field in the microinstruction should be 0100). The component a.pc indicates that the A field should contain the number of the pc register The component b.1 indicates that the B field should contain the register number of the register whose name is "1". c.pc indicates that the C field should contain the number of the pc register. rd indicates that the rd field should contain 1. This instruction does not specify values for the other fields of the microinstruction. For that reason, those fields default to all 0's. For example, the binary microinstruction will have 0000 in its cond field (the code for never branch). Thus, a branch will not occur when this microinstruction is executed. The wr field is also 0 so a write operation will not occur. Note that a comment in symbolic microcode starts with a semicolon.

To specify the ALU operation in a symbolic microinstruction, we use the mnemonic for the operation. For example, we use `add` for addition, `and` for bitwise AND, and `sext` for sign extension. See the file `microlevel.pdf` for a complete list of the ALU mnemonics.

To specify a read or write operation, we use the mnemonics `rd` or `wr`, respectively. For example, here is the two-instruction sequence of microinstructions that fetches the instruction in main memory that the `pc` register points to and increments the `pc`:

```
a.pc c.mar               ; load mar with contents of pc
a.pc add b.1 c.pc rd     ; read from address in mar and incr pc
```

In the first microinstruction above, we have not specified an ALU operation. Thus, the alu field defaults to 0000, which causes the ALU to let its left input pass through to its output unchanged. Since this instruction puts the `pc` register contents on the A bus which is connected to the left side of the ALU, the contents of the `pc` register pass unchanged to the output of the ALU, and then onto the C bus. Since the C field specifies the `mar`, the `mar` is loaded from the C bus, which is carrying the address from the `pc`. Thus, this microinstruction simply copies the address in the `pc` to the `mar`.

Before a main memory read operation can be performed, the `mar` has to be initialized with the address to read from. Thus, the `rd` operation in the sequence above cannot be specified in the first microinstruction above (the microinstruction that copies the address in the `pc` to the `mar`). However, a `rd` can occur simultaneously with the `add` operation. So the `rd` operation can appear in the second microinstruction. We could perform the same operations with three microinstructions:

```
a.pc c.mar               ; load mar with contents of pc
rd                       ; read from address in mar
a.pc add b.1 c.pc        ; increment pc
```

But this sequence is inefficient: It requires 50% more time (because it has an additional microinstruction) and occupies more space in microstore.

The fields of a microinstruction all default to all 0's if the symbolic microinstruction does not specify a value for them, *with one exception*. If the C field is not specified, it defaults to 11111 (31 decimal), which is the register number of the read-only register that contains 0. Because it is read only, it is not loaded with a new value when the C field contains its default value. Thus, if a symbolic microinstruction does not specify the C field, then no register in the register bank is loaded with a new value. For example, the only effect of the second microinstruction in the three-instruction sequence above is to read from memory—no register in the register bank is loaded with a new value.

To specify a branch in a microinstruction, we specify the mnemonic for the branch condition, "@", and the label on the instruction to branch to (for a list of the microcode branch-condition mnemonics, see the file `microlevel.pdf`). For example, the following instruction branches to the label L1 if the output of the ALU (which is equal to the current contents of the `mdr` register) is negative:

```
a.mdr add b.0 neg@L1     ; branch to L1 if mdr < 0
```

`neg` is the mnemonic for branch on negative. It is translated to 0011 and placed in the cond field of the microinstruction. The address corresponding to the label L1 is placed in the addr field of the microinstruction. The output of the ALU is equal to the contents of the `mdr` plus 0 (because the add operation adds the contents of the `mdr` on the A bus with 0 on the B bus). *We need the add operation here to force the ALU to set the flag registers based on the contents of the* `mdr` *so the* n *flag can be tested by the conditional branch.* The microinstruction

```
a.mdr c.ir neg@L1      ; does not set the flag registers
```

would not work because the default ALU operation does not set the flag registers.

The ALU operation occurs at T_2. At the start of T_3, the flag registers are loaded based on the current ALU output. Thus, the if `mdr` is negative, then the ALU output is negative, and the n flag register accordingly is set to 1. During the rest of T_3, the branch-control logic generates an output that depends on the flag registers and the cond field in the microinstruction. Because the cond field in this instruction specifies a branch on negative, the branch-control logic will output 1 if n = 1 and 0 otherwise. Then at T_4, if the branch-control logic outputs a 1 (which means n = 1, which means the `mdr` is negative), the branch-to address (the address in the addr field of the microinstruction that corresponds to the label `L1`) is loaded into the `mpc`, causing a branch to that location in the microcode. Thus, this microinstruction branches to `L1` if the `mdr` contents are negative. If, on the other hand, the `mdr` contents are not negative, then the microinstruction in the next higher location in microstore is executed next.

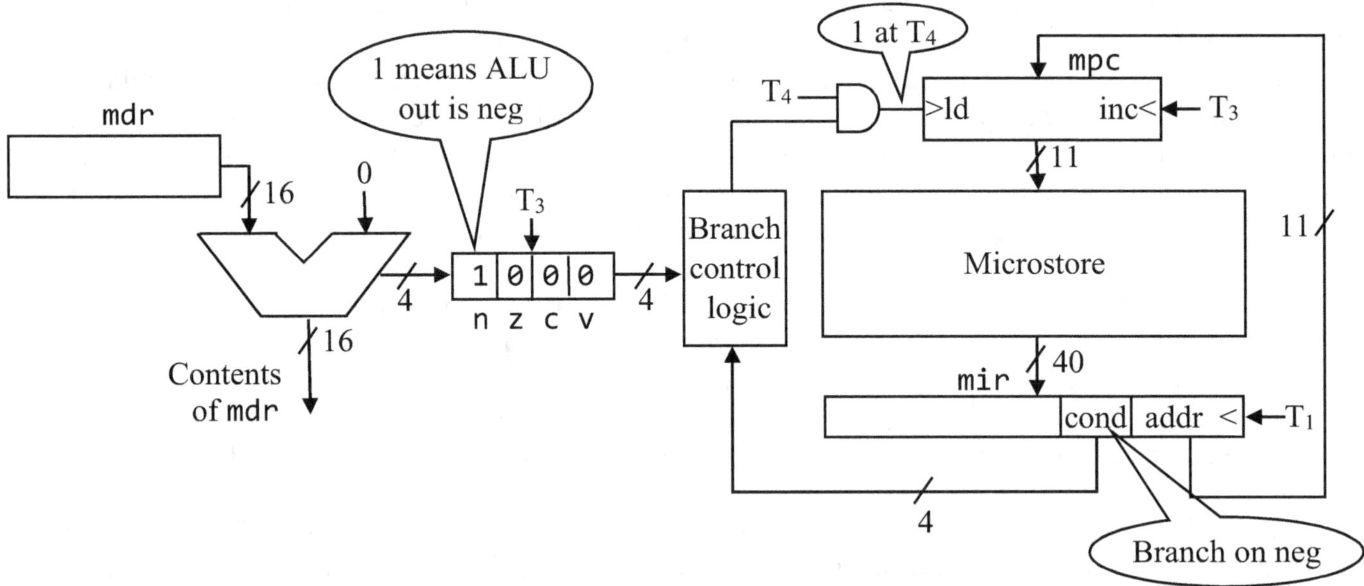

The components of a symbolic microinstruction can be in any order except for a label. If a symbolic microinstruction has a label, the label should be the first component and start in column 1. If the label is followed by a colon, it can start in any column, but it still must be the first component of the microinstruction. All the components of a symbolic microinstruction, except for a label, should not start in column 1. For example, here is an instruction with the label `fetch`:

```
fetch:    a.pc c.mar
```

Fetching a Machine Instruction and Decoding the Opcode

Recall that the CPU performs the following four steps repeatedly:

1. Fetch machine instruction that `pc` register points to.
2. Increment the `pc` register.
3. Decode the opcode.
4. Execute the instruction just fetched.

Here is the microcode that performs steps 1 and 2 (with line numbers added):

```
1 fetch     a.pc c.mar                  ; copy address in pc to mar
2           a.pc add b.1 c.pc rd        ; increment pc, start read
```

The microinstruction on line 1 causes the `pc` register to drive the A bus and the `mar` to be loaded from the C bus. Because an ALU operation is not specified, the default operation is in effect: namely, whatever enters the left side of the ALU appears unchanged on its output. The A bus drives the left side of the ALU, and the ALU output drives the C bus. Thus, whatever is placed on the A bus (which for this instruction is the contents of the `pc` register) appears unchanged on the C bus. Because the instruction on line 1 loads the `mar` from the C bus, its net effect is to load the `mar` from the `pc` register.

Line 1 loads the `mar` with the address of the machine instruction to be executed next. Line 2 then performs the read operation. Specifically, it reads the instruction into the `mdr` from the address provided by the `mar`. Recall that we first have to load the `mar` with the desired address. Then perform the read. Thus, line 1 cannot both load the `mar` and perform the read.

Now that we have the machine instruction in the `mdr` and have incremented the `pc`, the next step is to decode its opcode. The opcode is in the machine instruction's leftmost four bits. Its first bit resides in the sign-bit position. Thus, to determine the first bit of an opcode, we can simply use a microinstruction that passes the instruction through the ALU so that the n flag register reflects the leftmost bit of the instruction. We can then use that microinstruction to branch if $n = 1$ or fall through to the next instruction if $n = 0$. Then to determine each of the remaining bits in the opcode, we use microinstructions that shift the machine instruction left one position (so that the next opcode bit occupies the sign-bit position) and repeat the preceding test. We call this process *decoding the opcode*.

Let's examine the microinstructions that determines the initial bits of the opcode:

```
3           a.mdr add b.0 c.ir neg@L1       ; add 0 to set flag registers
4 L0:       a.ir sll b.1 c.dc neg@L01       ; shift left 1 position
5 L00:      a.dc sll b.1 c.dc neg@L001      ; shift left 1 position
```

Line 3 copies the contents of the `mdr` (which contains the machine instruction) via the ALU to the `ir`. Thus, the n flag register reflects the leftmost bit of the machine instruction. The `add` in this microinstruction *is necessary*. If omitted, the default ALU operation is in effect in which case the ALU will not set the flag registers. The conditional branch on line 3 branches to `L1` if the n flag is 1 (which means the first bit of the opcode is 1), or it falls through to the next instruction if the n flag is 0 (which means the first bit of the opcode is 0). The labels we use reflect what the opcode must be at that label. For example, if we reach the microinstruction at the label `L00`, the first two bits of the opcode must be 00— hence, the label `L00`.

Line 4 loads the `dc` (decoding) register with the machine instruction now in the `ir`. But the ALU performs a `sll` operation as the machine instruction passes through the ALU. The B bus provides the shift count. Line 4 puts 1 on the B bus, which results in a shift of one position. Thus, the leftmost bit in the output of the ALU is now the second bit of the opcode, and the `dc` register is loaded with the shifted instruction. The conditional branch instruction on line 4 tests the n flag, which now reflects the second bit of the opcode. It branches to `L01` if the second bit is 1, or it falls through to the next instruction whose label is `L00`. Thus, if we reach the label `L01`, then the first two opcode bits are 01; if we reach the label `L00`, the first two opcode bits are 00.

This process of shifting the machine instruction and then testing its leftmost bit is continued until all four bits of the opcode have been determined. Each opcode causes the decoding process to end up at the label for that opcode. For example, if the opcode is 0000, then the decoding process ends up at the label `L0000`; if the opcode is 0001, then the decoding process ends up at the label `L0001`, and so on.

The shifting occurs in the `dc` register—not the `ir` register. To execute the machine instruction, the microprogram needs the original unshifted machine instruction. Using the `dc` register for shifts leaves the original machine instruction unchanged in the `ir`.

Here is the microcode for the entire `fetch`, increment `pc`, and decoding processes (the microcode that interprets the machine instructions is not included):

```
             ;================================================
             ; Fetch machine instruction, increment pc
Fetch:       a.pc c.mar
             a.pc add b.1 c.pc rd


             ;================================================
             ; Decode instruction
             a.mdr add b.0 c.ir neg@L1
L0:          a.ir sll b.1 c.dc neg@L01
L00:         a.dc sll b.1 c.dc neg@L001
L000:        a.dc sll b.1 c.dc neg@L0001
             br@L0000


L1:          a.ir sll b.1 c.dc neg@L11
L10:         a.dc sll b.1 c.dc neg@L101
L100:        a.dc sll b.1 c.dc neg@L1001
             br@L1000


L01:         a.dc sll b.1 c.dc neg@L011
L010:        a.dc sll b.1 c.dc neg@L0101
             br@L0100


L11:         a.dc sll b.1 c.dc neg@L111
L110:        a.dc sll b.1 c.dc neg@L1101
             br@L1100


L001:        a.dc sll b.1 c.dc neg@L0011
             br@L0010


L011:        a.dc sll b.1 c.dc neg@L0111
             br@L0110


L101:        a.dc sll b.1 c.dc neg@L1011
             br@L1010


L111:        a.dc sll b.1 c.dc neg@L1111
             br@L1110
```

```
        ;=====================================================
        ; Interpret machine instruction
L0000:  ; ld =================================================
                .

                .

                .
L1111:  ; trap ===============================================
        br@fetch ; only microcode needed for opcode 1111
```

Interpreting Machine Instructions with Microcode

When we say that the CPU is *executing* a machine language instruction, it is really *interpreting* the instruction. That is, it is executing the sequence of *microinstructions* that have the effect the machine language instruction is supposed to have. A machine language instruction, in effect, is a call of the sequence of microinstructions that interpret it..

To complete the microcode for the basic instruction set, we have to provide a sequence of microinstructions for each machine language instruction that interprets that machine instruction. For example, if the machine instruction is a `st` instruction, its opcode is 0001. Thus, the decoding process ends up at the label `L0001`. At this label, we need the microcode that interprets the `st` instruction.

The `st` instruction has the address in its rightmost 12 bits to which it is to store. The address is extracted from the instruction in the `ir`, zero-extended to 16 bits, and loaded into the `mar`. The `ac` register contents are then moved into the `mdr`, in preparation for a write operation. Finally, the write operation performs the write of the data in the `mdr` (which came from the `ac`) to the address in the `mar` (which came from the instruction in the `ir`). The net effect is to store the `ac` into memory at the address specified by the `st` instruction. Sounds complicated, but the microcode is actually fairly simple:

```
L0001:  ; st ================================================
        a.ir and b.m12 c.mar    ; extract address, move into ir
        a.ac c.mdr              ; move ac contents into mdr
        wr br@fetch             ; write, branch back to fetch
```

The first microinstruction extracts the address in the machine instruction (which is in the `ir`) by ANDing it with `m12`. Recall that `m12` is the name of the register that contains 0fff. The ANDing process in effect zeros out the opcode bits in the machine instruction obtained from the `ir` (because the leftmost four bits of `m12` are 0000). This microinstruction then loads the extracted address into the `mar` in preparation for a write operation. The second microinstruction copies the contents of the `ac` register into the `mdr`. The third microinstruction performs the write, which completes the interpretation of the `st` instruction. The unconditional branch in the third microinstruction then branches back to `fetch`, where the fetch-increment-decode-execute cycle repeats for the next machine language instruction.

Let's look at the microcode for the `str` instruction. The `str` instruction stores the `ac` register contents at the address in the `sp` register plus the relative address in the `str` instruction. For example,

```
        str 3
```

stores the `ac` register contents into the location whose address is the address in `sp` plus 3. Here is the required microcode:

```
L0101:      ; str ============================================
            a.ir and b.m12 c.mar   ; extract rel addr from str inst
            a.mar add b.sp c.mar   ; add the contents of sp to it
            a.ac c.mdr             ; load mdr from ac
            wr br@fetch            ; perform write and start next fetch
```

The **call** instruction is an interesting instruction because it involves a push operation (of the **pc** register contents). Here is its microcode:

```
L1010:      ; call ============================================
            a.sp sub b.1 c.sp               ; decrement sp
            a.sp c.mar                       ; load mar from sp
            a.pc c.mdr                       ; load mdr with return addr in pc
            a.ir and b.m12 c.pc wr br@fetch ; load pc, write, branch to subrt
```

Recall that in a push operation, first the **sp** register is decremented, then the value to be pushed is stored in the location the **sp** register points to. The first microinstruction above decrements the **sp** register. The next two instructions prepare the **mar** and the **mdr** for the write operation in the fourth microinstruction that completes the push operation. The final microinstruction initiates a write, loads a new address into the **pc**, and branches back to **fetch**. The new address in the **pc** (the address of the subroutine called) causes a branch *in the machine code* to that address. Recall the address in the **pc** determines which machine instruction is fetched next. Thus, the new address in the **pc** causes a branch to that instruction.

The **call** instruction performs an unconditional branch. Here the microcode for the conditional branch instruction **brz**:

```
L1110:      ; brz ============================================
            a.ac add b.0 !zer@fetch      ; start fetch of next inst if ac != 0
            a.ir and b.m12 c.pc br@fetch ; branch to address in brz inst
```

In the first microinstruction, a register is not specified for the C field. Thus, the C field defaults to 31, which is the number of the read-only register. Thus, no register is loaded from the C bus. Nevertheless, the contents of the **ac** register still go through the ALU, causing the setting of the **z** flag register. The conditional branch in the first instruction branches back to **fetch** if $z = 0$, which is the case if the **ac** register contents are not zero (**!zer** is the mnemonic for branch on not zero). Thus, if the **ac** register is not zero, the branch to **fetch** occurs. The result is the machine instruction in main memory following the **brz** is fetched and executed next. If, however, the **ac** register is zero, then the branch in the first microinstruction is not taken. Instead, the second microinstruction is executed. It loads the **pc** register with the address in the 12 rightmost bits of the **brz** instruction. Thus, on the branch back to **fetch**, the instruction at the address *in* the **brz** instruction is fetched and executed next.

A **trap** machine instruction (opcode 1111) is essentially a call of a service module in the operating system that performs an I/O operation or a **halt**. It is *not* implemented in microcode. The only microinstruction required for the trap instruction is an unconditional branch back to **fetch**:

```
L1111:      ; trap ============================================
            br@fetch ; only microcode needed for opcode 1111
```

Assembling and Using Microcode

You should now complete the microcode implementation for the basic instruction set in the file `b.sm` by adding the microcode needed for each machine instruction. Next, assemble it by entering

        `micro b.sm`   (on Windows)

or

        `./micro b.sm`   (on Linux, Mac OS X, or Raspberry Pi)

The `micro` program responds by assembling the code in `b.sm` to binary and outputting the binary form to the file `b.m`. It also displays the files it uses:

```
Symbolic microcode file: b.sm
Binary microcode file:    b.m
List file:                b.lst
```

The file `b.m` contains the translated microcode. The file `b.lst` is a text file that includes the source microcode and its translated form in hex.

   Next, test your microcode by assembling the basic assembly language program in the file `btest.a` by entering

        `basic btest.a`   (on Windows)

or

        `./basic btest.a`   (on Linux, Mac OS X, or Raspberry Pi)

Note: For convenience, you can also invoke the basic program by entering "b" in place of "`basic`".

The `basic` program translates the assembly language program in `btest.a` to binary and outputs the binary form to the file `btest.e`. Finally, run the machine language program in `btest.e` on the LCC simulator by entering

        `sim btest.e`   (on Windows)

or

        `./sim btest.e`   (on Linux, Mac OS X, or Raspberry Pi)

You should see on the screen the following (which `sim` also writes the to the file `btest.log`):

```
sim Simulator Ver 3.0    Sun Mar 13 11:12:34 2022
DosReis Anthony J.   ← your name here


================================================== output
Correct if 1 to 10 displayed
12345678910
================================================= statistics
Machine code size              =      74 (dec)
Machine instructions executed =      39 (dec)
Microcode size                 =      71 (dec)
Microinstructions executed     =     266 (dec)
Load point                     =       0 (hex)
```

If you do not see on your screen the numbers from 1 to 10, then your microcode has a bug. If you want to revert back to the correct binary microcode provided by the software package, copy `bsave.m` to `b.m`.

Debugging Microcode

The microlevel debugger works the same way the machine-level debugger works. Most of the commands are identical and have the same effect. Two debugger commands, `p` and `t`, and the `-t` command line argument, however, are case sensitive: The uppercase versions are for the machine level; the lowercase versions are for the microlevel. For example, `P5` sets a breakpoint at the *main memory* address 5, but `p5` sets a breakpoint at the *microstore* address 5.

   If you include the argument `-t` (lowercase) on the command line when you invoke `sim`, the debugger is activated with the microlevel trace function on. For example, to run the executable file in `btest.e` with the debugger activated with the trace function on, enter on the command line

       sim btest.e -t   (use lowercase t)

`sim` will then execute and trace only one microinstruction each time you hit the Enter key. The trace includes the microinstruction itself and its effect. If instead of immediately hitting the Enter key, you first enter a positive integer, then thereafter `sim` will execute that number of microinstructions each time you hit the enter key. If you enter **g**, your program runs to the next breakpoint, or if none, then to completion. If you enter **t**, the trace function is turned off (if it is on) or on (if it is off). If you enter lowercase **p** followed by a microcode address, a breakpoint is set at that address (execution is paused whenever a breakpoint is reached). If you enter **q**, the run is terminated. The trace that appears on the screen is also written to the ".`log`" file that `sim` creates.

   The following is a sample of the trace output that appears on the display screen when the program in `btest.e` runs with the microlevel debugger active. On the first prompt in this example, we hit the Enter key without first entering any characters, causing a trace of one microinstruction. On the next prompt, we entered 2, causing the trace of two microinstructions before the next prompt (thereafter, hitting just the Enter key causes the trace of two microinstructions). Finally, we entered q, terminating the run.

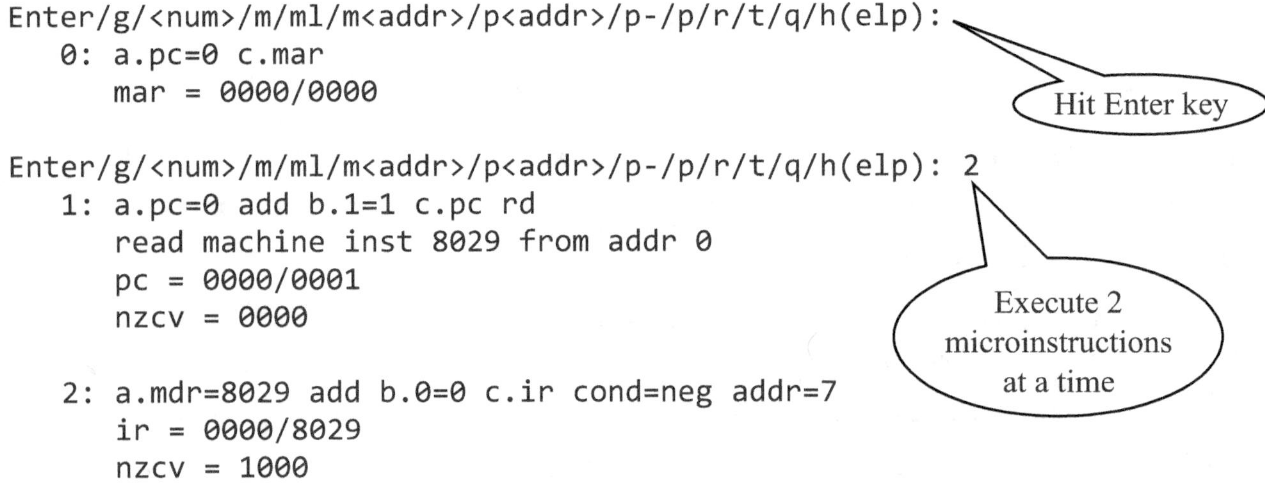

```
Enter/g/<num>/m/ml/m<addr>/p<addr>/p-/p/r/t/q/h(elp):
   0: a.pc=0 c.mar
      mar = 0000/0000

Enter/g/<num>/m/ml/m<addr>/p<addr>/p-/p/r/t/q/h(elp): 2
   1: a.pc=0 add b.1=1 c.pc rd
      read machine inst 8029 from addr 0
      pc = 0000/0001
      nzcv = 0000

   2: a.mdr=8029 add b.0=0 c.ir cond=neg addr=7
      ir = 0000/8029
      nzcv = 1000

Enter/g/<num>/m/ml/m<addr>/p<addr>/p-/p/r/t/q/h(elp): q
```

The trace shows the before and after contents of registers that are changed. For example,

```
ir = 0000/8029
```

indicates that the contents of `ir` have changed from 0000 to 8029. The trace also shows the contents of registers that are used. For example,

```
1: a.pc=0 add b.1=1 c.pc rd
```

indicates that at the time of the add operation, the `pc` register contained 0, and the register named "1" contained 1.

The debugger machine-level breakpoint command, P, can also be helpful in debugging microcode. Here is how you might use the P command. The `btest.e` program displays the numbers 1 to 10 if the microcode for the basic instruction set is correct. But suppose for your microcode, only the numbers 1 to 4 are displayed. Thus, the microcode that is executed after 4 is displayed has a bug. To zero in on the bug in your microcode, invoke `sim` with the `-t` command line argument. Use the P command to set a *machine-level* breakpoint immediately after the `dout` instruction that displays 4 (get the breakpoint address from the lst file that the `basic` assembler produces when it assembles `btest.a`). Then enter g to go to the breakpoint. `sim` will pause just before the problem area in your microcode is executed. At the pause, enter 1 (or some other small positive number). Then hit the Enter key repeatedly to trace the problem area of your microcode. By examining the trace, you should be able to identify the bug in the microcode.

A second approach to debugging microcode is to write a simple assembly language test program for each machine instruction. Then test the microcode for each machine instruction separately, moving on to the test for the next machine instruction only when the instruction under test works correctly. A third approach is to activate the debugger by entering `-t` on the command line when invoking `sim`. Next, enter g to execute the program to its termination. Then examine the entire trace that is recorded in the log file that `sim` creates.

Compiling C Code to the Basic Instruction Set

To see how good the basic instruction set is, let's see how well is supports code written in C. Let's translate the following C program to the basic instruction set:

```
 1 // e0701.c
 2 #include <stdio.h>
 3 int s;                   // global variable
 4 int sum(int x, int y)
 5 {
 6     return x + y;        // return the sum of of x and y
 7 }
 8 int main()
 9 {
10     s = sum(5, 7);       // call sum passing it 2 and 3
11     printf("%d\n", s);
12     return 0;            // return 0 to startup code
13 }
```

To create an executable file from this program, it has to be compiled to assembly language, assembled to machine language, and linked, all done by a C compiler. The link step combines the machine code produced by the assembly step with *startup code* and any other module required by the program. Startup code gets control first when the program is invoked on the command line. It calls `main`. When `main` finishes, it returns to startup code. Startup code then returns to the operating system (but as you will see, our simplified startup code simply halts).

When our C program is executed, startup code gets control first. It calls `main`. On line 10 in the C program, `main` calls the `sum` function, passing it the arguments 5 and 7 to the parameters x and y. To do this, `main` pushes the arguments in reverse order (first 7, then 5) onto the stack. For example, to push 7 onto the stack, `main` first decrements `sp` to reserve a slot on the stack. Then it stores 7 in that slot using a `str 0` instruction (the most recent slot created on the stack always has the relative address 0):

```
asp -1        ; decrement sp by adding -1 to it
ldi 7         ; load ac with 7
str 0         ; store ac at relative address 0
```

The push of the of the argument 7 *creates on the stack the parameter* y. The subsequent push of the argument 5 *creates on the stack the parameter* x.

Important observation: The calling sequence in the *calling* function creates the parameters in the *called* function by pushing the values of the arguments in the call onto the stack.

On entry into the `sum` function, the stack looks like this:

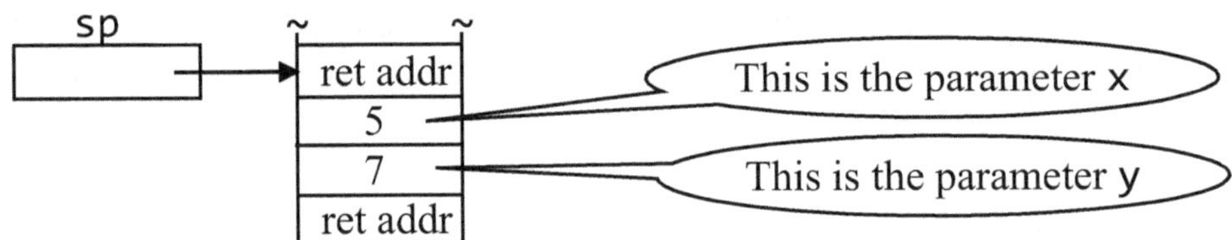

Recall that the stack grows in the downward direction. Thus, the return address pushed by the `call` instruction in startup code (the first item pushed) is in the location with the highest address, then 7, then 5, then the return address pushed by the `call` instruction in `main`. The relative address of y (the slot with 7) is 2; the relative address of x (the slot with 5) is 1. The `sum` function accesses x and y with two relative instructions:

```
ldr 1         ; load x
addr 2        ; add y
```

Note that there are *no x and y labels* in the assembly language program. The parameters x and y are dynamically created (i.e., created during run time) by push operations—not by `.word` directives with the labels x and y.

After computing the sum of x and y, the `sum` function returns to `main` by executing a `ret` instruction, which pops the return address off the stack and into the `pc` register. But the x and y parameters are still on the stack. Thus, the first action by `main` on return from `sum` is to pop x and y off the stack by adding 2 to the `sp` register:

```
asp 2         ; pop x and y parameters
```

`main` then stores the value returned by `sum` that is in the `ac` register into the global variable `s`:

```
        st s            ; assign the returned value to s
```

Next, `main` displays the value in `s` with a `dout` instruction, and moves the cursor to the next line (the C program does all this by calling the C library function `printf`, but we will simply use a `dout`, `nl` sequence):

```
        ld s            ; load ac from s
        dout            ; display value in s
        nl              ; move cursor to next line
```

Here is the assembly language code for the entire program including startup code with decimal line numbers on the left, *not hex addresses*:

```
 1 ; e0701.a
 2 startup:   call main       ; pushes return address
 3            halt
 4 ; =============================================
 5 s:         .word 0         ; global variable
 6 sum:       ldr 1           ; load x
 7            addr 2          ; add y
 8            ret             ; return with sum in ac
 9 ; =============================================
10 main:      asp -1          ; decrement sp by adding -1
11            ldi 7           ; load ac with 7
12            str 0           ; store ac at rel addr 0
13            asp -1          ; decrement sp by adding -1
14            ldi 5           ; load ac with 5
15            str 0           ; store ac at rel addr 0
16            call sum        ; pushes return address
17            asp 2           ; pop x and y parameters
18            st s            ; store value returned into s
19            ld s            ; load ac from s
20            dout            ; display value in s
21            nl              ; move cursor to next line
22            ldi 0           ; load ac with 0
23            ret             ; return 0 to startup code
```

Based on this program, the basic instruction set does a good job in supporting C code. However, this program uses only a very small subset of C. It turns out that the basic instruction set has major flaws. It, in fact, does *not* do a good job in supporting C code. In the next chapter, we will expose some of its flaws, and microcode a completely different instruction set that is not as flawed as the basic instruction set.

Global variables in C are variables declared outside a function definition and are mapped to `.word` directives. *Local variables* are variables declared *within* a function and, like parameters, are dynamically created on the stack. They are *not* created by `.word` directives. If a function has local variables, they are created by that function when it is called (by decrementing the `sp` register) and are destroyed by that function (by incrementing the `sp` register) just before the function returns to its caller. Let's look at a simple C program that has a local variable `y`:

```
 1 // e0702.c
 2 #include <stdio.h>
 3 void f(int x)
 4 {
 5         int y;                  // local variable created here
 6         y = x;
 7         printf("%d\n", y);
 8 }                              // local variable destroyed here
 9 int main()
10 {
11     f(3);   // parameter x created here before call, destroyed after call
12     return 0;
13 }
```

The calling sequence in `main` corresponding to line 11 creates the parameter x by pushing 3 onto the stack. On return from f, the parameter x is destroyed by `main` by incrementing the `sp` register. On line 5, the f function creates the local variable y by decrementing the `sp` register. Just before returning to `main`, the f function destroys y by incrementing the `sp` register. Here is the corresponding assembler code:

```
 1 ; e0702.a
 2 startup:  call main       ; pushes return address
 3           halt
 4 ; ===============================================
 5 f:        asp -1          ; create local variable y
 6           ldr 2           ; get x
 7           str 0           ; store into y
 8           ldr 0           ; get y
 9           dout            ; display y
10           nl
11           asp 1           ; destroy y
12           ret             ; return to main
13 ; ===============================================
14 main:     asp -1          ; create x on the stack
15           ldi 3           ; get 3
16           str 0           ; store 3 into x
17           call f
18           asp 1           ; destroy x
19           ldi 0           ; return 0 to startup code
20           ret
```

Local variable y created and destroyed by *called* function

Parameter x created and destroyed by *calling* function

Note that there are no labels for the parameter x or the local variable y. Parameters and local variables are not accessed by name (because they have no name at the assembly level) *but by their relative addresses*. For example, on line 6, x in the function f is accessed with a `ldr` instruction which specifies the relative address 2 (at relative addresses 0 and 1 are the local variable y and the return address from the `call` instruction, respectively).

Problems

1) Complete the microcode for the basic instruction set in the file `b.sm`. Test your microcode by entering on the command line

    ```
    micro b.sm
    basic btest.a
    sim btest.e
    ```

    Prefix these commands with "`./`" on a Linux, Mac OS X, or Raspberry Pi system. Hand in the listing of the `btest.log` file created by `sim`.

2) How does the `sim` program know it should use the microcode in `b.m` when it runs the program in `btest.e`? *Hint*: What is in the first byte of `btest.e` (use the `see` program to examine `btest.e`).

3) Is `add` the only ALU operation that can be used in the microinstruction at the start of the decoding process that loads the `ir` from the `mdr` and sets the flag registers?

4) Is the `ld` instruction on line 19 in `e0701.a` necessary? If not, why is it there?

5) Assemble the following microinstructions to their 40-bit forms. Give your answers in hex.

    ```
    a.pc add b.1 c.pc rd
    a.mdr add b.0 c.ir neg@L1        ; L1 at address 00000000111
    a.ir sll b.1 c.dc neg@L01        ; L01 at address 00000001011
    ```

6) Give the symbolic form of the following microinstructions, which are from the basic instruction set microcode:

    ```
    d36d28180b
    000f878000
    ```

7) What is wrong with the following microinstruction: `a.1 c.mdr rd`

8) Modify the program in `e0701.c` by making the `s` variable a local variable within `main` by moving its declaration to just before the assignment to `s` in the `main` function. Translate the function to assembly language, assemble, and run on `sim`.

9) The symbolic microcode assembler (`micro`) is not case sensitive on labels, but the `basic` assembler is case insensitive on labels. Why the difference? *Hint*: Consider the C programming language.

10) Why are the arguments in a function call pushed in right-to-left order? *Hint*: Consider a function with a variable number of parameters (for example, `printf` in C).

11) Give the assembler code that creates an uninitialized local variable in C? Give the code that creates an initialized local variable in C. Is there a "cost" to initializing local variables?

12) Same as question 11 but for global variables in C. Does your answer suggest why global variables have a default value (0), but local variables do not?

13) Can the microinstructions that perform the decoding process be restructured so that some of the branching microinstructions can be eliminated, resulting in more efficient microcode?

14) Create a file `p0714.a` that contains the basic instruction set assembly code for the following C program. Assemble with the `basic` program and run on `sim`. Comment your assembly code with the corresponding C code (see `comment.txt`). Hand in the listing of the `p0714.log` file created by `sim`.

```c
// p0714.c
#include <stdio.h>
int y = 7, z;
int add10(int x)
{
    return x + 10;
}
int main()
{
    z = add10(y + 3);
    printf("%d\n", z);
    return 0;
}
```

15) Create a file `p0715.a` that contains the basic instruction set assembly code for the following C program. Assemble with the `basic` program and run on `sim`. Comment your assembly code with the corresponding C code (see `comment.txt`). Hand in the listing of the `p0715.log` file created by `sim`.

```c
// p0715.c
#include <stdio.h>
int a, y = 7;
void f(int x, int y, int z)
{
    int result;
    result = x + y - z;
    printf("%d\n", result);
}
int main()
{
    int b = 7, c;
    a = 1;
    c = a + b + y;
    f(a, b, c);
    return 0;
}
```

16) Create a file `p0716.a` that contains the basic instruction set assembly code for the following C program. Assemble with the `basic` program and run on `sim`. Comment your assembly code with the corresponding C code (see `comment.txt`). Hand in the listing of the `p0716.log` file created by `sim`.

```c
// p0716.c
#include <stdio.h>
void g(int x)
{
    printf("%d\n", x);
}
void f(int x)
{
    g(x - 2);
}
int main()
{
    f(5);
    return 0;
}
```

17) Create a file `p0717.a` that contains the basic instruction set assembly code for the following C program. Assemble with the `basic` program and run on `sim`. Comment your assembly code with the corresponding C code (see `comment.txt`). Hand in the listing of the `p0717.log` file created by `sim`.

```c
// p0717.c
#include <stdio.h>
int x = 5;
void f(int *p)
{
    printf("%d\n", *p);   // deferencing the address in p
    *p = *p + 1;
}
int main()
{
    f(&x);                     // passing address of x
    printf("%d\n", x);
    return 0;
}
```

8 Stack Instruction Set

Using the Stack Instruction Set

To assemble and run a program written using the stack instruction set, use the `stack` assembler (or equivalently, the `s` assembler) to assemble it. Then use `sim` to run the executable file created by the `stack` assembler. For example, to assemble and run the stack instruction set program `stest.a`, enter

```
stack stest.a          (creates the executable file stest.e)
sim stest.e            (runs stest.e using the microcode in s.m)
```

To use your own microcode for the stack instruction set instead of the provided microcode, complete the symbolic microcode in `s.sm` that implements the stack instruction set. Then translate the symbolic microcode in `s.sm` to binary using the `micro` program:

```
micro s.sm             (overlays the provided binary microcode in s.m)
```

`sim` will then use your microcode in `s.m` when it executes a stack instruction set program. To revert back to the provided microcode, copy `ssave.m` to `s.m`.

Pointers in C and C++

C and C++ support pointers. A pointer is a variable that contains an address. For example, suppose x is a variable at the memory address 100 that contains the constant 5, and p is a variable that has the address of x:

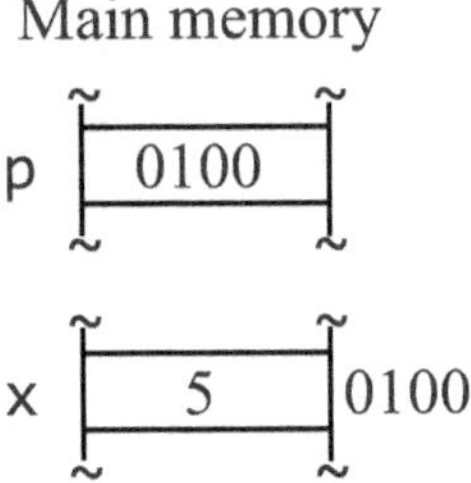

Then we say that "p points to x." We typically represent the address in p with an arrow from p to x:

In C and C++, to assign the address of x to p, we use the address-of operator "&":

```
p = &x;     // assign p the address of x
```

To get the address in p, we use p itself. For example, to assign q the address in p, we use

```
q = p;      // assign q the address in p, q now also points to x
```

But to access what p is pointing to, we use the *dereferencing operator* "*". For example, to assign y what p is pointing to, we use

```
y = *p;     // assign y what p is pointing to
```

Thus, if p is pointing to x, and x contains 5, then 5 is assigned to y. If we access what p is pointing to, as in the preceding example, we say we are *dereferencing* p.

We also dereference p to assign a new value to the location p is pointing to. For example, to assign 7 to the memory location p is pointing to, we use

```
*p = 7;     // assign 7 to what p is pointing to
```

Thus, if p is pointing to x, then 7 is assigned to x.

In the examples above, x and y hold integers, and p and q hold pointers to integers. In C, these variables have to be declared appropriately before they are used. Here are the required declarations:

```
int x = 5, y;   // declare x and y to be type int, initialize x to 5
int *p, *q;     // declare p and q to be type int pointer
```

Read "int *" as "integer pointer." Thus, int *p declares p to be an integer pointer. Note that when it appears in a declaration, the asterisk is *not* the dereferencing operator—it is used simply to indicate that a variable is a pointer.

Most programming languages do not support pointers as extensively as C and C++. But virtually all languages use pointers, although their use may be hidden. For example, a reference variable in an object-oriented programming language is a pointer—it points to an object.

Because of the ubiquity of pointers in programming languages, any worthwhile instruction set must provide good support for pointers. Specifically, the machine code for the following C statements should be simple and efficient both for variables created with .word directives (e.g., global variables) and for variables created on the stack (e.g., function parameters and local variables):

```
p = &x;    // assign p the address of x
*p = 5;    // assign 5 to the location p points to
y = *p;    // assign y what p points to
```

Let's see how the basic instruction set handles these statements if x, y, and p are created with .word directives:

```
x          .word 0
y          .word 0
p          .word 0
```

It is easy to get and store the address of x using the basic instruction set. We simply use the `ldi` instruction and then `st` to store the address in p:

```
ldi x          ; get address of x
st p           ; store address into p
```

Recall that the assembler translates labels to their corresponding addresses. Thus, the immediate field in the `ldi` instruction above contains the address of x. When executed, the `ldi` instruction loads the immediate value it contains (which is the address of x) into the `ac` register. The `st` instruction then stores the address into p.

How does the basic instruction set handle dereferencing pointers? We can easily load the address in p into the `ac` register using a `ld` instruction (or a `ldr` instruction if the pointer is on the stack):

```
ld p
```

But we have no simple way to get to the location at the address in the `ac` register. Thus, with the basic instruction set, there is *no simple way to dereference pointers*. Moreover, with the basic instruction set, there is no simple way to get the address of a variable on the stack. For example, suppose x is a parameter or a local variable (in which case it is on the stack and is not created with a `.word` directive). We have no easy way of getting its address. For example, suppose x has the relative address of 5. Then its actual 16-bit main memory address is given by the contents of the `sp` register plus 5. But with the basic instruction set, we have no way of accessing the contents of the `sp` register. Thus, we have no way of getting the address of a parameter or a local variable. In view of the limitations of the basic instruction set on handling pointers, we conclude that it is an *unacceptable instruction set* for any practical use.

Non-Constant Relative Addresses

Suppose in a C++ program you have the following sequence of statements within a function, where x is a variable on the stack with relative address 2 (*note*: a variable declaration following executable code, as in the following example, is allowed in C++ but not in C):

```
x = 5;       // relative address of x is 2
int z;       // decrement sp to reserve slot on stack for z
z = x;       // relative address of x is now 3
```

Here is the corresponding assembler code produced by a non-optimizing compiler:

```
ldi 5          ; get 5
str 2          ; store 5 in x
asp -1         ; reserve slot on stack for z
ldr 3          ; get x
str 0          ; store in z
```

Wrong relative address?

You might think that there is a bug in the `ldr` instruction above. It is supposed to get `x`. The relative address of `x` is 2 but the `ldr` instruction is using the relative address 3. But, in fact, 3 is the correct relative address. The declaration of `z` causes the `sp` register to be decremented by 1 to reserve a slot on the stack for `z`. This change in the stack causes the relative address of each item on the stack to be increased by 1. Thus, the relative address of `x` changes from 2 to 3.

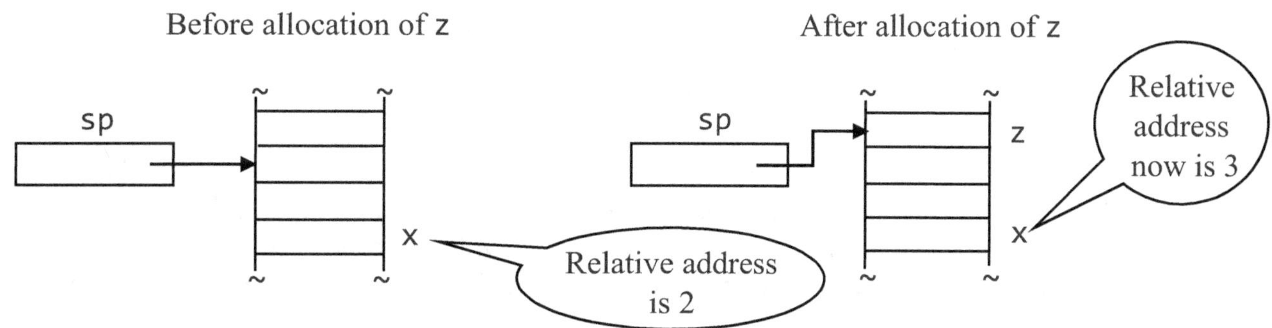

Non-constant relative addresses make writing assembler code or writing compilers that generate assembler code unnecessarily difficult. The solution to this problem is to use two registers—the `sp` register to keep track of the top of the stack and a second register—let's call it `fp` (frame pointer)—to provide the base address for the relative addresses. Then changes to the `sp` register will not affect relative addresses.

Stack Architecture

From the preceding discussion, we can see that the basic instruction set is seriously flawed. Let's now turn our attention to a better instruction set—*the stack instruction set*—that uses the top of the stack in place of the `ac` register. Unlike the basic instruction set, it can dereference pointers, and relative addresses do not change during the execution of a function.

In the stack instruction set, there is no `ac` register. If, for example, we want to display a value with the `dout` instruction, the value must be on top of the stack. The `dout` instruction then pops and displays that value. To add two values, the two values must be the top two values on the stack. The `add` instruction then pops both values, adds them, and pushes the sum back onto the stack.

Because the stack is central to the operation of the LCC with the stack instruction set, we say that the LCC with the stack instruction set has a *stack architecture*. The LCC with the basic instruction set has a *register architecture* (because the `ac` register is central to its operation). Thus, the same computer type can have more than one architecture depending on the instruction set it uses.

Here is the stack instruction set code that pushes 20000 and 3, adds them, and displays the result using the `dout` instruction:

```
        p @20000     ; push constant at label @20000 onto the stack
        pi 3         ; push 3 onto the stack
        add          ; pop twice, add, push sum back onto to stack
        dout         ; pop and display sum
           ⋮
@20000:    .word 20000
```

The `p` and `pi` instructions are like the `ld` and `ldi` instructions, respectively, in the basic instruction set except that they push a value onto the stack instead of loading a register. Note that the add instruction consists of just the mnemonic. The two operands are on the stack and the sum goes back onto the top of the stack. Thus, neither the operands nor the location for the result are specified in the instruction.

To assign a value to a variable, the top of the stack must have the value and just below it the target address. The `stav` instruction pops the value and the target address, and then stores the popped value at the popped address. For example, here is the code that assigns 5 to x (where x is a variable created by a `.word` directive):

```
pi x          ; push address of x onto the stack
pi 5          ; push 5 onto the stack
stav          ; pop twice and store value at address
```

The assembler translates labels to addresses. Thus, in the first `pi` instruction above, the assembler translates the label x to the address of x and places the address in the immediate field of the instruction. Thus, when executed, the `pi` instruction pushes the immediate value (the address of x) onto the stack.

If x is a stack variable with a relative address, say 3, then we assign 5 to it with the following sequence:

```
cora 3        ; convert rel addr 3 to abs addr, push abs addr
pi 5          ; push 5 onto the stack
stav          ; pop twice and store value at address
```

The `cora` (convert relative address) instruction specifies a relative address. It converts that relative address to the corresponding absolute address by adding the relative address and the contents of the `fp` register. It then pushes the resulting address onto the stack. Thus, when the `stav` instruction in the sequence above is executed, the value 5 is on top of the stack and just under it is the absolute address of x. Thus, the `stav` instruction stores 5 into x. The "av" in the mnemonic `stav` indicates you must first push an **a**ddress and then a **v**alue before a `stav` instruction is executed.

Frame Pointer Register

With the basic instruction set, the `sp` register has a dual purpose: to keep track of the top of the stack and to provide the base address for the relative instructions. This dual use of the `sp` register has a major disadvantage: The relative addresses of variables on the stack (parameters and local variables) change whenever a push or pop operation occurs. Non-constant relative addresses make writing assembler code or writing a compiler that generates assembler code unnecessarily difficult. The fix for this problem— which we incorporate in the stack instruction set—is to continue to use the `sp` register to keep track of the top of the stack but to use a new register—the `fp` (frame pointer) register—to provide the base address for the relative instructions. Then pushes and pops will not affect relative addresses.

The items on the stack corresponding to the call and execution of a function (the parameters, return address, and local variables) collectively are called a *stack frame*. When a function is executing, the `fp` register should point to its stack frame.

Consider a program that consists of a `main` function and an `f` function. When the `main` function is executing, the `fp` register should point to `main`'s stack frame. When `main` calls `f`, `fp` should then point to `f`'s stack frame. When `f` returns to `main`, the `fp` register must be restored so that it again points to `main`'s stack frame:

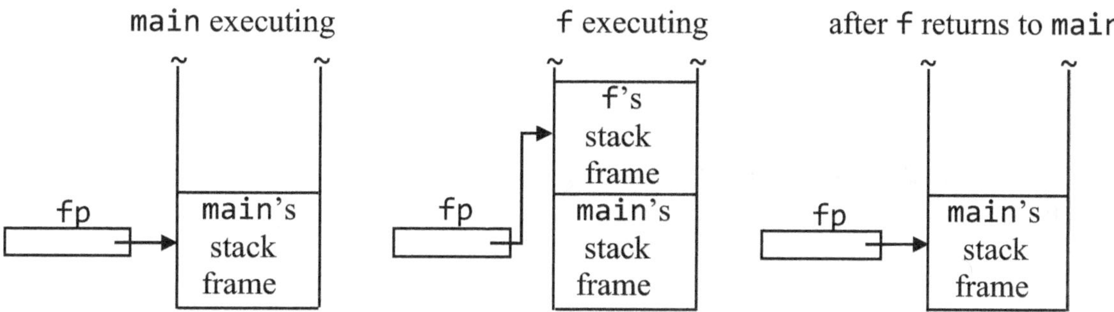

To restore `fp` so that it points to `main`'s stack frame requires that the `fp` register be saved when `main` calls `f`. The saving of the `fp` register is performed by the `esba` (establish base address) instruction. The `esba` instruction is executed at the very beginning of every function. It saves the frame pointer of its caller by pushing it onto the stack. The restoring of the `fp` register that occurs when a function is about to return to its caller is performed by the `reba` (restore base address) instruction. The `reba` instruction is executed at the end of every function, just before the `ret` instruction. Here is the form of a program in which `main` calls `f`:

```
startup:   asp -1; reserve space on stack for return code from main
           call main
           halt
; ==============
f:         esba   ; saves main's frame pointer, loads fp with f's
           ⋮
           reba   ; removes locals (if any), restores main's frame pointer
           ret
; ==============
main:      esba   ; saves startup's frame pointer, loads fp with main's
           ⋮
           reba   ; removes locals (if any), restores startup's frame pointer
           ret
```

The `reba` instruction also removes local variables, if any, from the stack before a function returns to its caller.

Here is the sequence of events that creates the stack frame for a function using the stack instruction set:

1. If the *called* function returns a value, the *calling* sequence starts by decrementing the `sp` register. This reserves the slot on the stack that receives the value returned by the called function.
2. The calling sequence then pushes the values of the arguments, if any, in right-to-left order, thereby creating the parameters in right-to-left order. Thus, the first parameter (i.e., leftmost) is located at the lowest memory address.
3. Next, the calling sequence executes a `call` instruction, which pushes the return address onto the stack and passes control to the called function.
4. The called function executes an `esba` instruction, which saves the frame pointer of the calling function by pushing it onto the stack and then loads `fp` from `sp` (so `fp` points to the stack frame for the called function).
5. Finally, the called function creates its local variables, if any, by decrementing the `sp` register.

Thus, in order of increasing addresses, a stack frame consists of

1. local variables, if any
2. the frame pointer for the calling function
3. return address (i.e., address in the calling function to return to)
4. parameters, if any
5. a reserved slot if the called function returns a value to its caller

During the execution of a function, the `fp` register points to the stack frame for that function—specifically to the slot in its stack frame that holds the frame pointer for the calling function:

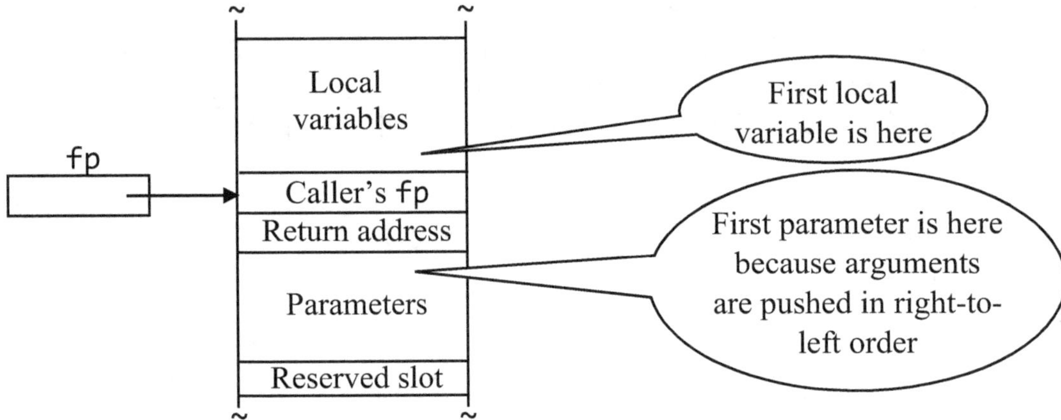

The `fp` register points *to the middle* of the stack frame, below which are the local variables and above which are the parameters. Thus, local variables have *negative* relative addresses, and parameters have *positive* relative addresses. The relative address of the first local variable is always −1; the relative address of the first parameter is always 2.

Let's examine in detail what happens on the stack when the following program is executed:

```
1 // e0801.c
2 #include <stdio.h>
3 void f(int x)
4 {
5     int y;   // local variable created here
6     y = x;
7     printf("%d\n", y);
8 }   // local variable destroyed here
9 int main()
10 {
11     f(3);   // param x created here before call, destroyed after call
12     return 0;
13 }
```

The program starts with startup code reserving a slot on the stack for the return code that `main` returns on line 12. It then calls `main`, which pushes the return address—the address in startup code that `main` returns to—onto the stack. On entry, `main` executes an `esba` instruction which pushes the `fp` register (which contains 0 because there is no stack frame for our highly simplified startup code) onto the stack. The `esba` instruction also loads the `fp` register from the `sp` register, so that both the `sp` and `fp` registers point to the same slot on the stack. The stack at this point looks like this:

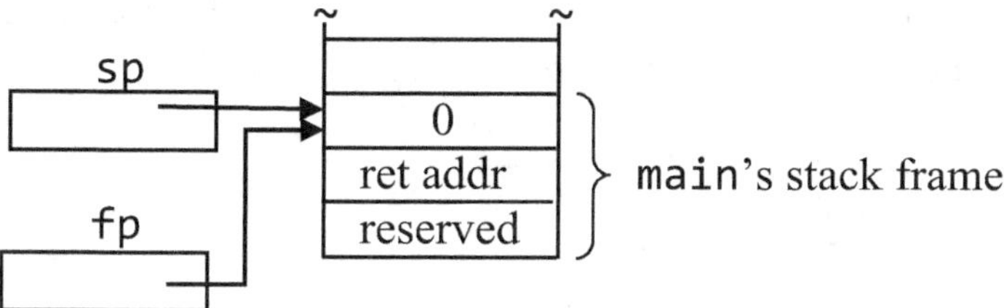

The calling sequence corresponding to line 11 pushes 3 onto the stack (which creates the parameter `x`). It then calls `f` with the `call` instruction, which pushes the return address (the address in `main` that `f` returns to) onto the stack. Thus, the stack on entry into `f` looks like this:

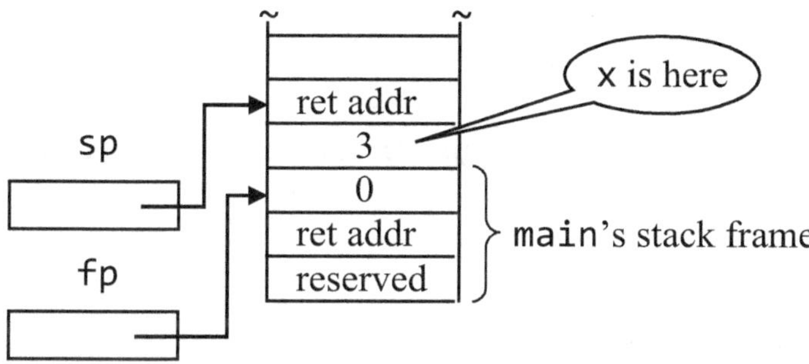

Immediately on entry, `f` executes an `esba` instruction. It first saves `fp` (which contains `main`'s stack frame pointer) by pushing it onto the stack. It then loads `fp` with the current address in `sp`. The stack then looks like this:

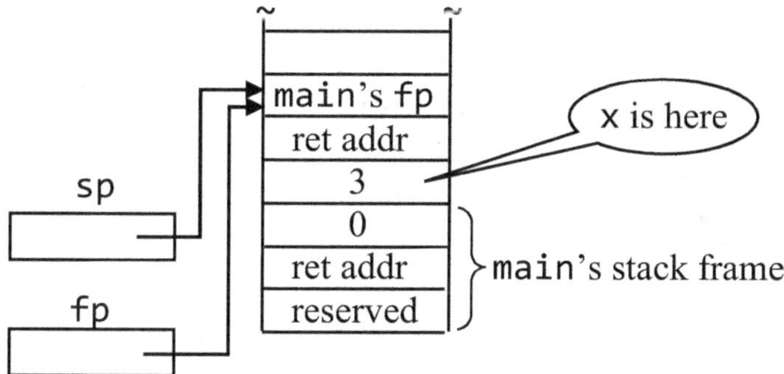

Next, `f` creates a slot on the stack for the local variable `y` by decrementing the `sp` register. We get

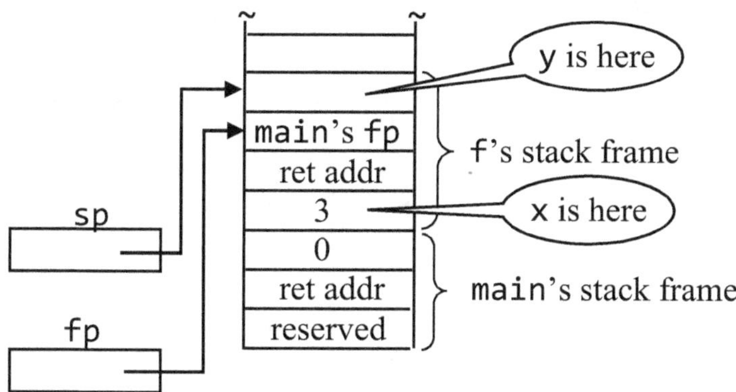

Note that when f is executing, fp does not point to the location in the stack frame for f with the lowest address. The local variable y is below the location fp points to and the parameter x is above it. Thus, the relative address of y is negative (it is −1), and the relative address of x is positive (it is +2).

After assigning x to y and displaying y, f executes the reba instruction. The reba instruction first loads sp from fp. The effect is to remove the local variable y from the stack. We get

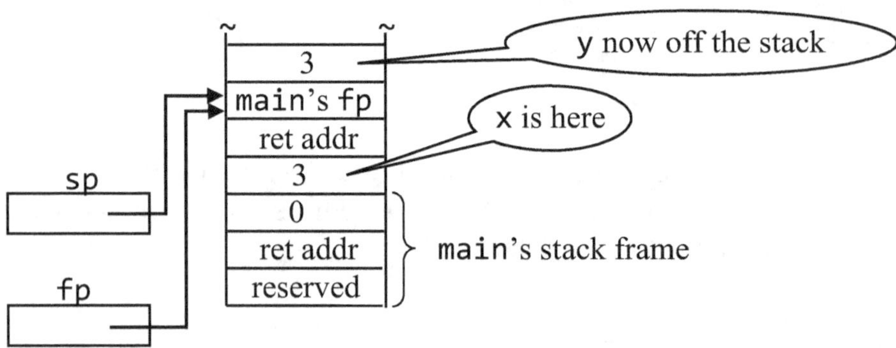

The reba instruction then pops the top of the stack into the fp register. This has the effect of restoring fp with main's stack frame pointer. We get

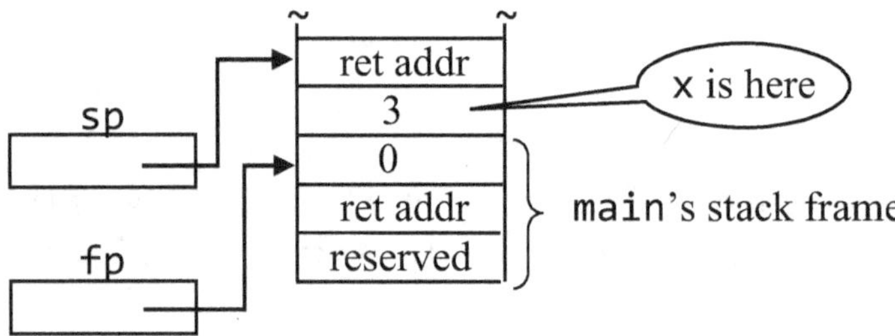

After the reba instruction, f executes the ret instruction which pops the return address off the stack into the pc register which causes a return to main. We get

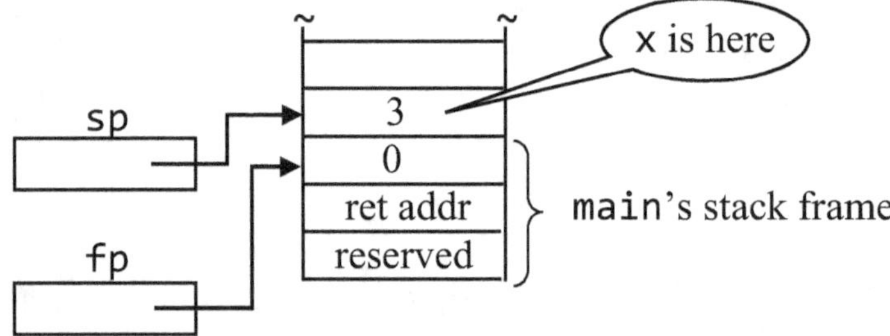

Back in main, main completes the calling sequence by removing the parameter x from the stack by incrementing the sp register. We get

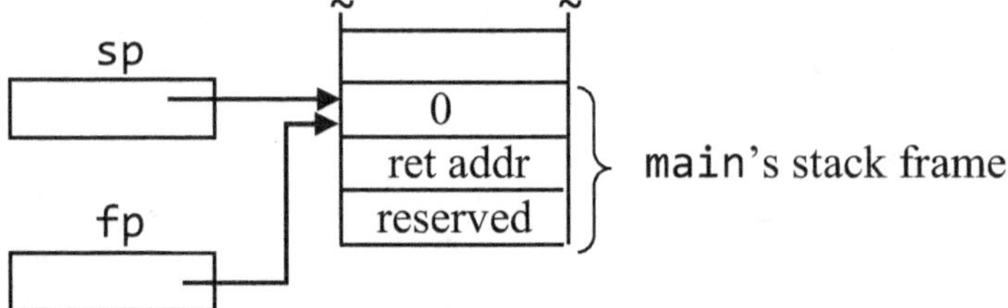

To return to startup code, `main` executes the following sequence of instructions:

```
cora 2; push address of reserved slot
pi 0   ; push return code
stav   ; store return code into reserved slot
reba
ret
```

The `cora` instruction pushes the absolute address corresponding to relative address 2 (which is the relative address of the stack location reserved for the return code). The `pi` instruction pushes a 0 return code (0 indicates a normal termination). The `stav` pops the return code and the address of the reserved slot, and then stores the return code at the popped address. The `reba` instruction then restores `fp` with startup code's stack frame pointer by popping the 0 (which is startup code's `fp` value) into the `fp` register. The return address is now on top of the stack. Finally, the `ret` instruction returns to startup code by popping the return address into the `pc` register. Note that real startup code would then return to the operating system, passing it the return code it received from `main`. But our simplified startup code simply halts.

Here is the assembler code with decimal line numbers for the program in `e0801.c`:

```
 1 ; e0801.a
 2 startup:   asp -1         ; space for return code
 3            call main       ; pushes return address
 4            halt
 5 ; =============================================
 6 f:         esba           ; saves main's frame pointer, loads fp with f's
 7            asp -1         ; create local variable y
 8            cora -1        ; push address of y
 9            pr 2           ; push value in x
10            stav           ; assign x to y
11            pr -1          ; push value in y
12            dout           ; display y
13            nl             ; move cursor to next line
14            reba           ; remove y, restore main's stack pointer
15            ret            ; return to main
16 ; =============================================
17 main:      esba           ; saves frame pointer, loads fp with f's
18            pi 3           ; push 3 (creates x)
19            call f         ; push return address, branch to f
20            asp 1          ; destroy x
21            cora 2         ; push address of reserved slot
22            pi 0           ; push 0 return code
23            stav           ; store return code in reserved slot
24            reba           ; restore startup's frame pointer
25            ret            ; return to startup code
```

Dereferencing Pointers in C and C++

Earlier, we saw that the basic instruction set cannot easily dereference pointers. Let's see if the stack instruction set does any better. Here is C code that uses pointers and its corresponding assembler code, assuming x, y, and p are created by .word directives:

```
        int x, y, *p;
x:          .word 0
y:          .word 0
p:          .word 0


        p = &x;
            pi p   ; push address of p
            pi x   ; push address of x
            stav   ; pop twice, store address of x into p


        *p = 5;
            p p    ; push the pointer in p
            pi 5   ; push 5
            stav   ; pop twice, store 5 where p points
```

In the following sequence, the dp (dereference pointer) instruction replaces the pointer on top of the stack with what the top of the stack is pointing to:

```
        y = *p;
            pi y   ; push the address of y
            p p    ; push pointer in p
            dp     ; dereference the pointer on top of the stack
            stav   ; pop twice, store what p points to into y
```

All the assembler code sequences to handle pointers are simple and efficient. Now let see if we get the same result if x, y, and p are variables on the stack. Suppose x, y, and p are local variable with relative addresses −1, −2, and −3, respectively.

```
        int x, y, *p;
            asp -1       ; create x, relative address = -1
            asp -1       ; create y, relative address = -2
            asp -1       ; create p, relative address = -3


        p = &x;
            cora -3      ; push address of p
            cora -1      ; push address of x
            stav         ; pop twice, store address of x in p


        *p = 5;
            pr -3        ; push the pointer in p
            pi 5         ; push 5
            stav         ; pop twice, store 5 where p points
```

```
y = *p;
    cora -2     ; push the address of y
    pr -3       ; push pointer in p
    dp          ; dereference the pointer on top of the stack
    stav        ; pop twice, store what p points to in y
```

Here again, all the assembler code sequences to handle pointers are simple and efficient. Thus, the stack instruction set fixes two of the major flaws in the basic instruction set:

1. the inability to handle pointers
2. non-constant relative addresses

Multiplying

The stack instruction set has two multiply instructions that work in exactly same way but are implemented differently. mhw (multiply by hardware) uses the multiply circuit within the ALU. mmc (multiply by microcode) uses a procedure in microcode consisting of shift and add operations within a loop. A real computer, of course, would not have two instructions that provide the same function. But the LCC does to illustrate an important point: A computational capability can be implemented in hardware. But it can also be implemented in microcode. The hardware approach is faster but more expensive.

Like the add instruction, the multiply instructions operate on the two numbers on top of the stack. To multiply 2 and 3 with the mhw instruction, we push 2 and 3 with pi instructions, then execute the mhw instruction. It pops the 2 and the 3, multiplies them, and pushes the result back onto the stack. We can then pop and display the result with the dout instruction:

```
pi 2   ; push 2
pi 3   ; push 3
mhw    ; pop twice, multiply, push result
dout   ; pop result and display
nl     ; move cursor to start of next line
```

Here is the microcode for the mhw instruction in the stack instruction set:

```
a.sp c.mar                 ; get address of top of stack into mar
a.sp add b.1 c.sp rd       ; read top of stack and increment sp
a.mdr c.temp               ; save in temp
a.sp c.mar                 ; prepare to read 2nd operand, don't incr sp
rd                         ; read 2nd operand into mdr
a.mdr mul b.temp c.mdr     ; multiply, put sum in mdr
wr br@fetch                ; replace top of stack with sum in mdr
```

It pops off the stack the first operand of the multiplication operation. The second operand is then on the top of the stack. Because it will be replaced by the product, it is unnecessary (and inefficient) to pop it off the stack by incrementing sp. Thus, the sp register is *not* incremented a second time.

The microcode for the mmc instruction is more complex. It uses a loop that repeatedly performs add and shift operations. It multiplies the same way we multiply with a pencil and paper. For example, let's multiply 00011 (3 decimal) by 00101 (5 decimal). The multiplicand (the top number) is multiplied by each bit of the multiplier (the bottom number). The partial products are either equal to the multiplicand (if the multiplying bit is 1) or 0 (if the multiplying bit is 0). The sum of the partial products appropriately shifted is the product. We get the product 01111 (15 decimal). We can perform this process in microcode with a loop that adds and shifts. Here is our pencil and paper multiplication:

```
        00011 multiplicand
        00101 multiplier
       00011
      00000
     00011       Partial products
    00000
   00000
   000001111 product
```

Here is the pseudocode for the microcode we need:

```
 1                 pop stack into temp (temp is the multiplicand)
 2                 pop stack into mdr (mdr is the multiplier)
 3                 set ac to 0
 4 loop:           if mdr (the multiplier) = 0 branch to done
 5                 if rightmost bit of mdr (the multiplier) = 0 branch to skip
 6                 add temp (the multiplicand) to ac
 7 skip:           shift mdr (the multiplier) right one position
 8                 shift temp (the multiplicand) left one position
 9                 branch to loop
10 done:          push ac (the product)
11                 branch to fetch
```

Each time through the loop, the `mdr` register (the multiplier) is shifted right one position (line 7). Thus, the test of the rightmost bit of `mdr` on line 5 tests a different bit in the multiplier each time it is executed. `temp` (the multiplicand) is shifted left on line 8 each time through the loop. Thus, whenever it is added to the `ac` register on line 6, it is in the appropriately shifted position. At the conclusion of the loop, the `ac` register holds the product. The `ac` register here is used simply as another temporary register in which to accumulate the sum of the multiplicands. It is not accessible at the machine level. In place of the `ac` register, we could have used any other available register, such as `r1`.

Adding Opcodes

With four bits to represent opcodes, we can represent only 16 opcodes. However, some of the instructions in the stack instruction set do not specify any operands. Thus, their rightmost 12 bits are unused and, therefore can be used as an extension of the opcode (only the rightmost four bits are needed). For example, in the stack instruction set, `ret`, `esba`, `reba`, `mhw`, and `mmc` all have the four-bit opcode 1010, but have different opcode extensions in their rightmost four bits:

	Opcode (hex)	Unused (hex)	Opcode Extension (hex)
ret	a	00	0
esba	a	00	1
reba	a	00	2
mhw	a	00	4
mmc	a	00	8

The opcode extensions for these instructions are decoded in microcode with a succession of shift right operations that test the bits in the opcode extension from right to left. Each right shift operation shifts the next bit in the extended opcode into the carry flag. The conditional branch in each shift instruction branches if the bit shifted into the carry flag is 1:

```
L1010:     ; ret, esba, reba, mhw, mmc ============================
           a.ir and b.m12 zer@ret     ; branch if opcode extension = 0
           a.ir srl b.1 c.dc cy@esba ; branch if bit 0 in opcode ext = 1
           a.dc srl b.1 c.dc cy@reba ; branch if bit 1 in opcode ext = 1
           a.dc srl b.1 c.dc cy@mhw  ; branch if bit 2 in opcode ext = 1
           a.dc srl b.1 c.dc cy@mmc  ; branch if bit 3 in opcode ext = 1
           br@fetch
ret:       ; microcode for ret
              ⋮
esba:      ; microcode for esba
              ⋮
reba:      ; microcode for reba
              ⋮
mhw:       ; microcode for mhw
              ⋮
mmc:       ; microcode for mmc
              ⋮
```

Stack Instruction Set Summary

Opcode	Format		Description
0	p	x	mem[--sp] = mem[x];
1	pi	x	mem[--sp] = x;
2	pr	s	mdr = mem[fp + s]; mem[--sp] = mdr;
3	cora	s	mdr = fp + s; mem[--sp] = mdr;
4	stav		temp = mem[sp++]; mem[mem[sp++]] = temp;
5	dp		mem[sp] = mem[mem[sp]];
6	asp	s	sp = sp + s;
7	add		temp = mem[sp++]; mem[sp] = mem[sp] + temp;
8	sub		temp = mem[sp++]; mem[sp] = mem[sp] - temp;
9	call	x	mem[--sp] = pc; pc = x;
a000	ret		pc = mem[sp++];
a001	esba		mem[--sp] = fp; fp = sp;
a002	reba		sp = fp; fp = mem[sp++];
a004	mhw		temp = mem[sp++]; mem[sp] = mem[sp] * temp;
a008	mmc		temp = mem[sp++]; mem[sp] = mem[sp] * temp;

```
b          brp    x     if (mem[sp++] > 0) pc = x;
c          br     x     pc = x;
d          brn    x     if (mem[sp++] < 0) pc = x;
e          brz    x     if (mem[sp++] == 0) pc = x;
f          trap   y     see below
```

```
halt   or trap 0        Terminate program
nl     or trap 1        Output newline character
dout   or trap 2        Pop and display signed number in decimal
udout  or trap 3        Pop and display unsigned number in decimal
hout   or trap 4        Pop and display number in hex
aout   or trap 5        Pop and display ASCII character
sout   or trap 6        Pop address and display string at that address
din    or trap 7        Read decimal number from keyboard and push
hin    or trap 8        Read hex number from keyboard and push
ain    or trap 9        Read character from keyboard and push
sin    or trap 10       Pop address and read in string to that address
bp     or trap 14       Breakpoint
```

```
x:     bits 0 to 11 in machine instruction zero-extended to 16 bits
s:     bits 0 to 11 in machine instruction sign-extended to 16 bits
y:     bits 0 to 7 in machine instruction zero-extended to 16 bits
sp:    stack pointer
fp:    frame pointer register
mdr:   memory data register
temp: temporary register
```

Directives: `.word`/`.fill`, `.zero`/`.blkw`, `.string`/`.stringz`/`.asciz`, `.start`

In our preceding discussion, we saw that the stack instruction set can handle pointers, but the basic instruction set cannot. Moreover, the stack instruction set has the `brp` (branch on positive) instruction as well as the `brn` and `brz` conditional branch instructions. The basic instruction set has only the `brn` and `brz` conditional branch instructions. Thus, the stack instruction set provides more function than the basic instruction set even though its instructions have the same number of bits (16 bits). How is this possible? By comparing the two instruction sets, we find the answer: To perform add and store operations, the basic instruction set needs four instructions: `add` and `st` (for variables defined by `.word` directives), and `addr` and `str` (for variables on the stack). But the stack instruction set needs only two: `add` to add and `stav` to store. Moreover, the stack instruction set has more instructions amenable to opcode extensions—that is, more instructions which do not use their rightmost 12 bits, which therefore can be used for opcode extensions.

There is, however, a downside to the stack instruction set. Its instructions use the stack which is in main memory. Accessing memory takes considerably more time that accessing registers. Let's compare the code sequences for the two instruction sets that add `x` and `y` and store the result in `z`:

```
   Basic Instruction Set       |  Stack Instruction Set
              Memory           |             Memory
             accesses          |            accesses
    ld x   ;   1               |   pi z  ;   1          store address of z
    add y  ;   1               |   p x   ;   2          get x, push x
    st z   ;   1               |   p y   ;   2          get y, push y
                               |   add   ;   3          pop, pop, push
                               |   stav  ;   3          pop, pop, push
```

The basic instruction set code makes three main memory accesses plus three more to fetch the instructions. The stack instruction set code makes 11 memory accesses plus five more to fetch the instructions. Six memory accesses total for the basic instruction set versus 16 total for the stack instruction set. Quite a substantial difference! The inherent run-time inefficiency of a stack architecture is the reason why most computers have a register architecture rather than a stack architecture.

Problems

1) Complete the microcode for the stack instruction set in the file named `s.sm`. Test your microcode by entering on the command line

```
micro s.sm          (overlays provided microcode in s.m but backup is in ssave.m)
stack stest.a
sim stest.e
```

Hand in the listing of the `stest.log` file created by `sim`.

2) Do the multiply instructions work for both positive and negative numbers? Confirm you answer by running several test cases.

3) When two 16-bit signed numbers are multiplied, what is the maximum number of bits required by the product?

4) The opcode extensions for the machine instructions with opcode 1010 are powers of 2 (0, 1, 2, 4, 8). . Why not 0, 1, 2, 3, 4? Any advantage of one over the other?

5) What stack assembler code corresponds to the following C statement, where `p` and `y` are variables created with `.word` directives:

```
y = **p;
```

Hint: `**p` accesses the location pointed to by the location `p` points to. `p` is a *pointer to a pointer*. It should be declared this way:

```
int **p;
```

This declaration consists of two parts: "`int *`" and "`*p`". Read "`*p`" as "p is a pointer" and "`int *`" as "to an `int` pointer." Thus, `p` is a pointer to an `int` pointer.

6) What stack assembler code corresponds to the following C statement, where p and y are variables created with .word directives:

```
y = **p + 1;
```

7) What stack assembler code corresponds to the following C statement, where p and y are variables created with .word directives:

```
y = *(*p + 1);
```

8) What stack assembler code corresponds to the following C statement, where p and y are variables created with .word directives:

```
y = **(p + 1);
```

9) What stack assembler code corresponds to the following C statement, where p is a variable created with a .word directive:

```
**p = 5;
```

10) What stack assembler code corresponds to the following C statement, where p is a variable created with a .word directive:

```
*(*p + 1) = 5;
```

11) What stack assembler code corresponds to the following C statement, where p is a variable created with a .word directive:

```
**(p + 1) = 5;
```

12) Create a file p0812.a that contains the stack instruction set assembly code for the following C program. Assemble with the stack program and run on sim. Comment your assembly code with the corresponding C code (see comment.txt). Hand in the listing of the p0812.log file created by sim.

```c
// p0812.c
#include <stdio.h>
int y = 7, z;
int add10(int x)
{
    return x + 10;
}
int main()
{
    z = add10(y + 3);
    printf("%d\n", z);
    return 0;
}
```

13) Create a file `p0813.a` that contains the stack instruction set assembly code for the following C program. Assemble with the `stack` program and run on `sim`. Comment your assembly code with the corresponding C code (see `comment.txt`). Hand in the listing of the `p0813.log` file created by `sim`.

```c
// p0813.c
#include <stdio.h>
int a, y = 7;
void f(int x, int y, int z)
{
    int result;
    result = x + y - z;
    printf("%d\n", result);
}
int main()
{
    int b = 7, c;
    a = 1;
    c = a + b + y;
    f(a, b, c);
    return 0;
}
```

14) Create a file `p0814.a` that contains the stack instruction set assembly code for the following C program. Assemble with the `stack` program and run on `sim`. Comment your assembly code with the corresponding C code (see `comment.txt`). Hand in the listing of the `p0814.log` file created by `sim`.

```c
// p0814.c
#include <stdio.h>
void g(int x)
{
    printf("%d\n", x);
}
void f(int x)
{
    g(x - 2);
}
int main()
{
    f(5);
    return 0;
}
```

15) Create a file `p0815.a` that contains the stack instruction set assembly code for the following C program. Assemble with the `stack` program and run on `sim`. Comment your assembly code with the corresponding C code (see `comment.txt`). Hand in the listing of the `p0815.log` file created by `sim`.

```c
// p0815.c
#include <stdio.h>
int y = 7;
void f(int *p)
{
    *p = *p + 1;
}
int main()
{
    f(&y);
    printf("%d\n", y);
    return 0;
}
```

16) In the microcode for the 1010 instructions, can the number of microinstructions that decode the opcode-extension be reduced?

17) Write a program that multiplies 2 by 16000 using the `mhw` instruction. Repeat but use the `mmc` instruction. Compare runtimes (runtime is given by the number of microinstructions executed).

18) Same as problem 17 but multiply 16000 by 2. Why are the runtimes different from the runtimes in problem 17?

19) Modify your microcode for `mmc` so it repeatedly adds the multiplicand the number of times specified by the multiplier. For example, to multiply 2 by 16000, `mmc` adds 2 to the `ac` register (initialized to 0) 16000 times. Redo problems 17 and 18, but with your new microcode for `mmc`

20) A stack instruction set program will not execute properly if the microcode filename does not start "s". Why not? *Hint*: Consider the I/O instructions.

21) Write and run a C program that uses the shift-add approach to multiply. Test your program by multiplying 3 by 5, -3 by 5, 3 by -5, and -3 by -5. Translate your C program to the stack assembly language (use the file `p0821.a`), assemble, and run on `sim`. Comment your assembly code with the corresponding C code (see `comment.txt`). Hand in the listing of the `p0821.log` file created by `sim`.

9 Register Instruction Set

Using the Register Instruction Set

To assemble and run a program written using the register instruction set, use the `register` assembler (or equivalently, the `r` assembler) to assemble it. Then use `sim` to run the executable file created by the `register` assembler. For example, to assemble and run `rtest.a`, enter

```
register rtest.a         (creates the executable file rtest.e)
sim rtest.e              (runs rtest.e using the microcode in r.m)
```

To use your own microcode instead of the provided microcode for the register instruction set, complete the symbolic microcode in `r.sm` that implements the register instruction set. Then translate the symbolic microcode in `r.sm` to binary using the `micro` program:

```
micro r.sm               (overlays the provided binary microcode in r.m)
```

`sim` will then use your microcode in `r.m` when it executes a register instruction set program. To revert back to the provided microcode, copy `rsave.m` to `r.m`.

In the I/O trap instructions in the register instruction set, you can specify a register, in which case the I/O operation uses that register. For example,

```
dout r3
```

displays the contents of `r3`. If a register is not specified, it defaults to `r0`. `sim`—not microcode—handles the trap instructions so you do not have to write any microcode to support this feature.

Flaws in the Stack Instruction Set

Although the stack instruction set is an improvement over the basic instruction set, it still has some flaws. For example, the address fields in the stack instruction set, like the address fields in the basic instruction set, are 12 bits wide. With 12 bits, only the lowest 4K (4096) of memory can be addressed. The stack grows downward from the top of main memory. But the size of the stack at its largest is generally very small—typically less than 20 words. Thus, a program written with the stack instruction set (or the basic instruction set) can take advantage of only a small portion of main memory (the lowest 4K and the stack in high memory). In this chapter we introduce a new instruction set, the *register instruction set*, that can access all of main memory.

A more serious flaw in both the basic and stack instruction sets is their inability to correctly compare two signed numbers. To compare two signed numbers, the bottom number is subtracted from the top number. If the result is negative, then the top number is less than the bottom number. For example, to determine if x is less than y with the stack instruction set, we push x, push y, and then subtract. If the result is negative, then x < y. In the following code, a branch to `less` occurs if x < y:

```
p x              ; push x
p y              ; push y
sub              ; compute x - y
brn less         ; branch if x < y
```

Unfortunately, this approach does not work if overflow occurs during the subtraction. For example, suppose x is 0111111111111111 (32767 decimal) and y is 1111111111111111 (−1 decimal). To subtract, the LCC adds the two's complement of y to x:

```
    0111111111111111  (32767)
  + 0000000000000001  (two's complement of −1)
    1000000000000000  (−32768)
```

The result is negative, which *incorrectly* indicates x (which is 32767) is less than y (which is −1). The result of the subtraction should be +32768 (note that 32767 − (−1) = +32768). But because this value is out of the range of 16-bit two's complement numbers, the computed result is incorrect, which results in an incorrect compare operation. Moreover, we do not have any easy way with both the stack and basic instruction sets to determine if overflow occurs. Thus, we cannot easily modify our approach to comparing numbers so that it always yields a correct compare.

Out next instruction set, the *register instruction set*, fixes both flaws discussed above. We call it the register instruction set because it takes advantage of the multiple registers in the LCC.

Instruction Set Architecture

The *instruction set architecture* (ISA) of a computer is the collection of the features of the computer that are "visible" at the machine-instruction level. For example, the ISA of the LCC with the basic instruction set consists of the 64K main memory, the ac, pc, and sp registers, and its machine instruction set. Let's now look at the ISA of the LCC with the register instruction set. It consists of the 64K main memory, eight registers, named r0 to r7, the pc and flag registers, and its machine instruction set. Registers r5, r6, and r7 have the alternate names fp (frame pointer), sp (stack pointer), and lr (link register), respectively:

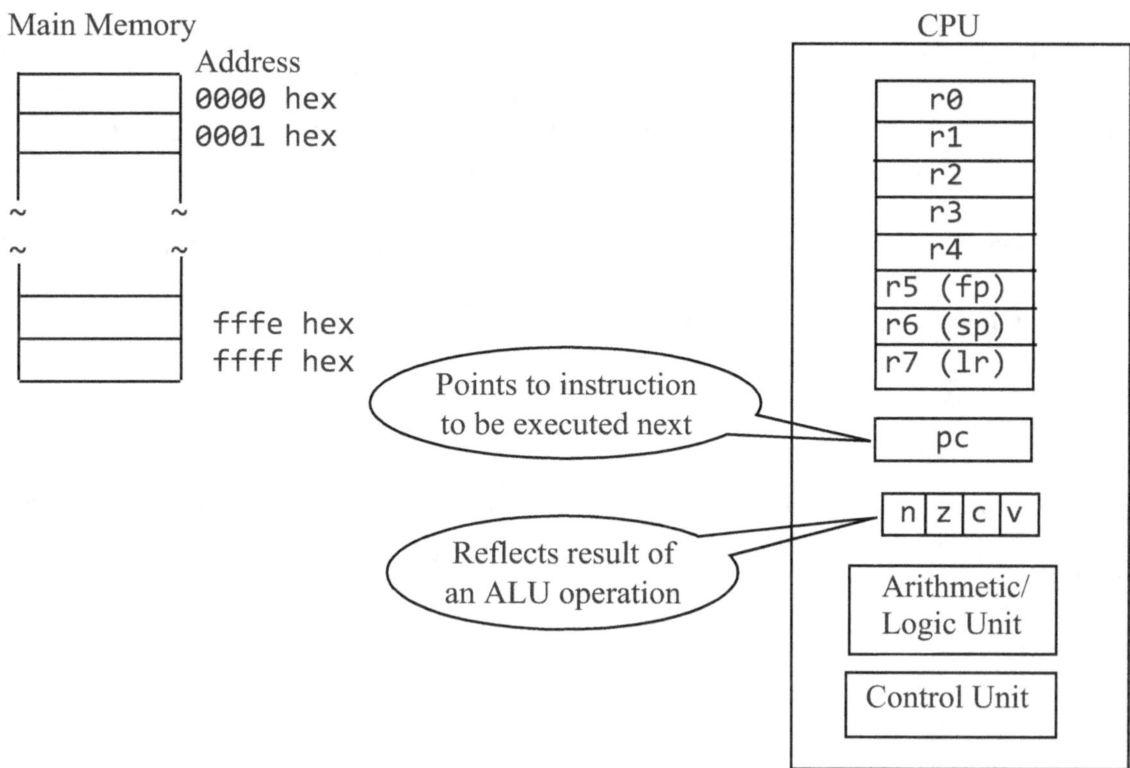

The register instruction set uses pc-*relative addresses* (also called *pc-offsets*). That is, the addresses within instructions are relative to the location that the pc register is pointing to. When executed, an instruction with a pc-relative address accesses the memory location whose address is given by the current address in the pc register plus the pc-relative address in the instruction:

(address in pc) + (pc-relative address)

We call result resulting address the *absolute* or *effective address*. It is the address that is actually sent to the memory unit on a read or write operation. For example, if an instruction at address 2 has a pc-relative address 5, the absolute address is $3 + 5 = 8$. That is, the instruction accesses the memory location at the address $3 + 5 = 8$. Why $3 + 5$ and not $2 + 5$? Recall that the CPU increments the pc register *before* it executes the instruction. When an instruction with a pc-relative address is executed, the pc register has already been incremented so that it is pointing to the next instruction. Thus, a pc-relative address in an instruction is *not* relative to the address of the instruction but *to the address of the next instruction*.

The assembler for the register instruction set computes pc-relative addresses for us—we do not have to do it. For example, consider the following code:

```
        ld r1, x
        ⋮
x:          .word 5
```

Suppose the ld (load) instruction is at location 2 and x is at location 8. The assembler determines the pc-relative address by computing

pc-relative address = (address of x) − (address of ld + 1) = $8 - (2 + 1) = 5$

A relative address is the number of words between two points in a program (from the location right after the instruction to the target label). It *does not depend on the load point*. Thus, unlike the absolute addresses in the basic and stack instruction sets, relative addresses do not have to be adjusted according to the load point. If a program with the code above were loaded into memory so that the ld instruction is at address 1002, then x would be at the address 1008. The correct relative address is still 5:

1003 (address in pc when the ld executed) + 5 (relative address) = 1008 (address of x)

The ld instruction is one of the instructions in the register instruction set that has a pc-relative address. Here is its format:

0010 C pcoffset9

It consists of a four-bit opcode (0010), the C field (the three-bit number of the destination register), and pcoffset9 (a nine-bit pc-relative address). For example, if the pc-relative address of x in the following instruction is 5,

```
ld r1, x
```

then its machine language version is

```
opcode   C      pcoffset9
0010    001    000000101
```

or 2205 in hex. The pcoffset9 field is treated as a signed number. Thus, it can be positive, zero, or negative. It can range from −256 to 255. The st (store) instruction has the same format as the ld instruction.

The lea (load effective address) instruction has the same format as the ld instruction. When executed, it loads the destination register with the absolute address corresponding to its pcoffset9 relative address. That is, it loads the destination register with

(contents of pc register) + pcoffset9

Thus, the ld instruction

```
ld r0, x
```

loads r0 with the value at x, but

```
lea r0, x
```

loads r0 with the 16-bit main memory address of x.

The ldr (load relative) instruction loads the destination register from the address given by a register plus an offset (which can be positive, zero, or negative). For example,

```
ldr r3, fp, -2     (fp is r5)
```

load r3 from the address given by the contents of fp (which is r5) plus −2. Here is its format:

        0110 C A offset6

Its C field contains the number of the destination register; its A field contains the number of the register with the address. For example, the assembler instruction above is translated to

        `0110 011 101 111110`

The offset6 field is six bits wide. Its range is from −32 to +31. The `str` (store relative) instruction has the same format at the `ldr` instruction (the C field in the `str` instruction specifies the register to be stored).

The `mvi` (move immediate) instruction moves its nine-bit immediate value (signed extended) to the destination register specified by the C field. Here is its format:

        1101 C imm9

For example,

        `mvi r3,-2`

moves −2 into `r3`. The imm9 can range from −256 to +255

The `add` instruction has two formats:

        0001 C A 0 00 B

and

        0001 C A 1 imm5

In the first format, the C, A, and B fields are all three-bit register fields. The B field is in positions 0 to 2 in the instruction, the A field in positions 6 to 8, and the C field is in positions 9 to 11. Here is an assembler instruction that is translated to the first format:

        `add r0, r1, r2`

It adds the contents of `r1` and `r2` (the registers specified by the A and B fields) and loads `r0` (the register specified by the C field) with the sum. The second format includes an immediate value in place of the third register:

        `add r0, r1, -3`

This instruction adds the contents of `r1` and the immediate value −3 and loads `r0` with the sum. The immediate value is in the imm5 field of the instruction. Because imm5 is only 5 bits wide, its range is from only −16 to + 15.

The `sub` (subtract) and the `and` instructions have the same two formats that the `add` instruction has. The `and` instruction performs a bitwise AND operation. The `cmp` instruction subtracts just like the `sub` instruction. But unlike the `sub` instruction, it does not load a destination register with the result (its only function is to set the flag registers). Thus, its format is the same as the format for the `sub` instruction except that the C field is not used (it contains 000)

The `bl` (branch and link) or equivalently `jsr` (jump to subroutine) instruction branches to the specified subroutine after loading the return address into the link register `lr` (`r7`). Here is its format:

    0100 1 pcoffset11

The branch-to address is provided by the 11-bit `pc`-relative address in the instruction. For example, the following instruction branches to the subroutine at the label `sub` after loading `lr` with the return address:

```
bl sub; load lr with return address, branch to sub
```

The `blr` (branch and link register) or equivalently `jsrr` (jump to subroutine register) instruction branches to the subroutine at the address in the specified register after loading `lr` with the return address. The branch-to address is provided by the register specified by the A field in the instruction plus an offset if one is specified. For example, the following instruction branches to the address in `r1` (plus an optimal offset6) after loading `lr` with the return address:

```
blr r1, 3  ; load lr with ret address, branch to address in r1+3
```

The format of the `blr` instruction is

    0100 000 A offset6   (offset6 defaults to 0 if omitted in the assembly language instruction)

Because the `bl` and `blr` instructions load `lr` with the return address (they do not push it onto the stack like the `call` instruction in the basic and stack instruction sets), the `ret` instruction returns simply by copying the contents of `lr` to the `pc` register (instead of popping the top of the stack into `pc`).

The `not` instruction performs a bitwise NOT operation. It makes a copy of the contents of the register specified by its A field, performs a bitwise NOT operation on it, and moves the result into the destination register specified by its C field. For example,

```
not r1, r2
```

moves the bitwise NOT of the contents of `r2` into `r1`.

The `push` instruction pushes the contents of the specified register onto the stack. The pop instruction pops the top of the stack into the specified register. For example, the sequence

```
push r1     ; push contents of r1 onto stack
pop r2      ; pop top of the stack into r2
```

pushes the contents of `r1` onto the stack and then pops the top of the stack into `r2`.

The `br` (branch) instructions branch to the specified address if the condition specified by the 3-bit number in its *cc field* (condition code field) is true. Here is its format:

    0000 cc pcoffset9

The branching condition is specified at the assembly level by extending the `br` mnemonic with a suffix that represents the branching condition. For example

```
brn loop              ; branch on negative
```

branches on negative to the label `loop`. The condition code for `brn` is 010. Thus, its machine instruction would have 010 its condition code field. Here is a summary of the branching mnemonics, along with their codes and the condition tested:

Mnemonic	Condition Code	Condition Tested
brz or bre	000	z = 1
brnz or brne	001	z = 0
brn	010	n = 1
brp	011	n = z
brlt	100	n != v
brgt	101	n = v and z = 0
brc	110	c = 1
br or bral	111	branch always

The bre, brne, brlt, and brgt instructions are typically used right after a cmp (or sub) instruction. The cmp instruction (the two-register form) subtracts the contents of the register specified by its B field from the register specified by its A field, and sets the flag registers n, z, c, and v to reflect the result. The branching instruction then branches or not depending on the condition code in the instruction and the flag registers. For example, here is a sequence that branches to dog if the signed number in r1 is less than the signed number in r2:

```
cmp r1, r2  ; subtract r2 from r1, set flags
brlt dog    ; branch if r1 < r2
```

The branch to dog occurs if the condition for the brlt instruction (n ! = v) is true. If n != v, then either n = 1 and v = 0, or n = 0 and v = 1.

Case 1: n = 1 and v = 0
v = 0 so signed overflow did not occur when the cmp instruction subtracted r2 from r1. Thus, n = 1 indicates that the true result of the subtraction is negative. A negative result in a subtraction indicates that the top number (the contents of r1 in this example) is less than the bottom number (the contents of r2).

Case 2: n = 0 and v = 1
v = 1 so signed overflow occurred. Thus, n reflects the sign of the computed result—not the true result. The sign of the true result is 1, which indicates that the true result of the subtraction is negative, again indicating that the top number is less than the bottom number.

Thus, the brlt instruction works correctly whether or not overflow occurs when the cmp or sub instruction that precedes it is executed. Similarly, brgt (branch on greater) works correctly whether or not overflow occurs in the cmp or sub instruction that precedes it.

The basic and stack instruction sets also have no easy way to compare unsigned numbers. But we can do so easily with the register instruction set. Recall from chapter 1 that the c flag acts like a borrow flag on a subtraction. In a subtraction of two *unsigned* numbers, if the top number less than the bottom number, then a borrow into the leftmost position occurs, resulting is the setting of the c flag register to 1. Thus, if c = 1 after a cmp or sub instruction, the top number is less than the bottom number. For example, in the following sequence, suppose r0 and r1 hold unsigned numbers. Then the branch to bird occurs if the r0 number is less than the r1 number:

```
cmp r0, r1 ; unsigned compare
brc bird   ; branch to bird if r0 < r1
```

An alternate mnemonic for `brc` is `brb` (branch on below). Use `brc` or `brb` for "less than" unsigned comparisons and `brlt` for "less than" signed comparisons.

The register instruction set has three types of instructions that transfer control: the branch instructions, the branch and link instructions (`bl` and `blr`), and the `jmp` instruction. The `jmp` instruction unconditionally jumps to the absolute address in the specified register plus an offset if one is specified. For example, the following instruction jumps to the absolute address in `r3`:

```
jmp r3
```

Recall that the two principal flaws in the stack instruction set (which are also in the basic instruction set) are its inability to correctly compare numbers and its inability to access the full 64K of main memory. Our register instruction set, however, has neither of these flaws. With a `cmp` instruction followed by a conditional branching instruction, we can easily and correctly compare numbers, both signed and unsigned. Because the addresses within instructions are `pc`-relative addresses, a register instruction set program can be loaded anywhere into memory and still work correctly. If a program is loaded into high main memory, it can still directly access its data and call its subroutines, assuming they are in range of its `pc`-relative addresses. Even if data or subroutines are out of range, they can still be accessed. For example, suppose the data at `x` is out of range. We can access it with

```
        ld r1, ax        ; load r1 with address of x
        ldr r0, r1, 0     ; load r0 from x
          ⋮
ax:     .word x          ; ax within range of the ld instruction
```

At run time, the location corresponding to the label `ax` will have the 16-bit absolute address of `x`. The `ld` instruction loads this address into `r1`. Then the `ldr` instruction loads `r0` from the address in `r1` to get `x`. As long as `ax` is within range of the `pc`-relative address in the `ld` instruction, this sequence will work. The label `x` *can be anywhere*. We can similarly call a subroutine regardless of its location with the following sequence:

```
          ld r1, asub      ; load r1 with address of sub
          blr r1           ; branch and link to subroutine whose addr in r1
            ⋮
asub:     .word sub        ; asub is within range of the ld instruction
```

We can also unconditionally jump to any location with

```
            ld r1, aabort    ; load r1 with address of aabort
            jmp r1           ; jump to address in r1
              ⋮
aabort:     .word abort      ; aabort is within range of the ld instruction
```

Register Instruction Set Summary

Mnemonic		Format		Flags	Description	
br--	0000	cc pcoffset9			if cc, pc = pc + pcoffset9	
add	0001	C A 0 00 B		nzcv	C = A + B	
add	0001	C A 1 imm5		nzcv	C = A + imm5	
ld	0010	C pcoffset9			C = mem[pc + pcoffset9)	
st	0011	A pcoffset9			mem[pc + pcoffset9] = A	
bl	0100	1 pcoffset11			lr = pc; pc = [pc + pcoffset11]	
blr	0100	0 00 A offset6			lr = pc; pc = A	
and	0101	C A 0 00 B		nz	C = A & B	
and	0101	C A 1 imm5		nz	C = A & imm5	
ldr	0110	C A offset6			C = mem[A + offset6]	
str	0111	C A offset6			mem[A + offset6] = C	
cmp	1000	000 A 0 00 B		nzcv	A - B	(set flags)
cmp	1000	000 A 1 imm5		nzcv	A - imm5	(set flags)
not	1001	C A 0 00000		nz	C = ~A	
push	1010	C 00000 0000			mem[--sp] = C	(push C-field reg)
pop	1010	C 00000 0001			C = mem[sp++];	(pop into C-field reg)
srl	1010	C 00000 0010		nzc	C >> 1	(0 inserted on left, c=last out)
sra	1010	C 00000 0100		nzc	C >> 1	(sign bit replicated, c=last out)
sll	1010	C 00000 1000		nzc	C << 1	(0 inserted on right, c=last out)
sub	1011	C A 0 00 B		nzcv	C = A - B	
sub	1011	C A 1 imm5		nzcv	C = A - imm5	
jmp	1100	000 A offset6			pc = A + offset6	
ret	1100	000 111 offset6			pc = lr	
mvi	1101	C imm9			C = imm9	
lea	1110	C pcoffset9			C = pc + pcoffset9	
trap	1111	0000 trapvec8			OS call	

mov C, imm9 is a pseudo-instruction translated to the machine language instruction mvi C, imm9
mov C, A is a pseudo-instruction translated to the machine language instruction add C, A, 0
C, A, and B are 3-bit register fields.
cc is the 3-bit condition code field in branch instructions.
pcoffset9, pcoffset11, imm5, imm9, offset6 are signed number fields of the indicated length.
If offset6 is omitted in an assembly language instruction, it defaults to 0.

Trap Instructions

Mnemonic		Format		Flags	Description
halt	1111	000 0	00000000	none	Stop execution, return to OS
nl	1111	000 0	00000001	none	Output newline character
dout	1111	C 0	00000010	none	Display signed number in C in decimal
udout	1111	C 0	00000011	none	Display unsigned number in C in decimal
hout	1111	C 0	00000100	none	Display number in C in hex
aout	1111	C 0	00000101	none	Display ASCII character in C
sout	1111	C 0	00000110	none	Display string C points to
din	1111	C 0	00000111	none	Read decimal number from keyboard into C
hin	1111	C 0	00001000	none	Read hex number from keyboard into C
ain	1111	C 0	00001001	none	Read ASCII character from keyboard into C
sin	1111	C 0	00001010	none	Input string into buffer C points to
bp	1111	000 0	00001110	none	Breakpoint, pause execution

If C is omitted in a trap assembly language instruction, it defaults to r0 (000).

Branch Instruction Condition Codes

brz or bre	000	z == 1	(branch on zero, branch on equal)
brnz or brne	001	z == 0	(branch on nonzero, branch on not equal)
brn	010	n == 1	(branch on negative)
brp	011	n == z	(branch on positive)
brlt	100	n != v	(branch on less than in signed comparison)
brgt	101	(n == v) && (z == 0)	(branch on greater than or equal in signed comparison)
brc or brb	110	c = 1	(branch on carry/below in unsigned comp)
br or bral	111		(branch always)

Assembler Directives

Directive	Description
.word <value>	Create word initialized to <value>
.fill <value>	Same as .word
.zero <size>	Create block of <size> words initialized to 0
.space <size>	Same as .zero
.blkw <size>	Same as .zero
.string <string>	Create null-terminated ASCII <string>
.stringz <string>	Same as .string
.asciz <string>	Same as .string
.start <label>	Specify <label> as entry point (or use the label "_start" on entry point)
.global <var>	Specify <var> is a global variable
.globl <var>	Same as .global
.extern <var>	Specify <var> is an external variable

The mov instruction (not listed above) is really just an **add** instruction in which the immediate value is 0. For example, the mov instruction

```
mov r1, r2        ; move contents of r2 into r1
```

is really this **add** instruction

```
add r1, r2, 0
```

which adds the contents of r2 and 0 and moves the result into r1. Thus, its effect simply is to move the contents of r2 into r1. The mov instruction is not a distinct instruction but just an easy way to represent another instruction. For this reason, we call it a *pseudo-instruction* ("pseudo" means "fake").

If the second operand in a mov pseudo-instruction is a register, it is translated to an add instruction, as illustrated above. However, if the second operand is an immediate value, then it is translated to a mvi instruction. For example,

```
mov r1, 3
```

is really the instruction

```
mvi r1, 3
```

Thus, whenever we have to do a move operation, we can simple use the "mov" mnemonic followed by the appropriate operands—either two registers or a register and an immediate value. We will use it often.

Programming with the Register instruction Set

To get a feel for the register instruction set, let's examine an assembler program that passes and dereferences addresses. Before you study this program, be sure you understand how the ldr instruction works. It and the str instruction are the instructions that dereference pointers. For example, suppose r0 contains a pointer. Then

```
ldr r0, r0, 0
```

loads r0 from the address given by its second are third operands (r0 and 0). The address given by the contents of r0 plus 0 is, of course, just the address in r0. Thus, the instruction loads r0 from the location r0 is pointing to. In other words, it dereferences the pointer in r0. The effect of this instruction is to replace the pointer in r0 with the value the pointer is pointing to.

In the following program, main passes the address of x to the parameter p in the function f. f then dereferences p twice—once to access the location p points to (to get the value in x) and once to store a new value in the location p points to (to store a new value in x). The effect is to increment x by 1. The comments in the program show the corresponding C code.

On line 25, main saves lr because the bl instruction on line 31 modifies lr. Thus, if main did not save lr, it would lose the return address it needs to return to startup code. To return to startup code, main restores lr by popping the saved return address into lr (line 41). It then executes a ret instruction, which moves the now correct return address in lr into the pc register, causing a return to startup code. f, however, does not similarly need to save and restore lr because it does not execute a bl instruction or otherwise modify lr. Because the save and restore of lr in f is unnecessary, most compilers would *not* generate the push of line 6 and the pop on line 22. But we are assuming our compiler does not have a lookahead capability. That is, when translating a line of C code, it does not look ahead in the C source code to determine the optimal way to translate the current line of code. Thus, when the compiler starts the translation of f, it does not know if f modifies lr. So it always generates the instructions to save and restore lr.

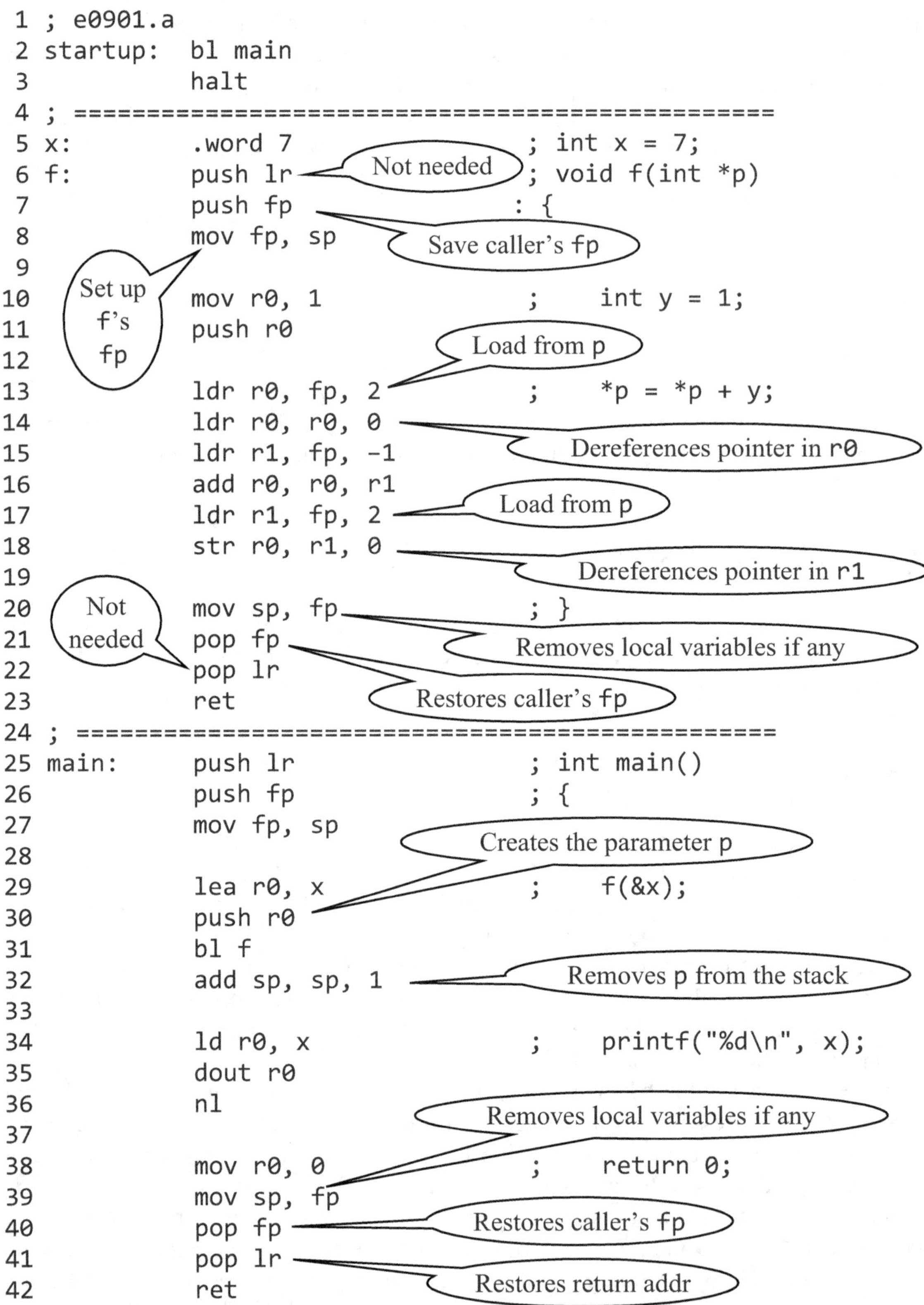


```
 1 ; e0901.a
 2 startup:  bl main
 3           halt
 4 ; ===============================================
 5 x:        .word 7            ; int x = 7;
 6 f:        push lr            ; void f(int *p)
 7           push fp            : {
 8           mov fp, sp
 9
10           mov r0, 1          ;     int y = 1;
11           push r0
12
13           ldr r0, fp, 2      ;     *p = *p + y;
14           ldr r0, r0, 0
15           ldr r1, fp, -1
16           add r0, r0, r1
17           ldr r1, fp, 2
18           str r0, r1, 0
19
20           mov sp, fp         ; }
21           pop fp
22           pop lr
23           ret
24 ; ===============================================
25 main:     push lr            ; int main()
26           push fp            ; {
27           mov fp, sp
28
29           lea r0, x          ;     f(&x);
30           push r0
31           bl f
32           add sp, sp, 1
33
34           ld r0, x           ;     printf("%d\n", x);
35           dout r0
36           nl
37
38           mov r0, 0          ;     return 0;
39           mov sp, fp
40           pop fp
41           pop lr
42           ret
```

On line 29, the `lea` instruction loads the address of `x`. The `push` on line 30 then pushes it, thereby creating the parameter p. Thus, the parameter p points to x. On line 31, the `bl` loads the return address in the `pc` register into `lr` and then branches to `f`. On line 6, the `push` instruction saves the return address in `lr` by pushing it onto the stack. Then, if the address in `lr` is corrupted during the execution of `f` (it is not for this function), the return address is still available on the stack.

The two instructions on lines 7 and 8 (and 26 and 27) together do what the `esba` instruction does in the stack instruction set: They save the caller's frame pointer and then load `fp` with the pointer to the stack frame of the called function (by loading `fp` from `sp`).

Line 11 creates and initializes the local variable `y` by pushing 1 onto the stack. The stack at this point looks like this:

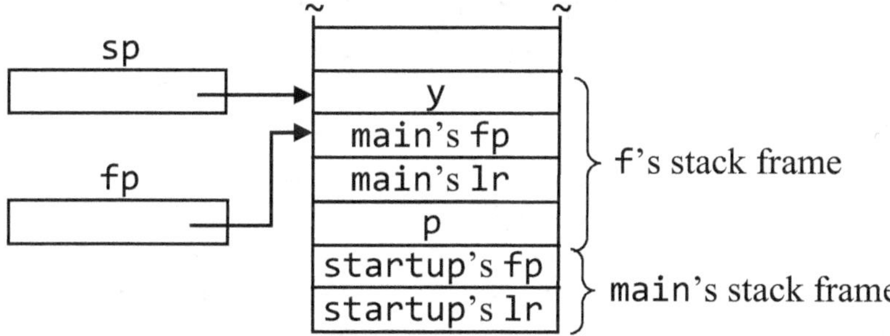

The parameter `p` has the relative address 2 (relative to the address in `fp`). The local variable `y` has the relative address −1. Thus, the `ldr` instruction on line 13 loads `r0` from `p` (so now both `r0` and `p` point to `x`). The `ldr` instruction on line 14 dereferences the pointer in `r0`. Specifically, it loads `r0` from the location `r0` points to (so it loads `x`). The `ldr` instruction on line 15 loads `r1` from `y`, and line 16 adds the value in `r0` (which is the value of `x`) and value in `r1` (which is the value of `y`) and leaves the sum in `r0`. The `ldr` on line 17 loads `r1` from `p` (recall the relative address of `p` is 2). So `r1` points to `x`. The `str` on line 18 stores `r0` (which contains the sum of `x` and `y`) in the location `r1` points to (which is `x`).

The `mov` instruction on line 20 has the effect of removing the local variable `y` from the stack. The `pop` instructions on line 40 and 41 restore `fp` and `lr` with the addresses they had on entry into `f`. Finally, the `ret` instruction on line 42 returns to startup code (by loading the `pc` register from `lr`). Saving and restoring `lr` in `f` (lines 6 and 22) are not necessary because `f` does not call a function, which would modify `lr`, or otherwise modify `lr`.

Amux, Bmux, and Cmux Multiplexers

The `ld` instruction in the basic instruction set loads an operand from memory into the `ac` register. For example,

```
ld x
```

loads the operand at the label `x` into the `ac` register. Thus, after reading the operand from memory into the `mdr`, the microcode for the `ld` instruction transfers the operand in the `mdr` to the `ac` register. Here is the microcode for the `ld` instruction in the basic instruction set:

```
L0000:     ; ld ================================================
           a.ir and b.m12 c.mar     ; move address in inst to mar
           rd                       ; read operand from memory
           a.mdr c.ac br@fetch      ; load ac from operand in mdr
```

The `ld` instruction in the register instruction set is more complex. It specifies not only the operand to be loaded but the register to load. For example,

```
ld r3, x
```

loads the operand at the label x into r3. The microcode for this instruction reads the memory operand into the mdr. But how does it get the contents of the mdr into r3? We can use

```
a.mdr c.r3 br@fetch      ; load r3 from operand in mdr
```

But this microinstruction is correct only if the ld instruction loads r3. What if the ld instruction loads any one of the other seven registers—for example,

```
ld r5, x
```

Note that the C field *of the microinstruction* above specifies the register to be loaded from the C bus. But we want the C field *of the machine instruction* to specify the register to be loaded. Then if the ld instruction is

```
ld r3, x
```

r3 is loaded (because the number of r3—011—is in the C field *of machine instruction*). But if the ld instruction is

```
ld r5, x
```

then r5 is loaded (because the number of r5—101—is in the C field of the *machine instruction*).

When we write microcode, sometimes we want a microinstruction that loads the register specified by the C field of the microinstruction in the mir. But at other times, as illustrated by the ld instruction in the register instruction set, we want a microinstruction that loads the register specified by the C field of the machine instruction in the ir. How do we provide the LCC this capability? Recall that the C decoder determines which register is loaded from the C bus. We simply add a multiplexer that drives the C decoder. The multiplexer selects either the C field in the microinstruction in the mir or the C field of the machine instruction in the ir. Let's call this multiplexer Cmux (sim supports this extended model of the LCC):

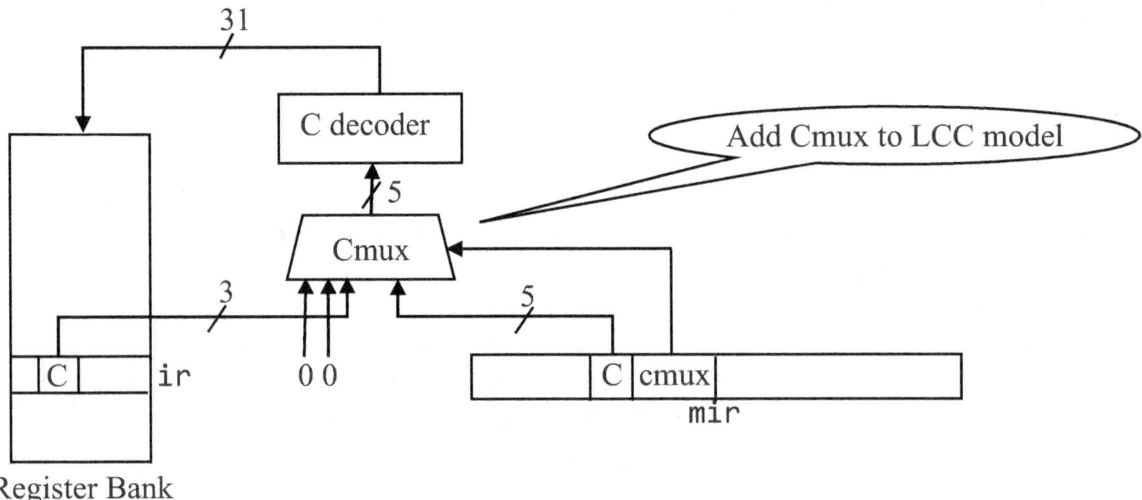

The Cmux multiplexer selects between the C field of the machine instruction and the C field in the microinstruction. The Cmux multiplexer has two five-line inputs. Because the C field in the machine instruction has only three bits, it is extended on the left with two 0's. The cmux field in the microinstruction (a one-bit field) determines which C field passes through to the C decoder. If cmux = 1, the C field in the machine instruction passes through; if cmux = 0, the C field in the microinstruction passes through.

In a symbolic microinstruction, if `cmux` is specified, then cmux = 1. Otherwise, cmux = 0. In the microcode for the basic and stack instruction sets, the register to load from the C bus is always specified by the C field in the microinstruction. Thus, we never need to specify `cmux` in the microcode for those instruction sets.

By selectively using the cmux field in a microinstruction, we can now microcode the `ld` instruction in the register instruction set:

```
L0010:     ; ld ===============================================
           a.ir sext b.m9 c.temp     ; get relative address
           a.temp add b.pc c.mar     ; convert to absolute address
           rd                        ; read operand from memory
           a.mdr cmux br@fetch       ; load destination reg from operand in mdr
```

The first microinstruction above extracts the pcoffset9 relative address from the instruction. The relative address is a signed number. Thus, we have to use the sext operation to extract it. The second microinstruction adds the relative address and the current contents of the `pc` to get the absolute address. The third microinstruction reads the main memory operand into the `mdr`. In the fourth microinstruction, no ALU operation is specified. Thus, the contents of the `mdr` (which are on the A bus) pass unchanged through the ALU to the C Bus. Because `cmux` is specified, the register specified by the C field in the *machine instruction* is loaded from the C bus.

The A decoder is configured with a multiplexer in the same way the C decoder is configured: The C decoder is driven by the Cmux multiplexer. Similarly, the A decoder is driven by the Amux multiplexer. The Amux multiplexer selects for output either the A field from the microinstruction or the A field in the machine instruction. The Cmux multiplexer is controlled by the cmux field in the microinstruction; the Amux multiplexer is controlled by the amux field in the microinstruction. The B decoder has a similar setup.

Let's take another look at the format of a microinstruction:

A	amux	B	bmux	C	cmux	ALU	u	rd	wr	cond	addr	
5	1	5	1	5	1	4	1	1	1	4	11	width

Note that it has the amux, bmux, and cmux fields that control the Amux, Bmux, and Cmux multiplexers. If these fields contain 1, then their corresponding multiplexers select the corresponding field in the machine instruction—not in the microinstruction. Armed with this knowledge, we can now write the microcode for the `add` instruction:

```
L0001:     ; add ===============================================
           a.ir and b.bit5 !zer@add1        ; determine which type of add
add0:      amux add bmux cmux u br@fetch     ; add two regs
add1:      a.ir sext b.m5 c.temp             ; extract immed value
           amux add b.temp cmux u br@fetch ; add reg and immed value
```

The first microinstruction extracts bit 5 of the machine instruction. This bit determines the type of **add** instruction. If it is 1, a branch to **add1** occurs. If it is 0, then the microinstruction at **add0** is executed. Note that the microinstruction at **add0** specifies **amux**, **bmux**, and **cmux**. Thus, it is the machine instruction, not the A, B, and C fields in the microinstruction, that determines which registers are involved in the add operation. The microinstruction at **add1** is executed if the **add** instruction has an immediate operand. This microinstruction extracts the immediate operand and places it in the **temp** register. Then the next microinstruction performs the add operation. Note that it specifies **amux**. Thus, the operand to be added with the immediate value comes from the register specified by the A field in the machine instruction. Because **cmux** is specified, the destination register is determined by the C field in the machine instruction—not the C field in the microinstruction.

You may have noticed that u appears in two of the microinstructions above. We will explain its effect in the section below on user and system flag registers.

Complication with the st, str, push, and Shift Instructions

Consider the following **st** instruction in the register instruction set:

```
st r1, x
```

It stores the contents of **r1** at the location corresponding to **x**. To do this, the microcode for the **st** instruction has to route the contents of **r1** down the A bus, through the ALU, to the **mdr**, in preparation for a memory write operation. The problem with doing this is that the register specified in a **st** instruction is *in its C field*, but we want it to drive the A bus. If we specify **amux** in a microinstruction, that causes the register in the A field—not the C field—of the machine instruction to drive the A bus.

The solution to this problem is quite simple: We shift the machine instruction in the **ir** three position to its right so that the register number specified in its C field ends up in the A field of the **ir**. Then a microinstruction with **amux** specified will drive the A bus with the register originally specified by the C field of the **ir**. Here is the microcode we need for the **st** instruction:

```
L0011:     ; st ================================================
           a.ir sext b.m9 c.temp    ; get relative address
           a.temp add b.pc c.mar    ; convert to absolute address
           a.ir srl b.3 c.ir        ; shift reg number in C field to A field
           amux c.mdr               ; move reg contents to mdr
           wr br@fetch              ; perform write operation
```

In this example, we use **srl** to shift the **ir** three positions. We could also use **ror** to shift the **ir**. Using **ror** would be necessary if the machine instruction used microcode that needed the **ir** restored to its original contents after the right shift. In that case, to restore **ir**, simply follow the **ror** instruction with a **rol** instruction that has the same shift count (3). For the **st** instruction, we do not need to restore **ir**. Thus, we can use the **srl** instruction.

User and System Flag Registers

Whenever the ALU performs an operation, it sets the flag registers according to the results of the operation. For example, when an `add` machine instruction is executed, the ALU adds the two operands specified in the instruction. It sets n to 1 if the result is negative, z to 1 if the result is zero, c to 1 if a carry out of the leftmost position occurs, and v to 1 if signed overflow occurs. A conditional branch instruction can then test the flag registers and respond according to their settings. For example, consider the following sequence:

```
add r0, r0, r1
brp cat
```

The `add` instruction adds the contents of r0 and r1 and sets the flag registers according to the result. The `brp` instruction then branches if n = z. Because the result cannot simultaneously be both negative and zero, n and z cannot both be 1. Thus, if n = z, they both must be 0. But this implies the result of the addition is not negative (because n = 0) and not zero (but z = 0), and therefore is positive. Thus, the `brp` instruction branches if and only if the result of the addition is positive.

For the code sequence above to work correctly, the flag registers *must* remain unchanged from the time they are set by the `add` instruction to the time they are tested by the `brp` instruction. But before the `brp` instruction tests the flag registers, the CPU has to perform the fetch of the `brp` instruction, the incrementation of the pc register, and the decoding of the `brp` instruction. The incrementation of the pc register *sets the flag registers*. The decoding process uses `sll` instructions, *which also set the flag registers*.

So how can the flag registers remain unchanged, *as they must if our machine code is to work correctly,* from the time they are set by the `add` instruction to the time they are tested by the `brp` instruction? Here is the answer: They can remain unchanged because there are two sets of flag registers: a user set and a system set. When the `add` instruction performs the add operation, it sets the user flag registers. The incrementation of the pc register and the decoding process sets the system flag registers. Thus, when the `brp` instruction tests the flag registers (it tests the user set), they are unchanged from the time they were set by the `add` instruction.

The u field in a microinstruction determines which set of flag registers are used and set. If u = 1, the user set is used; if u = 0, the system set is used. For example, the add operation for the instruction

```
add r0, r0, r1
```

is performed by the microinstruction at the label `add0` in the following microcode:

```
L0001:    ; add ================================================
          a.ir and b.bit5 !zer@add1        ; determine which type of add
add0:     amux add bmux cmux u br@fetch    ; add two regs
add1:     a.ir sext b.m5 c.temp            ; extract immed value
          amux add b.temp cmux u br@fetch  ; add reg and immed value
```

Because u is specified in the microinstruction at `add0`, its u field contains 1 (if u is omitted, the u field in the binary microinstruction defaults to 0). Thus, the microinstruction sets the user flag registers. Now look at the microinstructions for the `brp` instruction:

```
        a.ir sext b.m9 c.temp
        u zer@fetch              ( No u )  ; go to next instruction if z = 1
        u neg@fetch                        ; go to next instruction if n = 1
        a.temp add b.pc c.pc br@fetch ; branch to address in brp inst
```

The second and third microinstructions test the flag registers. Because they have u, they test the user flag registers—the flag registers that were set by the add instruction. However, the first microinstruction above and the microinstruction that increments the pc at the beginning of the program do not have u:

```
        ;=================================================
        ; Fetch machine instruction, increment pc
fetch:  a.pc c.mar
        a.pc add b.1 c.pc rd   ( No u )
```

Nor do the decoding instructions, for example,

```
L0:        a.ir sll b.1 c.dc neg@L01   ( No u )
```

Thus, they set the system flag registers, leaving the user flag registers unchanged.

The trace that sim produces (recall that it is turned on if you enter "-t" on the command line when you invoke sim) labels the system flag registers with "nzcv" and the user flag registers with "NZCV".

Problems

1) Complete the microcode for the register instruction set in the file named r.sm. Test your microcode by entering on the command line

   ```
   micro r.sm
   register rtest.a
   sim rtest.e
   ```

   Hand in the listing of the rtest.log file created by sim.

2) Draw the circuit that controls which set of flag registers is used.

3) Would it be better if the shift instructions in the register instruction set had both C and A fields, like the not instruction? Would it be better if the shift instructions had a C field and an immediate field, where the immediate field would be the number of positions to shift? Write the microcode for both alternatives. Any tradeoffs?

4) The machine instructions in the register instruction set with opcode 1010 are distinguished by the rightmost 4 bits. Would it be better if the rightmost 3 bits were used instead with 000, 001, 010, 011, 101 for push, pop, srl, sra, and sll, respectively? Write the microcode for this modification.

5) What is the difference between a ret instruction and a jmp r7 instruction?

6) In the IBM mainframe computers, the base register for relative addresses is specified at the beginning of each module (by a USING statement). The base register is loaded with the address of the *beginning* of the module. Thus, relative addresses are all non-negative. Compare this approach to the `pc`-relative addressing used by the register instruction set. Discuss advantages/disadvantages of each approach.

7) How could the unused bits in the shift instructions be used?

8) Of the four steps, fetch, increment, decode, execute, which takes the most time?

9) Create a file `p0909.a` that contains the register instruction set assembly code for the following C program. Assemble with the `register` program and run on `sim`. Comment your assembly code with the corresponding C code (see `comment.txt`). Hand in the listing of the `p0909.log` file created by `sim`.

```c
// p0909.c
#include <stdio.h>
int y = 7, z;
int add10(int x)
{
    return x + 10;
}
int main()
{
    z = add10(y + 3);
    printf("%d\n", z);
    return 0;
}
```

10) Create a file `p0910.a` that contains the register instruction set assembly code for the following C program. Assemble with the `register` program and run on `sim`. Comment your assembly code with the corresponding C code (see `comment.txt`). Hand in the listing of the `p0910.log` file created by `sim`.

```c
// p0910.c
#include <stdio.h>
int a, y = 7;
void f(int x, int y, int z)
{
    int result;
    result = x + y - z;
    printf("%d\n", result);
}
int main()
{
    int b = 7, c;
    a = 1;
    c = a + b + y;
```

```
    f(a, b, c);
    return 0;
}
```

11) Create a file `p0911.a` that contains the register instruction set assembly code for the following C program. Assemble with the `register` program and run on `sim`. Comment your assembly code with the corresponding C code (see `comment.txt`). Hand in the listing of the `p0911.log` file created by `sim`.

```c
// p0911.c
#include <stdio.h>
void g(int x)
{
    printf("%d\n", x);
}
void f(int x)
{
    g(x - 2);
}
int main()
{
    f(5);
    return 0;
}
```

12) Create a file `p0912.a` that contains the register instruction set assembly code for the following C program. Assemble with the `register` program and run on `sim`. Comment your assembly code with the corresponding C code (see `comment.txt`). Hand in the listing of the `p0912.log` file created by `sim`.

```c
// p0912.c
#include <stdio.h>
int y = 7;
void f(int *p)
{
    *p = *p + 1;
}
int main()
{
    f(&y);
    printf("%d\n", y);
    return 0;
```

10 Optimal Instruction Set and Fast Opcode Decoding

Using the Optimal Instruction Set

To assemble and run a program written using the optimal instruction set, use the `optimal` assembler (or equivalently, the `o` assembler) to assemble it. Then use `sim` to run the executable file created by the `optimal` assembler. For example, to assemble and run `otest.a`, enter

```
optimal otest.a          (creates the executable file otest.e)
sim otest.e              (runs otest.e using the microcode in o.m)
```

To use your own microcode instead of the provided microcode for the optimal instruction set, complete the symbolic microcode in `o.sm` that implements the optimal instruction set. Then translate the symbolic microcode in `o.sm` to binary using the `micro` program:

```
micro o.sm               (overlays the provided binary microcode in o.m)
```

`sim` will then use your microcode in `o.m` when it executes an optimal instruction set program. To revert back to the provided microcode, copy `osave.m` to `o.m`.

New and Modified Instructions in the Optimal Instruction Set

The register instruction set is a good instruction set, but it has one significant shortcoming: It does not take advantage of all the operations that the ALU can perform, such as multiplying, dividing, and the bitwise and rotate operations. Fortunately, this shortcoming can be remedied easily, giving us an improved (and perhaps truly optimal) instruction set, which we appropriately call the *optimal instruction set* (this is the instruction set used exclusively in *C and C++ Under the Hood*).

The optimal instruction set is the register instruction set modified as follows:

Mnemonic	Format	Flags		Description
srl	1010 C ct 0 0010	nzc	C >> ct	(0 inserted on left, c=last out)
sra	1010 C ct 0 0011	nzc	C >> ct	(sign bit replicated, c=last out)
sll	1010 C ct 0 0100	nzc	C << ct	(0 inserted on right, c=last out)
rol	1010 C ct 0 0101	nzc	C << ct	(rotate bit 15 to bit 0, c=last out)
ror	1010 C ct 0 0110	nzc	C << ct	(rotate bit 0 to bit 15, c=last out)
mul	1010 C A 0 0 0111	nz	C = C * A	(integer multiply)
div	1010 C A 0 0 1000	nz	C = C / A	(integer division)
rem	1010 C A 0 0 1001	nz	C = C % A	(remainder)
or	1010 C A 0 0 1010	nz	C = C | A	(bitwise OR)
xor	1010 C A 0 0 1011	nz	C = C ^ A	(bitwise exclusive OR)
mvr	1010 C A 0 0 1100		C = A	(copy A-field reg to C-field reg)
sext	1010 C A 0 0 1101	nz	C-field reg sign extended, A- field reg specifies field to extend	

- The shift instructions and the new rotate instructions include a four-bit `ct` (count) field that determines the number of positions the instruction shifts or rotates. In the register instruction set, the shift instructions could shift only one position although the ALU is capable of performing multiple-position shifts.
- For all the instructions with opcode 1010, the extended opcodes are five bits and range from 00000 to 01101. With five bits, we can have up to 32 distinct opcode-1010 instructions. In the register instruction set, the extended opcodes are only four bits, and each hold a power of 2: 0000, 0001, 0010, 0100, and 1000, which limits the number the number of opcode-1010 instructions to five.
- The rotate instructions are the "musical chairs" shift instructions. The bits that are shifted out of one side of a register are inserted into the other side of the register.
- The `div` divides and provides the quotient; `rem` divides and provides the remainder.
- The `or` and `xor` instructions perform the bitwise OR and the bitwise XOR operations, respectively, on the registers specified in the C and A fields.
- The `mvr` instruction copies the contents of one register to another (recall in the register instruction set that to perform a register copy, we have to use an `add` instruction that adds zero).
- The `sext` instruction sign extends the number in the register specified by the C field. The bits to extend are specified by the mask in the register specified by the A field. For example, suppose the mask is 0000000000011111. Because the mask's five rightmost bits are 1, then the five rightmost bits in the number in the register specified by the C field are sign extended.

With these new and modified instructions, we can take full advantage of the capabilities of the ALU.

Fast Decoding

Replacing the register instruction set with the optimal instruction set provides a major improvement of the LCC. However, the most significant improvement we can make is fast opcode decoding. Moreover, it works for *any* of our instruction sets. The decoding process we have used up to now—the bit-by-bit examination of the opcode—requires an exorbitant amount of execution time. Thus, using fast decoding dramatically increases the speed of the LCC.

Fast decoding requires a few relatively minor modifications to the hardware of the LCC:

1. A one-bit field—the *mmux field*—is added to each microinstruction.
2. The addr field in each microinstruction is extended to 12 bits.
3. The size of microstore is increased to 4096.
4. A *transfer logic circuit* is added that transforms the 16-bit word *on the C bus* to a 12-bit microstore branch-to address. Its output is used *only* when a machine instruction is on the C bus. This circuit outputs the opcode, the extended opcode (if any) of the machine instruction, and the constant 8 (1000 binary) in the following format:

4 bits	4 bits	4 bits
opcode	extended opcode or 0000 if none	1000

5. A two-bus multiplexer that allows the microstore branch-to address to be either from the addr field of the current microinstruction in the `mir` or from the transfer logic circuit. If the mmux bit is 1 in the current microinstruction, then the 12-bit output of the transfer logic drives the `mpc` register. If the mmux bit is 0, then the branching mechanism functions as described in Chapter 6. Thus, if mmux is 0 and a branch occurs (it depends on the flag registers and the cond field in the current microinstructin), it is to the address in the addr field of the current microinstruction.

6. The branch control logic is modified so that if mmux is 1, it outputs a 1 no matter what is in the flag registers or in the cond field of the current microinstruction. Thus, when mmux is 1, a branch *always* occurs (at T_4) to the address that the transfer logic circuit outputs:

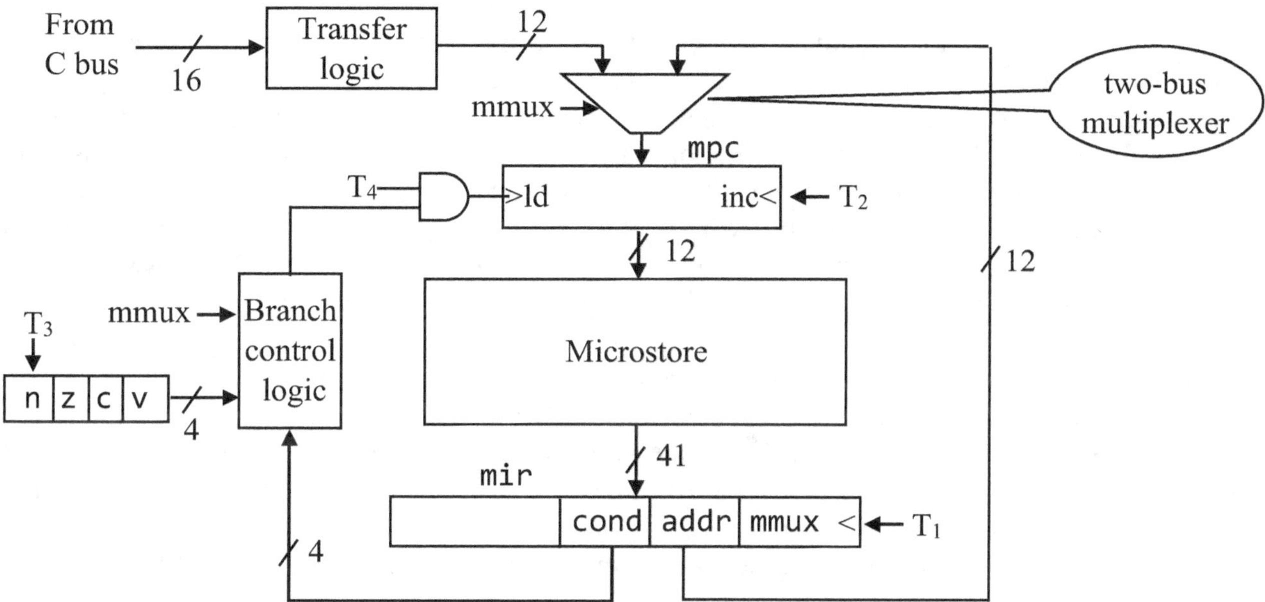

The transfer logic circuit transforms a machine instruction to the microstore address of the microcode sequence that interprets that machine instruction, thereby performing fast (essentially instantaneous) decoding. For example, suppose the 16-bit `st` machine instruction in the basic instruction set, 1005, is on the C bus and therefore inputted to the transfer logic circuit. The transfer logic circuit then outputs the 12-bit microstore address 108. The opcode for the instruction, 1, becomes the leftmost four bits of the outputted address. There is no extended opcode so the middle four bits are set to 0. The rightmost 4 bits are set to 8 (1000 binary):

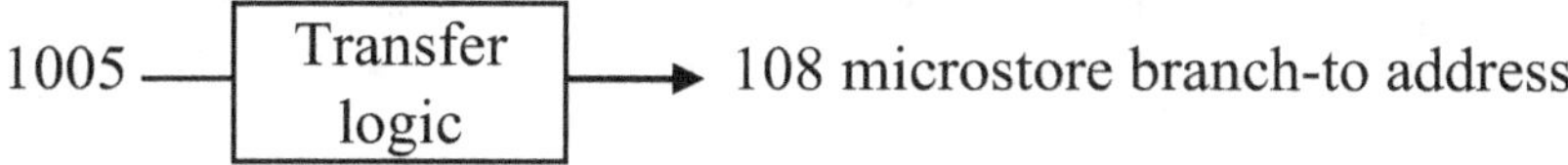

If mmux is 1, then 108 is loaded into the `mpc`, causing an immediate branch in microcode to the address 108 hex. The time-consuming bit-by-bit decoding process is eliminated. Of course, this mechanism requires the microcode for each instruction to be at specific addresses. For example, the microcode for the `st` instruction would have to start at the address 108 hex.

Fast decoding is not limited to the optimal instruction set. Given the appropriate microcode, we can use it for all the instruction sets we have studied. Let's examine the microcode that does fast decoding for the basic instruction set. It starts the usual way: It fetches the machine instruction pointed to by the `pc` and increments the `pc` register:

```
fetch:    a.pc c.mar
          a.pc add b.1 c.pc rd
```

The fetch reads the machine instruction into the `mdr`. Next, the machine instruction in the `mdr` is copied to the `ir`:

```
          a.mdr c.ir mmux       (no need to add 0 to set flag registers when mmux specified)
```

This microinstruction causes the machine instruction in the `mdr` to go down the A bus, through the ALU without modification, onto the C bus, and into the `ir`. Recall that the C bus drives the transfer logic circuit (see the preceding circuit diagram). Thus, because the machine instruction is on the C bus when this microinstruction is executed, the machine instruction is inputted to the transfer logic circuit. Because `mmux` is specified in this microinstruction (which sets the mmux bit in the corresponding binary microinstruction to 1), the output of the transfer logic circuit (which is the microstore branch-to address for this machine instruction) is loaded into the `mpc`, causing a branch in microcode to that address. Thus, while copying `mdr` to `ir`, this microinstruction performs essentially *instantaneous* decoding of the machine instruction's opcode.

The rest of the microcode for the basic instruction set simply consists of the sequences for each machine instruction. Each sequence has to start at a specific address (the address outputted by the transfer logic circuit for that instruction). To start a microcode sequence at a specific address, simply use the `.org` directive in the symbolic microcode source code followed the desired start address *in hex*. For example, the branch-to address of the opcode 0 machine instruction (the `ld` instruction) in the basic instruction set is 008. Thus, we start the microcode sequence for this machine instruction with `.org 008` (specify the address *in hex*):


```
.org 008 ; ld ===============================
a.ir and b.m12 c.mar
rd
a.mdr c.ac br@fetch
```

For the opcode 1 instruction, use `.org 108`:

```
.org 108 ; st ===============================
a.ir and b.m12 c.mar
a.ac c.mdr
wr br@fetch
```

Continue in this fashion up to the opcode e instruction:


```
.org e08 ; brz ==============================
a.ac add b.0 c.0 !zer@fetch
a.ir and b.m12 c.pc br@fetch
```

The `sim` program—not microcode—handles the opcode-f instructions (the trap instructions) so there is no microcode for these instructions. Simply use a microinstruction at address f08 that unconditionally branches back to `fetch`:

```
.org f08 ; trap instructions ===============
br@fetch
```

Fast Extended Opcode Decoding

The modifications to the LCC that support fast opcode decoding also support fast decoding of four-bit extended opcodes. The stack, register, and optimal instruction sets all have extended opcodes. In the stack instruction set, there are five instructions with opcode 1010 binary (a hex). Each has an extended opcode in its rightmost four bits: `ret` (a000), `esba` (a001), `reba` (a002), `mhw` (a004), and `mmc` (a008). In the register instruction set, the instructions with opcode 1010 also have the extended opcodes in their rightmost four bits. The extended opcodes in the optimal instruction set are five bits, *but only the four rightmost bits are needed* by the optimal instruction set. Thus, they can be treated as four-bit fields.

For the instruction sets with extended opcodes, the transfer logic circuit includes not only the opcode bits in the outputted address but also the four-bit extended opcode. The opcode bits go into the leftmost four bits of the 12-bit branch-to address; the extended opcode bits go into the middle four bits of the branch-to address. For example, if the `reba` instruction a002 in the stack instruction set is applied to the transfer logic circuit, the transfer logic circuit outputs the microstore branch-to address a28.

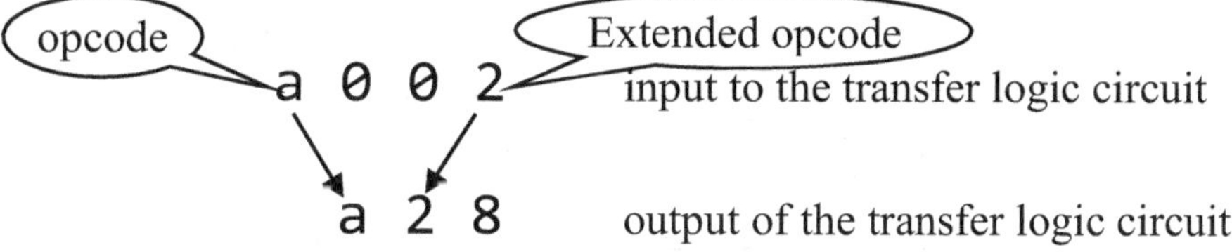

Thus, the microcode for this instruction must start at the microstore address a28 hex. Similarly, the microcode for `ret` (extended opcode 0), `esba` (extended opcode 1), `mhw` (extended opcode 4), and `mmc` (extended opcode 8) must start, respectively, at addresses a08, a18, a48, and a88:

```
.org a08 ; ret  ==============================
         ; microcode for the ret instruction

.org a18 ; esba ==============================
         ; microcode for the esba instruction

.org a28 ; reba ==============================
         ; microcode for the reba instruction

.org a48 ; mhw  ==============================
         ; microcode for the mhw instruction

.org a88 ; mmc  ==============================
         ; microcode for the mmc instruction
```

Fast Branch Instruction Decoding

The opcode 0000 instructions (the branch instructions) in the register and optimal instruction sets also have extended opcodes. Unfortunately, unlike the opcode 1010 instructions, they are *not* in the rightmost four bits of the instructions. Instead, they are in the three-bit condition code field that immediately follows the opcode. The condition code field specifies the condition for which the branch should occur. For these instructions, the transfer logic circuit places the extended opcode (i.e., the three-bit condition code field) zero-extended to four bits into the middle four bits of the microstore branch-to address it outputs. For example, the unconditional branch instruction 0ea3 whose condition code is 111 binary (7 hex) is transformed to the microstore branch-to address 078:

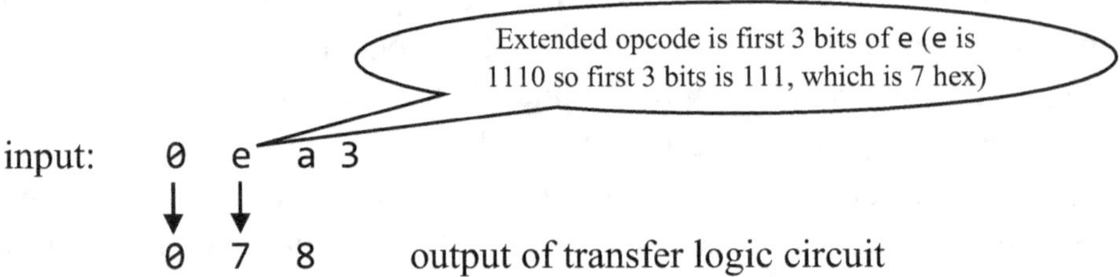

Incidentally, the 1000 (8 hex) in the rightmost four bits is necessary for the opcode 0 instructions. If 0000 were in the rightmost four bits, then the microcode for the opcode 0 instructions would have to start at the address 0. But the microcode that fetches and increments the **pc** starts at the address 0, so the microcode for any 0 opcode instruction cannot be there—hence the 1000 in the rightmost four bits.

Here are `.org` directives needed for the opcode 0 instructions in the register/optimal instruction sets:

```
.org 008 ; brz  ===============================
          ; microcode for the brz instruction

.org 018 ; brnz ===============================
          ; microcode for the brnz instruction

.org 028 ; brn  ===============================
          ; microcode for the brn instruction

.org 038 ; brp  ===============================
          ; microcode for the brp instruction

.org 048 ; brlt ===============================
          ; microcode for the brlt instruction

.org 058 ; brgt ===============================
          ; microcode for the brgt instruction

.org 068 ; brc  ===============================
          ; microcode for the brc instruction

.org 078 ; br   ===============================
          ; microcode for the br instruction
```

Comparing Microcode and Machine Language Programs

Suppose you want to compare the performance of the basic instruction set implemented with fast decoding with its performance without fast decoding. Let's assume `b.sm` contains the basic instruction set microcode without fast decoding, and `bf.sm` contains the microcode with fast decoding. Using the `micro` program, translate the microcode in `b.sm` and `bf.sm` to get `b.m` and `bf.m`, respectively. Run `btest.e` with the microcode in `b.m` the usual way:

```
sim btest.e
```

Because `btest.e` starts with the file signature "b", `sim` will load and use `b.m`. However, to run `btest.e` with the microcode in `bf.m`, you have to specify the `-m` command line argument followed by the microcode file name `bf.m` (you may omit the extension in `bf.m`—that is, specify just `bf`)

```
sim btest.e -mbf
```

After running `btest.e` with both versions of microcode, you can compare the performance statistics `sim` displays for each run. A precise measure of the run time of `btest.e` is given by the "`Microinstructions executed`" statistic displayed by `sim`. The size of the microcode (including any gaps between the sequences of microcode) is given by the "`Microcode size`" statistic. Between the two runs on `btest.e` (one using `b.m` and one using `bf.m`), be sure to copy `btest.log` to another file. Otherwise, the second run will overlay the `btest.log` file from the first run, in which case you will not have a record of the first run.

Using the statistics that `sim` displays, you can also compare two machine language programs. Suppose you have two machine language programs, and both solve the same problem. To determine which one is more efficient, refer to the "`Microinstructions executed`" statistic displayed by `sim`. It will give you a precise measure of run time. For example, if this statistic is 500 for one program and 1000 for the second program, then the second program takes exactly twice as long as the first program. Do *not* use the "`Machine instructions executed`" statistic. The execution times for machine instructions are not all the same. Thus, a program that executes more machine instructions could take less time than one that executes fewer machine instructions. Of course, when comparing machine language programs, you should use the same microcode for both.

Let's now examine the optimal instruction set assembly code for various structures in C and C++.

Name of an Array is a Pointer in C and C++

If the name of an array is not followed by square brackets, then the C/C++ compiler translates the name of the array to its address. In particular, it translates the name of the array to the address of the *first slot* of the array. In other words, if `a` is the name of an array, `a` is equivalent to `&a[0]`. For example, suppose `a` is declared with

```
int a[3];
```

Then `a` without the square brackets is a pointer to the first slot of `a`—that is, to `a[0]`. Each slot of `a` has type `int`. Thus, `a` without the square brackets is an `int` pointer.

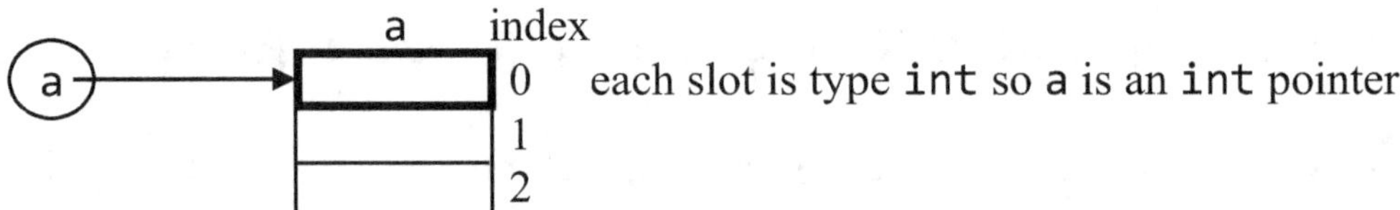

Suppose p is declared with

```
int *p;
```

Then the following statement makes perfectly good sense because the type of the left side matches the type of the right side (both have type int *):

```
p = a;      ; equivalent to p = &a[0];
```

We get

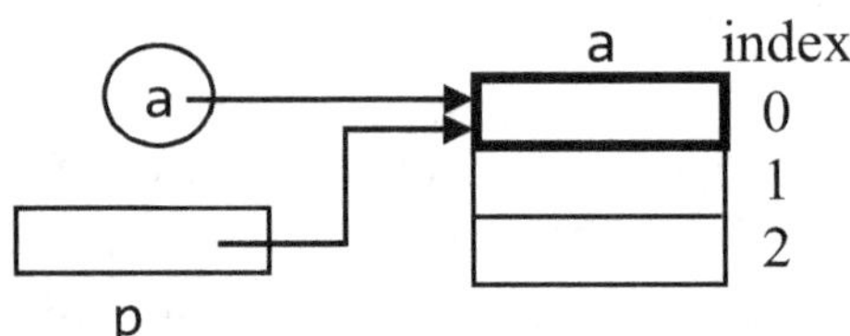

a and p have the *same type* (int *). After the assignment of a to p, a and p also have the *same value* (they both point to the first slot of the a array). *So we can use* a *and* p *interchangeably*. Specifically, we can use a as an array or as a pointer. Same for p. For example, the following two statements are equivalent:

```
a[2] = 10;
*(a+2) = 10;
```

We can also use p as an array or a pointer. For example, the following two statements are equivalent:

```
p[2] = 10;
*(p+2) = 10;
```

All four of the assignment statements above assign 10 to the slot in the a array with index 2. The only difference between a and p is that a is a constant pointer and p is not. We can assign p the address of any integer slot. But the value of a is fixed—its value is always the address of the first slot of the a array.

Important point: Because a pointer to the first slot of an array and the name of the array have the same type and the same value, a pointer to the first slot of an *array can be used as if it is the name of the array.* That is, it can be used with square brackets enclosing an index. For example, if p is pointing to the first slot of the a array, then the statement

```
p[2] = 10;
```

is legal, and it has the same effect as

```
a[2] = 10;
```

Passing an Array in a Function Call in C and C++

Suppose a is an array declared with

```
int a[3];
```

Suppose the call of the function f passes a:

```
f(a);
```

How should the parameter in f that corresponds to the argument a in the call of f be declared? The array name a without the square brackets is a pointer to the first slot of the a array. Each slot of a has the type int. Thus, *this call of f is passing an* int *pointer to* f. It is *not* passing the array itself. Thus, the parameter in f should be declared as an int pointer, like so:

```
void f(int *p)
{
    ...
}
```

Then when f is called, the parameter p receives the pointer to the first slot of the a array. Thus, on entry into f, we have the following configuration:

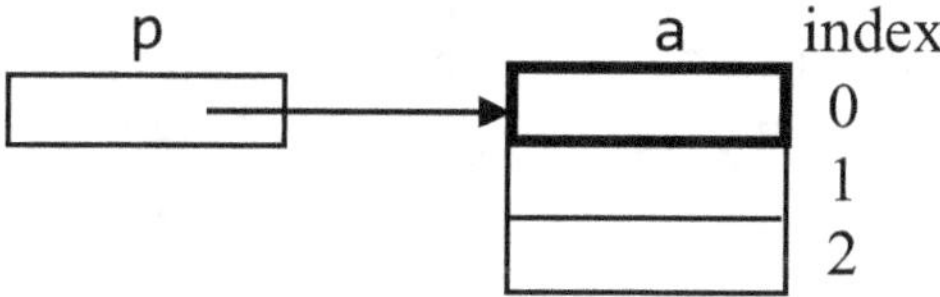

Because p points to the first slot of the array, we can use p as if it were the name of the array. For example, the following version of f assigns 99 to the slot of the array with index 2:

```
void f(int *p)
{
    p[1] = 99;    // use p as the name of an array
}
```

We, of course, can also use p as a pointer. For example, here is an equivalent version of f that uses p as a pointer:

```
void f(int *p)
{
    *(p+1) = 99; // use p as a pointer
}
```

Either way, we get the same optimal instruction set assembly code:

```
 1 f:            push lr            ; void f(int *p)
 2               push fp           ; {
 3               mov fp, sp
 4
 5               mov r0, 99        ;     p[1] = 99; or *(p+1) = 99;
 6               ldr r1, fp, 2
 7               str r0, r1, 1
 8
 9               mov sp, fp        ; }
10               pop fp
11               pop lr
12               ret
```


Because using p as if it were an array but declaring it as an `int` pointer might be confusing, C/C++ allows
p in the function header to be declared with square brackets instead of the asterisk. The `f` function rewritten
with this alternative is

```
void f(int p[])
{
    p[1] = 99;
}
```


The compiler generates exactly the same code for this version as the preceding two versions. The
declaration `int p[]` is just another way of indicating that p is an `int` pointer. Some C/C++ programmers
wonder why the declaration of the parameter is not `int p[3]`, where 3 is the size of the array, like so:

```
void f(int p[3])
{
    p[1] = 99;
}
```


The answer should now be obvious: p *is not an array* but a pointer to an array so it does not have a
dimension.

Rule: If empty square brackets follow the declaration of a parameter in a function definition, the brackets
indicate that the parameter variable is a pointer.

C and C++ argc and argv Parameters

In C, there is no string type. Instead, C uses `char` pointers. For example, consider the following C
statement:

```
p = "hello";        // p assigned addr of string, declare p as char *p
```

Wherever a string constant appears in a C program, the C compiler uses the *address of that string*. Thus, in place of the string constant in the preceding statement, the C compiler uses the address of the string—more precisely, it uses the address of the *first character* in the string. Thus, the preceding assignment statement does not move the string "hello" into p. Instead, it moves *the address of the first character in the string* into p. Thus, p should be declared as `char *p`. Here is the corresponding assembler code (assuming p is created with a `.word` directive):

```
        lea r0, greeting        // get addr of the string (optimal inst set)
        st r0, p                // store address in p
        :
greeting: .string "hello"       // define string at bottom of program
```

Now consider the following sequence in C:

```
        int *p;
        p =  "hello";           // p contains the address of the string
        printf("%s\n", p);      // for %s, printf expects a string address
```

When you use the `%s` conversion code in a `printf` statement, *you must provide the address of the string as the corresponding argument*. In the preceding `printf` statement, the argument p correctly provides the address of the string to be displayed. What about the following `printf` statement:

```
    printf("%s\n", "goodbye");    // displays "goodbye" (without the quotes)
```

Recall that in place of a string constant, the C compiler uses the address of the string. Thus, this `printf` statement is correctly passing the address of the string "goodbye", not the string itself.

When startup code calls `main` in a C/C++ program, it passes `main` the number of command line arguments (in `argc`) and a pointer (in `argv`) to an array of `char` pointers that in turn point to the command line arguments. `main` can then access the command line arguments via the `argv` pointer. For example, consider the following C program which is in the file `clargs.c`:

```
1 // clargs.c Displays all the command line arguments
2 #include <stdio.h>
3 int main(int argc, char *argv[])
4 {
5     int i;
6     for (i = 0, i < argc; i++)        // loop indexes through argv array
7         printf("%s\n", argv[i]);      // displays what argv[i] points to
8     return 0;
9 }
```

If we compile `clargs.c` with `gcc` (or another standard C compiler) and then invoke `clargs` with

```
    clargs dog bird
```

the startup code linked into the program by `gcc` (the real startup code—not the simplified version we have been using in our assembly language programs) configures `argc` and `argv` as follows and passes them to the `argc` and `argv` parameters in `main`:

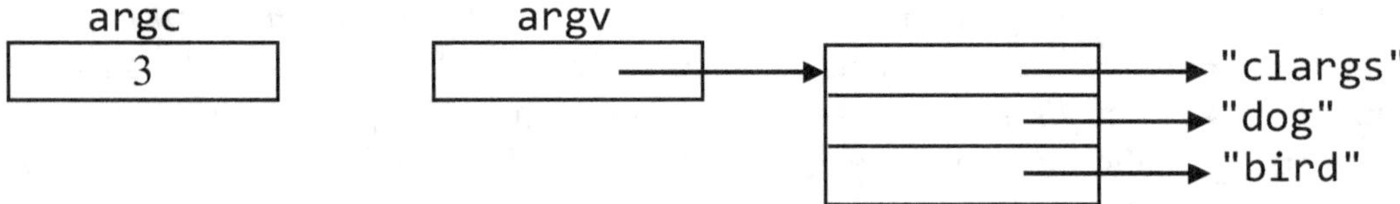

Important point: `argv` is a pointer to the first slot of an array. So we can use it as *if were the name of the array* (which we are doing with `argv[i]` in the `clargs` program on line 7). For example, to access the first slot of the array, we use `argv[i]`, where `i` is 0, which provides the address of the first command line argument (i.e., the address of "clargs").

How should `argv` be declared? `argv` is a pointer to the first slot of the array pictured above which in turn points to a character (the "c" in "clargs"). Thus, it is a pointer to a character pointer. Accordingly, the natural way to declare it is with

```
char **argv
```

In this declaration, read "`*argv`" as "`argv` is a pointer," and the initial "`char  *`" as "to a `char` pointer." But we declared `argv` differently on line 3 of the `clargs` program. Recall that using empty square brackets in a parameter declaration is an alternative way of indicating that a parameter is a pointer. In the `clargs` program, we are using this alternative declaration:

```
char *argv[]         // equivalent to char **argv
```

The empty square brackets in "`argv[]`" indicates that `argv` is a pointer. The initial "`char  *`" indicates that the `argv` pointer is pointing to a `char` pointer. Thus, these two ways of declaring `argv` are equivalent—either variation results in the same assembly/machine code.

One final point: On line 7 in the `clargs` program, `argv[i]` is passing the *address* of a string as required by the `%s` conversion code in the `printf`. Specifically, it is passing the address in the slot with index `i` of the array that `argv` is pointing to.

Function Name Overloading in C++

In C++ (but not C), a program can have multiple functions with the same name. We call this feature of C++ *function name overloading*. Functions with the same name must be distinguishable by their parameter lists. Specifically, the parameter list for each function must differ in order, number, or type from every other function that has the same name. For example, a C++ program can have the following two functions both named `f`:

```
    void f()
    {
        ⋮
    }
    void f(int x)
    {
        ⋮
    }
```

Because the parameter lists for these functions are distinguishable, the compiler can determine from the argument list in the call which f function should be called. For example, if the call is

```
f();
```

then obviously this is a call of the first f function above (the one that has no parameters). If, however, the call is

```
f(3);
```

then the second f function above should be called (the one that has a single int parameter).

   Although multiple functions can have the same name in a C++ program, they *cannot* have the same names at the assembler level. If they did, there would be multiple identical labels in the assembly language program which would cause an assembly-time error.

   How then should functions at the assembly level be named? Because C++ functions with overloaded names are distinguishable by their parameter lists, if the compiler includes an *encoding of the parameter list* in the name of the function at the assembly level, then each function will have a unique name. For example, we can encode an empty parameter list with "v" (for void) and a parameter list with a single int parameter with "i". Then the name of the following function

```
void f()
{
    ⋮
}
```

at the assembly level would be @f$v. The "v" indicates the function has no parameters. Preceding the parameter list encoding is the C++-level function name delimited with the "@" and "$" signs. Thus, this function is translated to

```
@f$v:      push lr
             ⋮
           ret
```

Similarly,

```
void f(int x)
{
    ⋮
}
```

is translated to

```
@f$i:      push lr
             ⋮
           Ret
```

These modified function names—like @f$i—are are called *mangled names*. *Note*: main is not mangled because only one main function is allowed in a C++ program. Thus, it never needs to be mangled.

Objects in C++

An *object* is a structure that contains both data and the functions that operate on that data. An object is created from a class. A *class* is a user-defined type that specifies the makeup of an object. A class is essentially the blueprint for an object. The data fields and the functions in an object are called *members* of the object.

In C++, an object can be created with a declaration, in which case the object gets the name provided by the declaration. The object is then accessed via its name. For example, suppose A is a class that specifies an x data field and a function `set`. Then the following declaration creates an A object named a:

```
A a; // creates an object named a from the class A
```

Here is a conceptual picture of the object we get from this declaration:

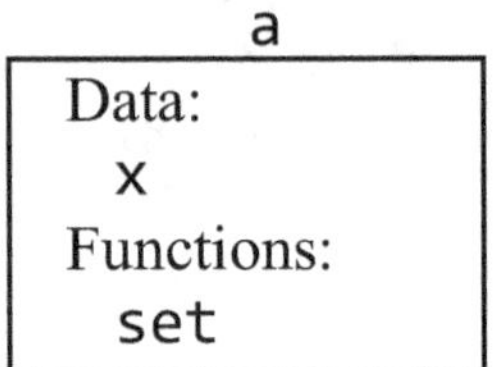

Functions and data in a class can be public or private. If a function or a data member is public, it can be directly accessed from outside the class. We invoke the public functions in the object via its name using the dot operator. For example, assuming `set` is public, the following statement invokes the `set` function in the a object passing it 5:

```
a.set(5);
```

The following statement assigns 10 to x in the a object assuming x is public:

```
a.x = 10;
```

An object can also be created by the executable instruction that uses the `new` operator. For example, the following statement creates an A object and assigns its address to the pointer variable `aptr`:

```
aptr = new A;
```

where `aptr` is declared with

```
A *aptr;
```

An object created with the `new` operator does not have a name. We access its members via the pointer to it. Here is a conceptual picture of the object we get for this example:

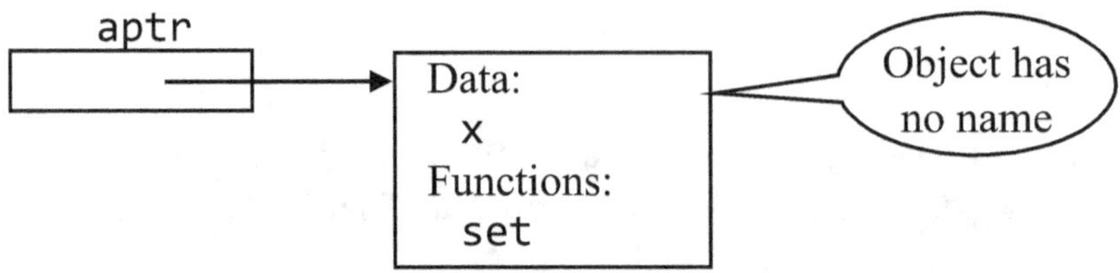

Although the object does not have a name, we can access its public members via the pointer `aptr` using the arrow operator (which consists of a hyphen and the greater than symbol). Assuming `set` is public, here is a statement that invokes the `set` function in the object to which `aptr` points:

```
aptr->set(5);    // invokes set function in object aptr points to
```

Similarly, if `x` is public, then accessing `x` is legal, as in the following statement:

```
y = aptr->x;    // access x in the object aptr points to
```

In C++, we need two notatios for accessing an object: the dot notation (for via name access) and the pointer notation (for via pointer access). But in Java, objects never have names. Thus, only one notation is needed for accessing an object. A potential source of confusion for programmers switching from C++ to Java or from Java to C++ is that in Java the dot operator—not the arrow operator as in C++—is used to access an object via a pointer to the object. For example, in Java, if `aptr` is a pointer to an object with a `set` function, we invoke the `set` function and pass it 5 with

```
aptr.set(5);    // calling set via the pointer aptr in Java
```

But in C++, this statement would be treated as the call of `set` in the object whose *name* is `aptr`. In C++, to call `set` via the pointer `aptr`, we use

```
aptr->set(5);    // calling set via the pointer aptr in C++
```

Let's now examine the program in `e1001.cpp`.

```
 1 // e1001.cpp  Objects in C++
 2 #include <iostream>
 3 using namespace std;
 4 class A
 5 {
 6     public:
 7         void set(int n, int m);
 8     private:
 9         int x;
10 };
11 void A::set(int n)
12 {
13     x = n;
14 }
15 int main()
16 {
17     A a, b;
18     a.set(5);
19     b.set(7);
20     return 0;
21 }
```

The class definition is on lines 4 to 10. It specifies what is in an object created from this class. Only the prototypes of the functions appear within the class definition. The definitions of the functions appear after the class definition. The `set` function is labeled `public`. Thus, it can be invoked from outside the class as well as from inside the class. The `x` field, however, is labeled `private`. Thus, it can be accessed directly only from a member within the class (as on line 13).

The definition for the `set` function in the class is on lines 11 to 14. Note that the name of the `set` function is qualified with the class name `A` (with a double colon separating the class name from the function name):

```
void A::set(int n)
```

More than one class in a program can have a `set` function. Thus, the name of a function in its definition must be qualified with the class name to distinguish it from identically named functions in other classes.

The declaration on line 17 creates two objects: one named `a`, the other named `b`. To call a function in an object, we qualify the function name with the object name using the dot operator. For example, to call the `set` function in the `a` object, we use on line 18

```
a.set(5);
```

Here is a conceptual picture of the `a` and `b` objects created by the preceding program.

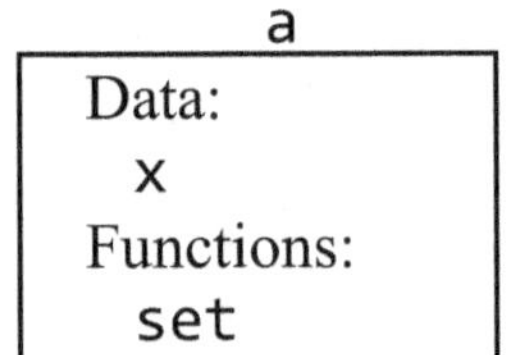

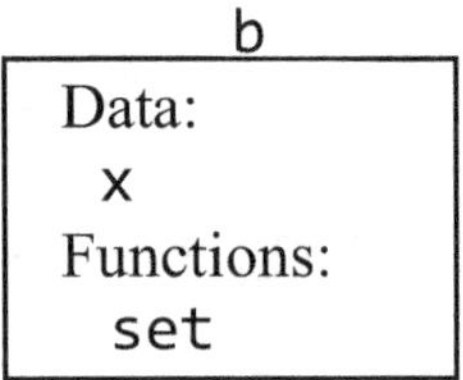

This conceptual view of the `a` and `b` objects leads to two questions:

1. Each object has its own `set` function. This is a very inefficient use of memory—to have multiple copies of the `set` function. What if we created 1 million A objects? We would then have 1 million copies of the `set` function.

2. The `set` functions in the `a` and `b` objects *are identical*. How then can the `set` functions have a different effect? For example, the call of the `set` function on line 18

   ```
   a.set(5);
   ```

   initializes the `x` *in the a object,* but the call of the *identical* `set` function on line 19

   ```
   b.set(7);
   ```

   initializes the `x` *in the b object.*

These questions are easily answered by examining the preceding program at the assembly level. At the assembly level, the `a` and `b` objects *contain only the x data field—no functions*. Separate from the `a` and `b` objects is a *single* `set` function:

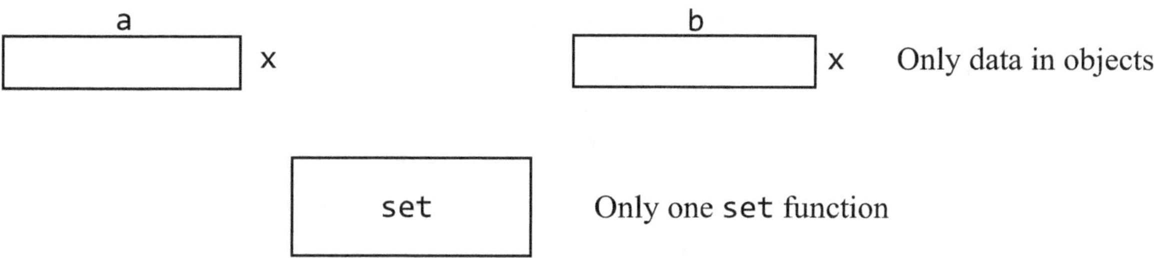

How then does the `set` function have a different effect depending on how it is called? If it is called with

```
a.set(5);
```

it is passed not only 5 but also the address of `a` (which is also the address of `x` in the `a` object). If it is called with

```
b.set(7);
```

it is passed not only 7 but also the address of `b` (which is the address of `x` in the `b` object). The `set` function dereferences the address it is passed to access `x`. Thus, if it is passed the address of `a`, it sets the `x` in the `a` object. But if it is passed the address of `b`, it sets the `x` in the `b` object. Thus, the `set` function really has two parameters created by the calling sequence corresponding to two arguments: (1) the address of the object and (2) the value inside parentheses in the calling statement. Both are pushed onto the stack by the calling sequence, thereby creating the two parameters of the `set` function.

Below in `e1001.a` is the assembler code for the preceding C++ program.

```
 1 ; e1001.a  Objects in C++
 2 startup:   bl main
 3            halt
 4 ;=================================================================
 5                             ; #include <iostream>
 6                             ; using namespace std;
 7                             ; class A
 8                             ; {
 9                             ;     public:
10                             ;         void set(int n);
11                             ;     private:
12                             ;         int x;
13                             ; };
14 ;=================================================================
15 @A@set$i:                   ; void A::set(int n)
16           push lr           ; {
17           push fp
18           mov fp, sp                   Get n into  r0
19
20           ldr r0, fp, 3     ;       x = n;
21           ldr r1, fp, 2                 Get x  addr into  r1
```

```
22              str r0, r1, 0
23                                      store n into x
24              mov sp, fp       ; }
25              pop fp
26              pop lr
27              ret
28 ;================================================================
29 main:        push lr          ; int main()
30              push fp          ; {
31              mov fp, sp
32
33              sub sp, sp, 1    ;     A a, b;
34              sub sp, sp, 1    ;
35
36              mov r0, 5        ;     a.set(5);
37              push r0
38              add r0, fp, -1            Create n
39              push r0
40              bl @A@set$i          Get address of a
41              add sp, sp, 2
42
43
44              mov r0, 7        ;     b.set(7);
45              push r0
46              add r0, fp, -2            Create n
47              push r0
48              bl @A@set$i          Get address of b
49              add sp, sp, 2
50
51              mov r0, 0        ;     return 0;
52              mov sp, fp
53              pop fp
54              pop lr
55              ret
56                               ; }
```

The calling sequence that starts on line 36 for

```
        a.set(5);
```

pushes on line 37 the argument 5 (which creates the parameter n). The offset -1 is the address of **a** relative
to pointer in the `fp` register so that the sum of the contents of the `fp` register and -1 is the address of **a**.
Thus, the instruction on line 38

```
        add r0, fp, -1      ; load r0 with the address of a
```

loads `r0` with the address of **a**, which is the address of **x** in the **a** object. This address is then pushed onto
the stack on line 39, creating a second parameter:

```
        push r0
```

On line 20, the `set` function loads `r0` from the parameter n (which has the relative address 3). On line 21, it loads `r1` with the address of the a object (which is also the address of x);

```
        ldr r0, fp, 3     ; r0 now contains 5
        ldr r1, fp, 2     ; r1 now contains the address of x in a object
```

It then initializes x in the a object with the contents of `r0` (5) with the `str` instruction on line 22:

```
        str r0, r1, 0     ; store r0 (5) in location r1 points to (x)
```

Problems

1) Implement the basic instruction set using fast decoding. Use the filename `bf.sm`. Compare the microcode size and the number of microinstructions executed with those statistics from your implementation that does not use fast decoding. Use `btest.a` in your comparison. Specify the `-mbf` command line argument when invoking `sim` so it uses the microcode in `bf.m`. Hand in the listing of the `btest.log` file created by `sim`.

2) Implement the stack instruction set using fast decoding. Use the filename `sf.sm`. Compare the microcode size and the number of microinstructions executed with those statistics from your implementation that does not use fast decoding. Use `stest.a` in your comparison. Specify the `-msf` command line argument when invoking `sim` so it uses the microcode in `sf.m`. Hand in the listing of the `stest.log` file created by `sim`.

3) Implement the register instruction set using fast decoding. Use the filename `rf.sm`. Compare the microcode size and the number of microinstructions executed with those statistics from your implementation that does not use fast decoding. Use `rtest.a` in your comparison. Specify the `-mrf` command line argument when invoking `sim` so it uses the microcode in `rf.m`. Hand in the listing of the `rtest.log` file created by `sim`.

4) Implement the optimal instruction set using fast decoding. Use the filename `of.sm`. Compare the microcode size and the number of microinstructions executed with those statistics from your implementation that does not use fast decoding. Use `otest.a` in your comparison. Specify the `-mof` command line argument when invoking `sim` so it uses the microcode in `of.m`. Hand in the listing of the `otest.log` file created by `sim`.

5) Complete the microcode for the optimal instruction set in the file named `o.sm`. Test your microcode by entering

```
        optimal otest.a
        micro o.sm
        sim otest.e
```

The `otest` program should display the integers 1 to 33. Hand in the listing of the of the `otest.log` file created by `sim`.

6) Write, assemble, and run an optimal instruction set assembly language program that adds two 32-bit numbers, 0002fff (hex) and 000010001 (hex), and subtracts the 32-bit number 00030001 (hex) from the 32-bit number 00050000 (hex). Display the sum and difference in hex. Display results as eight-digit hex numbers. Use `lcc` to assemble and run if you have not completed `o.sm`. Specify the `-x` command line argument when invoking `lcc` or `sim` so that `hout` always displays four hex digits.

7) In a computer with 32-bit instructions, all the instructions could have an eight-bit opcode with no extended opcodes. How would that simplify the transfer logic circuit?

8) In addition to slightly more complex and more costly hardware, what are the disadvantages, if any, of fast decoding? What are the advantages? Does fast decoding make it more difficult to change the instruction set architecture?

9) Why does the transfer logic circuit output an 8 in the rightmost four bits of its output?

10) Can an *add with carry* instruction be included in the optimal instruction set? It would be useful to have for problem 6. It can be one of the opcode 1010 instructions. It adds the current value (0 or 1) in the carry flag to the C-field register. It also adds the A-field register to the C-field register. It is difficult (or impossible?) to microprogram because it requires *two* add operations, each of which sets the flag registers. Thus, it may be impossible to microprogram the instruction so that the all the flag bits are set correctly. For example, if there is a carry out on the first addition but not on the second addition, the carry flag will be 0 at the conclusion of the instruction, but it should be 1.

11) If fast decoding is not used, what is the advantage of using powers of 2 for extended opcodes?

12) The add instruction, `add  r0,  r1,  0` has the effect of moving the contents of `r1` into `r0`. When would it be advisable to use this add instruction instead of `mvr  r0,  r1`?

13) Translate the program in `clargs.c` to the optimal instruction set. Use the file name `clargs.a`. Omit the inline startup code (instead link with the real startup code). Assemble, link with the real startup code in `su.o` (it creates and passes `argc` and `argv` to `main`), and execute by entering

```
optimal clargs.a            (assemble clargs.a)
optimal su.a                (assemble startup code in  su.a)
link clargs.o su.o -o clargs.e   (link clargs.o with real startup code in su.o)
sim clargs.e dog bird
```

14) Create a file `p1014.a` that contains the optimal instruction set version of the following C program. Comment your assembly code with the corresponding C code (see `comment.txt`). Assemble with `optimal` and run on `sim`. Hand in the listing of the `p1014.log` file created by `sim`.

```
// p1014.c  Passing an array
#include <stdio.h>
int a[3] = {10, 20, 30};   // initializes a array to 1, 2, 3
void f(int *p)
```

```cpp
{
    printf("%d %d %d\n", p[0], *(p+1), p[2]);
}
int main()
{
    f(a);          // passes f the address of the first slot of the a array
    return 0;
}
```

15) Create a file `p1015.a` that contains the optimal instruction set version of the following C++ program. Comment your assembly code with the corresponding C++ code (see `comment.txt`). Assemble with `optimal` and run on `sim`. Hand in the listing of the `p1015.log` file created by `sim`.

```cpp
// p1015.cpp  Creating an object with the new operator in C++
#include <iostream>
using namespace std;
class A
{
    public:
        void set(int n);
        void display();
    private:
        int x;
};
void A::set(int n)
{
    x = n;
}
void A::display()
{
    printf("%x\n", x);
}
int main()
{
    A* a = new A; // get mem for obj from locations following program
    a->set(5);
    a->display();
    return 0;
}
```

16) Create a file `p1016.a` that contains the optimal instruction set version of the following C++ program. Comment your assembly code with the corresponding C++ code (see `comment.txt`). Assemble with `optimal` and run on `sim`. Hand in the listing of the `p1016.log` file created by `sim`.

```cpp
// p1016.cpp  Function name overloading
#include <iostream>
```

```cpp
using namespace std;
void f()
{
    printf("void\n");                    // encode void with v
}
void f(int x)                            // encode int with i
{
    printf("int\n");
}
void f(char c)                           // encode char with c
{
    printf("char\n");
}
void f(int i, char c)                    // encode int, char with ic
{
    printf("int, char\n");
}
void f(char c, int i)                    // encode char, int with ci
{
    printf("char, int\n");
}
int main()
 {
    f()
    f(5);
    f('A');
    f(5, 'A');
    f('A', 5);
    return 0;
}
```

17) Create a file `p1017.a` that contains the optimal instruction set version of the following C++ program.
Comment your assembly code with the corresponding C++ code (see `comment.txt`). Assemble with
`optimal` and run on `sim`. Hand in the listing of the `p1017.log` file created by `sim`.

```cpp
// p1017.cpp  Creating and accessing objects in C++
#include <iostream>
using namespace std;
class A
{
    public:
        void set(int n, int m);
        void display();
    private:
        int x, y;
};
void A::set(int n, int m)
```

```
{
    x = n;
    y = m;
}
void A::display()
{
    printf("%d %d\n", x, y);
}
int main()
{
    A a;
    a.set(5, 10);
    a.display();
    return 0;
}
```

18) Rewrite `clargs.c` using `argv` as a pointer rather than as the name of an array. Compile and execute. If no command line arguments after the program name are entered, what happens? Fix this problem.

19) Implement the transfer logic circuit that the basic instruction set requires. Similarly for the stack, register, and optimal instruction sets.

20) Write a C program that displays the sum of two single-digit integers entered *on the command line* when the program is invoked. Use 3 and 5 to test your program. Omit the inline startup code (instead link with the real startup code). Use the file `p1020.a` for your assembly language program. Assemble, link with the real startup code in `su.o`, and execute by entering

```
optimal p1020.a               (assemble p1020.a)
optimal su.a                  (assemble startup code in su.a)
link p1020.o su.o -o p1020.e  (link p1020.o with the real startup code in su.o)
sim p1020.e 3 5
```

21) Project: Implement a C subset compiler that translates the example C programs in this textbook to the optimal instruction set. See *Writing Interpreters and Compilers for the Raspberry Pi Using Python*.

Epilog

Now that you have completed your study of the LCC from the transistor level to the assembly level, the next step is to read the two chapters in PDF form in the software package on linking and virtual memory. On completing those, read *C and C++ Under the Hood*, which emphasizes the software side of the LCC— specifically, C, C++, and the implementation of assemblers, linkers, machine interpreters, and file display programs.

Appendix A: ASCII

Hex	Decimal	
20	32	<blank>
21	33	!
22	34	"
23	35	#
24	36	$
25	37	%
26	38	&
27	38	'
28	40	(
29	41	)
2A	42	*
2B	43	+
2C	44	,
2D	45	-
2E	46	.
2F	47	/
30	48	0
31	49	1
32	50	2
33	51	3
34	52	4
35	53	5
36	54	6
37	55	7
38	56	8
39	57	9
3A	58	:
3B	59	;
3C	60	<
3D	61	=
3E	62	>
3F	63	?

Hex	Decimal	
40	64	@
41	65	A
42	66	B
43	67	C
44	68	D
45	69	E
46	70	F
47	71	G
48	72	H
49	73	I
4A	74	J
4B	75	K
4C	76	L
4D	77	M
4E	78	N
4F	79	O
50	80	P
51	81	Q
52	82	R
53	83	S
54	84	T
55	85	U
56	86	V
57	87	W
58	88	X
59	89	Y
5A	90	Z
5B	91	[
5C	92	\
5D	93	]
5E	94	^
5F	95	_

Hex	Decimal	
60	96	`
61	97	a
62	98	b
63	99	c
64	100	d
65	101	e
66	102	f
67	103	g
69	104	h
69	105	i
6A	106	j
6B	107	k
6C	108	l
6D	109	m
6E	110	n
6F	111	o
70	112	p
71	113	q
72	114	r
73	114	s
74	116	t
75	117	u
76	118	v
77	119	w
78	120	x
79	121	y
7A	122	z
7B	123	{
7C	124	|
7D	125	}
7E	126	~

Important Control Characters

Hex	Decimal		Meaning
0A	10	\n	Line feed (i.e., newline)
0D	13	\r	Carriage return

Appendix B: Basic Instruction Set Summary

Opcode	Format		Description
0	ld	x	`ac = mem[x];`
1	st	x	`mem[x] = ac;`
2	add	x	`ac = ac + mem[x];`
3	sub	x	`ac = ac - mem[x];`
4	ldr	x	`ac = mem[sp + x];`
5	str	x	`mem[sp + x] = ac;`
6	addr	x	`ac = ac + mem[sp + x];`
7	subr	x	`ac = ac - mem[sp + x];`
8	ldi	x	`ac = x;`
9	asp	s	`sp = sp + s;`
a	call	x	`mem[--sp] = pc; pc = x;`
b	ret		`pc = mem[sp++];`
c	br	x	`pc = x;`
d	brn	x	`if (ac == 0) pc = x;`
e	brz	x	`if (ac < 0) pc = x;`
f	trap	y	see below

halt	or trap 0		Terminate program
nl	or trap 1		Output newline character
dout	or trap 2		Output number in `ac` as signed decimal
udout	or trap 3		Output number in `ac` as unsigned decimal
hout	or trap 4		Output number in `ac` in hex
aout	or trap 5		Output character in `ac`
sout	or trap 6		Output string pointed to by `ac`
din	or trap 7		Input decimal number into `ac`
hin	or trap 8		Output hex number into `ac`
ain	or trap 9		Input character into `ac`
sin	or trap 10		Input string to address in `ac`
bp	or trap 14		Breakpoint

`x:` bits 0 to 11 in machine instruction zero-extended to 16 bits
`s:` bits 0 to 11 in machine instruction sign-extended to 16 bits
`y:` bits 0 to 7 in machine instruction zero-extended to 16 bits
`ac:` accumulator register
`pc:` program counter register
`sp:` stack pointer register

Directives: `.word/.fill,   .zero/.blkw,   .string/.stringz/.asciz,   .start`

Appendix C: Stack Instruction Set Summary

Opcode	Format		Description
0	p	x	`mem[--sp] = mem[x];`
1	pi	x	`mem[--sp] = x;`
2	pr	s	`mdr = mem[fp + s]; mem[--sp] = mdr;`
3	cora	s	`mdr = fp + s; mem[--sp] = mdr;`
4	stav		`temp = mem[sp++]; mem[mem[sp++]] = temp;`
5	dp		`mem[sp] = mem[mem[sp]];`
6	asp	s	`sp = sp + s;`
7	add		`temp = mem[sp++]; mem[sp] = mem[sp] + temp;`
8	sub		`temp = mem[sp++]; mem[sp] = mem[sp] - temp;`
9	call	x	`mem[--sp] = pc; pc = x;`
a000	ret		`pc = mem[sp++];`
a001	esba		`mem[--sp] = fp; fp = sp;`
a002	reba		`sp = fp; fp = mem[sp++];`
a004	mhw		`temp = mem[sp++]; mem[sp] = mem[sp] * temp;`
a008	mmc		`temp = mem[sp++]; mem[sp] = mem[sp] * temp;`
b	brp	x	`if (mem[sp++] > 0) pc = x;`
c	br	x	`pc = x;`
d	brn	x	`if (mem[sp++] < 0) pc = x;`
e	brz	x	`if (mem[sp++] == 0) pc = x;`
f	trap	y	`see below`

`halt`	or trap 0	Terminate program
`nl`	or trap 1	Output newline character
`dout`	or trap 2	Pop and display signed number in decimal
`udout`	or trap 3	Pop and display unsigned number in decimal
`hout`	or trap 4	Pop and display number in hex
`aout`	or trap 5	Pop and display ASCII character
`sout`	or trap 6	Pop address and display string at that address
`din`	or trap 7	Read decimal number from keyboard and push
`hin`	or trap 8	Read hex number from keyboard and push
`ain`	or trap 9	Read character from keyboard and push
`sin`	or trap 10	Pop address and read in string to that address
`bp`	or trap 14	Breakpoint

`x:`	bits 0 to 11 in machine instruction zero-extended to 16 bits
`s:`	bits 0 to 11 in machine instruction sign-extended to 16 bits
`y:`	bits 0 to 7 in machine instruction zero-extended to 16 bits
`sp:`	stack pointer
`fp:`	frame pointer register
`mdr:`	memory data register
`temp:`	temporary register

Directives: `.word`/`.fill`, `.zero`/`.blkw`, `.string`/`.stringz`/`.asciz`, `.start`

Appendix D: Register instruction Set Summary

Mnemonic	Format		Flags	Description	
br--	0000	cc pcoffset9		if cc, pc = pc + pcoffset9	
add	0001	C A 0 00 B	nzcv	C = A + B	
add	0001	C A 1 imm5	nzcv	C = A + imm5	
ld	0010	C pcoffset9		C = mem[pc + pcoffset9)	
st	0011	A pcoffset9		mem[pc + pcoffset9] = A	
bl	0100	1 pcoffset11		lr = pc; pc = [pc + pcoffset11]	
blr	0100	0 00 A offset6		lr = pc; pc = A	
and	0101	C A 0 00 B	nz	C = A & B	
and	0101	C A 1 imm5	nz	C = A & imm5	
ldr	0110	C A offset6		C = mem[A + offset6]	
str	0111	C A offset6		mem[A + offset6] = C	
cmp	1000	000 A 0 00 B	nzcv	A - B	(set flags)
cmp	1000	000 A 1 imm5	nzcv	A - imm5	(set flags)
not	1001	C A 0 00000	nz	C = ~A	
push	1010	C 00000 0000		mem[--sp] = C	(push C-field reg)
pop	1010	C 00000 0001		C = mem[sp++];	(pop into C-field reg)
srl	1010	C 00000 0010	nzc	C >> 1	(0 inserted on left, c=last out)
sra	1010	C 00000 0100	nzc	C >> 1	(sign bit replicated, c=last out)
sll	1010	C 00000 1000	nzc	C << 1	(0 inserted on right, c=last out)
sub	1011	C A 0 00 B	nzcv	C = A - B	
sub	1011	C A 1 imm5	nzcv	C = A - imm5	
jmp	1100	000 A offset6		pc = A + offset6	
ret	1100	000 111 offset6		pc = lr	
mvi	1101	C imm9		C = imm9	
lea	1110	C pcoffset9		C = pc + pcoffset9	
trap	1111	0000 trapvec8		OS call	

mov C, imm9 is a pseudo-instruction translated to the machine language instruction mvi C, imm9
mov C, A is a pseudo-instruction translated to the machine language instruction add C, A, 0
C, A, and B are 3-bit register fields.
cc is the 3-bit condition code field in the branch instructions.
pcoffset9, pcoffset11, imm5, imm9, offset6 are signed number fields of the indicated length.
If offset6 is omitted in an assembly language instruction, it defaults to 0.

Trap Instructions

Mnemonic		Format		Flags	Description
halt	1111	000 0	00000000	none	Stop execution, return to OS
nl	1111	000 0	00000001	none	Output newline character
dout	1111	C 0	00000010	none	Display signed number in C in decimal
udout	1111	C 0	00000011	none	Display unsigned number in C in decimal
hout	1111	C 0	00000100	none	Display number in C in hex
aout	1111	C 0	00000101	none	Display ASCII character in C
sout	1111	C 0	00000110	none	Display string C points to
din	1111	C 0	00000111	none	Read decimal number from keyboard into C
hin	1111	C 0	00001000	none	Read hex number from keyboard into C
ain	1111	C 0	00001001	none	Read ASCII character from keyboard into C
sin	1111	C 0	00001010	none	Input string into buffer C points to
bp	1111	000 0	00001110	none	Breakpoint, pause execution

If C is omitted in a trap assembly language instruction, it defaults to r0 (000).

Branch Instruction Condition Codes

brz or bre	000	z == 1	(branch on zero, branch on equal)
brnz or brne	001	z == 0	(branch on nonzero, branch on not equal)
brn	010	n == 1	(branch on negative)
brp	011	n == z	(branch on positive)
brlt	100	n != v	(branch on less than in signed comparison)
brgt	101	(n == v) && (z == 0)	(branch on greater than or equal in signed comparison)
brc or brb	110	c = 1	(branch on carry/below in unsigned comp)
br or bral	111		(branch always)

Assembler Directives

Directive	Description
.word <value>	Create word initialized to <value>
.fill <value>	Same as .word
.zero <size>	Create block of <size> words initialized to 0
.space <size>	Same as .zero
.blkw <size>	Same as .zero
.string <string>	Create null-terminated ASCII <string>
.stringz <string>	Same as .string
.asciz <string>	Same as .string
.start <label>	Specify <label> as entry point (or use the label "_start" on entry point)
.global <var>	Specify <var> is a global variable
.globl <var>	Same as .global
.extern <var>	Specify <var> is an external variable

Appendix E: Optimal Instruction Set Summary

Mnemonic	Format			Flags	Description	
br--	0000	cc pcoffset9			if cc, pc = pc + pcoffset9	
add	0001	C A 0 00 B		nzcv	C = A + B	
add	0001	C A 1 imm5		nzcv	C = A + imm5	
ld	0010	C pcoffset9			C = mem[pc + pcoffset9)	
st	0011	A pcoffset9			mem[pc + pcoffset9] = A	
bl	0100	1 pcoffset11			lr = pc; pc = [pc + pcoffset11]	
blr	0100	0 00 A offset6			lr = pc; pc = A	
and	0101	C A 0 00 B		nz	C = A & B	
and	0101	C A 1 imm5		nz	C = A & imm5	
ldr	0110	C A offset6			C = mem[A + offset6]	
str	0111	C A offset6			mem[A + offset6] = C	
cmp	1000	000 A 0 00 B		nzcv	A - B	(set flags)
cmp	1000	000 A 1 imm5		nzcv	A - imm5	(set flags)
not	1001	C A 0 00000		nz	C = ~A	
push	1010	C 0000 00000			mem[--sp] = C	(push C-field reg)
pop	1010	C 0000 00001			C = mem[sp++];	(pop into C-field reg)
srl	1010	C ct 00010		nzc	C >> ct	(0 inserted on left, c=last out)
sra	1010	C ct 00011		nzc	C >> ct	(sign bit replicated, c=last out)
sll	1010	C ct 00100		nzc	C << ct	(0 inserted on right, c=last out)
rol	1010	C ct 00101		nzc	C << ct	(rotate bit 15 to bit 0, c=last out)
ror	1010	C ct 00110		nzc	C << ct	(rotate bit 0 to bit 15, c=last out)
mul	1010	C A 0 00111		nz	C = C * A	(integer multiply)
div	1010	C A 0 01000		nz	C = C / A	(integer division)
rem	1010	C A 0 01001		nz	C = C % A	(remainder)
or	1010	C A 0 01010		nz	C = C | A	(bitwise OR)
xor	1010	C A 0 01011		nz	C = C ^ A	(bitwise exclusive OR)
mvr	1010	C A 0 01100			C = A	(copy A-field reg to C-field reg)
sext	1010	C A 0 01101		nz	C-field reg sign extended	(A-field reg specifies field to extend)
sub	1011	C A 0 00 B		nzcv	C = A - B	
sub	1011	C A 1 imm5		nzcv	C = A - imm5	
jmp	1100	cc A offset6			pc = A + offset6	
ret	1100	000 111 offset6			pc = lr	
mvi	1101	C imm9			C = imm9	
lea	1110	C pcoffset9			C = pc + pcoffset9	
trap	1111	0000 trapvec8			OS call	

mov C, imm9 is a pseudo-instruction translated to the machine language instruction for mvi C, imm9
mov C, A is a pseudo-instruction translated to the machine language instruction for mvr C, A
C, A, and B are 3-bit register fields.
cc is the 3-bit condition code field in the branch instructions.
ct is the 4-bit shift count field (if omitted at the assembly level, it defaults to 1).
pcoffset9, pcoffset11, imm5, imm9, offset6 are signed number fields of the indicated length.
If offset6 is omitted in an assembly language instruction, it defaults to 0.

Trap Instructions

Mnemonic		Format			Flags	Description
halt	1111	000	0	00000000	none	Stop execution, return to OS
nl	1111	000	0	00000001	none	Output newline character
dout	1111	C	0	00000010	none	Display signed number in C in decimal
udout	1111	C	0	00000011	none	Display unsigned number in C in decimal
hout	1111	C	0	00000100	none	Display number in C in hex
aout	1111	C	0	00000101	none	Display ASCII character in C
sout	1111	C	0	00000110	none	Display string C points to
din	1111	C	0	00000111	none	Read decimal number from keyboard into C
hin	1111	C	0	00001000	none	Read hex number from keyboard into C
ain	1111	C	0	00001001	none	Read ASCII character from keyboard into C
sin	1111	C	0	00001010	none	Input string into buffer C points to
bp	1111	000	0	00001110	none	Breakpoint, pause execution

If C is omitted in a trap assembly language instruction, it defaults to r0 (000).

Branch Instruction Condition Codes

brz or bre	000	z == 1	(branch on zero, branch on equal)
brnz or brne	001	z == 0	(branch on nonzero, branch on not equal)
brn	010	n == 1	(branch on negative)
brp	011	n == z	(branch on positive)
brlt	100	n != v	(branch on less than in signed comparison)
brgt	101	(n == v) && (z == 0)	(branch on greater than or equal in signed comparison)
brc or brb	110	c = 1	(branch on carry/below in unsigned comp)
br or bral	111		(branch always)

Assembler Directives

Directive	Description
.word <value>	Create word initialized to <value>
.fill <value>	Same as .word
.zero <size>	Create block of <size> words initialized to 0
.space <size>	Same as .zero
.blkw <size>	Same as .zero
.string <string>	Create null-terminated ASCII <string>
.stringz <string>	Same as .string
.asciz <string>	Same as .string
.start <label>	Specify <label> as entry point (or use the label "_start" on entry point)
.global <var>	Specify <var> is a global variable
.globl <var>	Same as .global
.extern <var>	Specify <var> is an external variable
.org <address>	Reset location counter to higher <address>
.extern <var>	Specify <var> is an external variable

Appendix F: Microinstruction Format

```
A     amux    B     bmux    C     cmux    alu    u     rd    wr    cond    addr
5     1       5     1       5     1       4      1     1     1     4       11      width
```

Field

A   Specifies register that inputs to the A multiplexer

amux   Controls A multiplexer:
        amux = 0 then A field in `mir` drives A decoder
        amux = 1 then A field in `ir` drives A decoder

B   Specifies register that inputs to the B multiplexer

bmux   Controls B multiplexer:
        bmux = 0 then B field in `mir` drives B decoder
        bmux = 1 then B field in `ir` drives B decoder

C   Specifies register that inputs to the C multiplexer

cmux   Controls C multiplexer:
        cmux = 0 then C field in `mir` drives C decoder
        cmux = 1 then C field in `ir` drives C decoder

alu   Specifies ALU operation:

F_3 F_2 F_1 F_0	Mnemonic	Output	Flags Set
0 0 0 0 (0)	nop	left	
0 0 0 1 (1)	not	~left	nz
0 0 1 0 (2)	and	left & right	nz
0 0 1 1 (3)	sext	left sign ext, (rt = mask)	nz
0 1 0 0 (4)	add	left + right	nzcv
0 1 0 1 (5)	sub	left − right	nzcv
0 1 1 0 (6)	mul	left * right	nz
0 1 1 1 (7)	div	left / right	nz
1 0 0 0 (8)	rem	left % right	nz
1 0 0 1 (9)	or	left | right	nz
1 0 1 0 (10)	xor	left ^ right	nz
1 0 1 1 (11)	sll	left << right (logical)	nzc
1 1 0 0 (12)	srl	left >> right (logical	nzc
1 1 0 1 (13)	sra	left >> right (arithmetic)	nzc
1 1 1 0 (14)	rol	left << right (rotate)	nzc
1 1 1 1 (15)	ror	left >> right (rotate)	nzc

u   User n, z, c, v flags used instead of system flags

rd   Initiates memory read from address in mar
wr   Initiates memory write of data in mdr to address in mar

cond   Specifies branch condition:

Mnemonic	Branch if	Branch on
0 nobr		never
1 zer	z = 1	zero or equal
2 !zer	z = 0	not zero or not equal
3 neg	n = 1	negative
4 !neg	n = 0	not negative
5 cy or <	c = 1	less than (unsigned cmp)
6 !cy or >=	c = 0	grt or eq (unsigned cmp/overflow)
7 v	v = 1	signed overflow
8 pos	n = z	positive
9 lt	n != v	less than (signed cmp)
10 le	n != v or z = 1	less than or equal (signed cmp)
11 gt	n = v and z = 0	greater (signed cmp)
12 ge	n = v	greater than or equal (signed cmp)
13 <=	c = 1 or z = 1	less than or equal (unsigned cmp)
14 >	c = 0 and z = 0	greater than (unsigned cmp)
15 br		always

addr   branch-to address

In the enhanced LCC (see Chapter 10),

- each microinstruction has a mmux bit in the rightmost position that controls the mpc multiplexer
- the mpc is 12 bits wide
- the addr field in each microinstruction is 12 bits wide
- microstore can hold up to 4096 microinstructions.

Appendix G: Register Names

Reg Num	Name	Initial Contents	Function
0	r0 or ac		accumulator register
1	r1		
2	r2		
3	r3		
4	r4		
5	r5 or fp		frame pointer register
6	r6 or sp		stack pointer register
7	r7 or lr		link register
8	r8 or 3	0x0003	
9	r9 or 4	0x0004	
10	r10 or 5	0x0005	
11	r11 or omask	0xf000	opcode mask
12	r12 or cmask	0x01e0	count mask (for shifts)
13	r13 or bit5	0x0020	
14	r14 or bit11	0x0800	
15	r15 or bit15	0x8000	
16	r16 or m3	0x0007	
17	r17 or m4	0x000f	
18	r18 or m5	0x001f	
19	r19 or m6	0x003f	
20	r20 or m8	0x00ff	
21	r21 or m9	0x01ff	
22	r22 or m11	0x07ff	
23	r23 or m12	0x0fff	
24	r24 or ir		machine instruction register
25	r25 or pc		program counter register
26	r26 or temp		
27	r27 or dc		decoding register
28	r28 or 1	0x0001	constant 1
29	r29 or mar		memory address register
30	r30 or mdr		memory data register
31	r31 or 0	0x0000	constant 0 (read-only register)

Index